DYING TO PLEASE YOU:

INDIGENOUS SUICIDE IN CONTEMPORARY CANADA

Copyright © 2nd Printing 2017
Library and Archives Canada Cataloguing in Publication
Chrisjohn, Roland David, author
Dying to please you : Indigenous suicide in contemporary
Canada / Roland D. Chrisjohn, Ph.D. and Shaunessy M. McKay
with Andrea O. Smith, M.Sc.

Includes bibliographical references.
ISBN 978-1-926886-46-6 (paperback)

1. Native peoples--Suicidal behavior--Canada. 2. Suicide--
Canada. I. McKay, Shaunessy M., author II. Smith, Andrea O.,
author III. Title.

E98.S9C57 2017   362.28089'97071   C2016-905821-2

Printed in Canada

Credits
Managing Editor: Gregory Younging
Peer Review: Lisa Monchalin

THEYTUS BOOKS

www.theytus.com
In Canada: Theytus Books, Green Mountain Rd.,
Lot 45, RR#2, Site 50, Comp. 8
Penticton, BC, V2A 6J7, Tel: 250-493-7181

 Canada Council   Conseil des arts
for the Arts   du Canada

This project has been made possible in
part by the Government of Canada.
Ce projet a été rendu possible en partie
grâce au gouvernement du Canada.

 Canadä

We acknowledge the financial support of
The Government of Canada through the
Department of Canadian Heritage and the
Canada Council for the Arts for our publish-
ing activities.

We acknowledge the financial support of The
Government of British Columbia through the
Arts Council for our publishing activities.

 BRITISH
COLUMBIA

 BRITISH COLUMBIA
ARTS COUNCIL
An agency of the Province of British Columbia

DYING TO PLEASE YOU:

INDIGENOUS SUICIDE IN CONTEMPORARY CANADA

Roland D. Chrisjohn, Ph. D.

and **Shaunessy M. McKay**

with

Andrea O. Smith, M. Sc., ABD

Theytus Books Ltd., Penticton, BC

Dedications:

By Roland Chrisjohn: *To the memory of my mother, Lasca Shannon Chrisjohn; and to the memory of my uncle, Irvin Chrisjohn; and to someone I never got the chance to know as well as I should have, Soup. Rest, my old friend.*

By Shaunessy McKay: *To my son Tyler, my family, and my friends; I couldn't have done this without you.*

By Andrea Smith: *To the memory of Sara Radcliffe.*

"They will not give a doit to relieve a lame beggar, but they will lay out ten to see a dead Indian."

~Shakespeare

TABLE OF CONTENTS

PREFACE

This book began more than 40 years ago now when a friend of the lead author ended his life over matters that even now seem far too trivial to have brought about that particular response. In such situations the feeling that you've failed a friend is impossible to shake; the need to find something to do about it, even though it is now far too late, never really diminishes.

It has taken this long for several reasons, the most important of which were (1) the thought that the position we've taken had been sufficiently clarified in 1996, (2) the further thought that someone else, someone that people would listen to this time, had gotten it right in 1999, and (3) the incredible capacity of academic and applied fields dedicated to the phenomenon of Native suicide to impose near-impenetrable layers of misunderstanding everywhere. This latter point was driven home to the lead author most forcefully when he realized near the end of his working time at a Native suicide crisis office that the "official" approach demanded he respond with obvious irrelevance to the suicidal Native bleeding in front of him.

Another start was made in 2002 by our third author, in her undergraduate thesis (which we've included here). Although it won international awards at the time, it has never received the circulation and exposure it deserved. And because the lead author's current posting didn't (and does not) have an attached graduate program, it wasn't possible to continue the collaboration as she has moved on to her doctoral studies.

Bits and pieces continued to be assembled by the lead author, and regularly teaching a course in Native Suicidology allowed him to keep up with the literature and even write large portions of this book as parts of lectures given. But it wasn't until the arrival of the second author that the book began to assemble itself. The second author hates disorder and does not tolerate it even in a thesis supervisor; so, as if she was completing a gigantic jig-saw puzzle, the various pieces went into the framework the lead author had developed 20 years before but hadn't put to proper use. Our second author is also a voracious reader; it was in her going through the collection of books and papers the lead author had assembled, and in being pushed along by her own thesis requirements, that the mess began to look like something.

Undergraduate students have the disadvantage of not knowing a lot about specific topics, but they have the advantage of the naiveté that goes with that lack; in short, they ask questions and demand answers where someone too close to the work has already moved past those concerns. Students in two courses in this last academic year (2014) put aside other concerns to concentrate on specific topics that have become parts of our Chapter 4; their efforts are acknowledged in this work, on the title page for that chapter.

Readers may discern that this book is, in reality, part of a much larger project. When serious work began, portions of this larger project kept intruding so frequently that for a time we considered writing a "super-book," to get it all down at once. But finally we decided to cut our work on indigenous suicide away from its sister works on (1) Canadian racism, (2) an alternative approach to psychological issues (autochthonology), and (3) methodology. Not only would the whole thing, taken together, have been unwieldy in the extreme, it would have put back the release of our work on Native suicide.

That would have been irresponsible on our part. The suicide plague is not going away, and, if there's anything to what we're saying, there are good reasons it's here to stay. We believe — and in here we argue — that the reactions to that plague now must change in fundamental ways. Even if we're wrong, it's time the conversation concerning "what's wrong with Indians" takes a different direction.

We take our audience to be *indigenous individuals with some concern (personal, professional, or otherwise) with the issue of Native suicide.* If our suspicion is right, this target audience can be reduced to *indigenous individuals.* We don't care if other, non-indigenous people read our work; we're concerned with Native people facing the challenge of unnecessary deaths, of themselves or of others around them. Our goal is to prevent such deaths, for at least long enough for the people involved to reach an understanding of what is really happening; for "reflection is a famous foe of violence," even self-violence.

Sooner or later we know we're going to hear the complaint that our work is "too difficult," "hard to understand," and that it "uses words that are too big." Well, tough. We're writing about life and death here, not an Archie comic book. Does anyone pretend that "the solution" to the "Native suicide crisis," even if our book isn't it, is going to be the intellectual equivalent of half an hour with Dr. Phil? Yes, it's hard; yes, it's going to take time to go through it; and yes, at least some of you are going to have to consult your dictionary. But the three of us are on the internet and we promise to answer our emails, as best we can.

Besides that, the people who complain our work is too difficult "for Indians" are making some extraordinary claims about Indians. If they really mean to say it's too difficult for *them*, then they should just say that rather than insult the whole lot of us. In any event, we *don't* think it's *too* difficult to understand. Yes, it's difficult. So will resolving any of the issues facing us indigenous peoples. But we either do the work or give up now.

Since we're focused on indigenous peoples — service providers, band officials, individuals with friends they worry about, individuals who worry about themselves — we don't much care about what others will have to say about this work. We have no intention to "defend" our beliefs, or argue about our analyses and conclusions. It's all there in black and white. And if you think we're wrong, then write your own book. If anyone claims they don't understand us and would like us to elaborate or explain, that's fine. That goes for Native and non-Native people alike. But we have no intention whatsoever to acknowledge mindless drivel, or to become mired in it; we have better things to do (for example, our books on racism and autochthonology).

This work has been accomplished without the support of any "official" institution.

We would like to thank our families, friends, and students for having put up with us during the trying period during which this work was completed.

August 20, 2014

DYING TO PLEASE YOU:

INDIGENOUS SUICIDE IN CONTEMPORARY CANADA

Chapter 1, Everything Old is Old Again

"Death Does Not End A Relationship"

Today and every day in Canada some Native woman, man, girl, or boy will die needlessly, perhaps by his or her own hand. That death won't just "touch" the friends and family members who were united in that individual: it will obliterate the relationships that existed and then demand that they be reconstructed on entirely different terms. Those relationships, as Robert Anderson observed, "struggle on in the survivor's mind toward some resolution which it may never find." To a great extent this is because the deceased is no longer there to assist us; but even were he or she present, there is no guarantee that closure could be achieved.

The evasiveness of definitive answers is particularly poignant when the death is self-inflicted. A death achieved by the deceased's own hand raises a host of issues, "why?" perhaps being the most persistent one that confronts us. Other issues — when, where, how, etc. — are obviously compelling to a host of different kinds of professionals, but "why?" isn't just a scientific question; for those of us left on this side of life, it almost scolds us. Why did "X" do it? Why wasn't I there to stop "X?" Why did "X" commit *suicide*, and not do something else? Why did this have to happen? This form of expression is less a search for a scientific answer to a clinical question than it is the expression of a yearning to understand.

In this work our aim is more to gratify the yearning than it is to satisfy the science, although we don't think the two programs necessarily conflict. Our parochial interest is self-inflicted death — suicide — in indigenous peoples in the geopolitical region widely known as Canada. We are arrogant enough to believe that what we have to say will bear on other populations in other lands, but we're neither intellectually nor emotionally invested beyond the limits we've specified here. Native individuals have been taking their own lives for some time now, and we think it high time real answers were given to real questions.

A Thousand Words on Indian Suicide

That is not to say that there aren't already plenty of answers out there. It is not difficult to find a large, perhaps (given the size of the indigenous population in Canada) even disproportionate, literature on Native suicide dating back 40 years or more. And its origin is surprising at least, if not downright mysterious.

Neither of us has any idea what the graph comparing Indian to non-Indian suicide rates was doing in the 1978 Department of Indian Affairs and Northern Development Annual Report,[1] but this picture is easily the single most compelling graphic ever produced concerning Native suicide. As we shall have cause to point out, there is good reason not to take the graph entirely at face value. Nevertheless, it is as hard now as it was then to dismiss the divergence between the two lines as some kind of statistical glitch. All subsequent summaries of Native/non-Native differences in suicide rates have reflected in a real way (and to a similar degree) its original result that indigenous peoples, depending on age and other demographic features, are three to ten times more likely to commit suicide than their non-indigenous age peers.

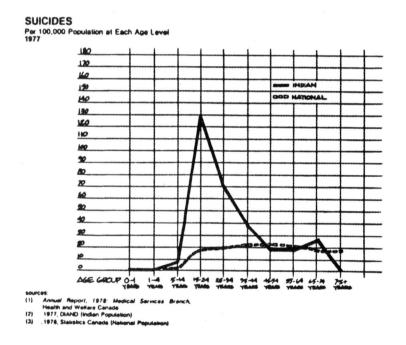

Figure 1. Graph comparing Indian and National suicide levels from 1978 DIAND Annual Report.

It was not just a conversation-stopper, it was an action-starter. It is likely that all along, at some level of consciousness, officialdom was aware of Native suicide as an issue; after all, suicides within specific

---

1   We hereby thank the person or persons responsible.

populations (for example, the Home Children) had previously been flash-points with respect to Canadian policy-making. And any data as detailed as presented in the 1978 report is unlikely to have dropped fully-formed from heaven. Even if it had, there would have been no necessity to include it in a report aimed largely at praising federal policy initiatives and successes; as a matter of fact, nowadays the pressure might well be to cover up this kind of information. So, the person or persons including the suicide graph in the report not only made it clear *that there was a problem*: they were announcing that at least some force within the federal government *was prepared to encourage action with regard to it.*

It was a propitious time for many: hairdressers were turning into cosmetologists, bartenders were mutating into mixologists, and the recently-contrived, self-certified discipline of suicidology was formalizing itself. Although various professionals had, by necessity, encountered suicide (and even Native suicide) as a feature of their day-to-day activities, the varied streams of results from numerous disciplines (social work, anthropology, psychiatry, psychology, epidemiology, etc.) had by the early '70's converged into its own specialization. The newly-identified "problem" of Native suicide thus had a pertinent, ostensibly scientific discipline already poised to spring into action with regard to it.

As with us here, the *why question* dominated, likely because, implicitly and explicitly, both lay and professional individuals assume then as now that knowing *why* something happens will tell us *what to do* to make it stop (or at least slow it down). Professionals, when working within their own disciplines, had for years been developing their ideas and had been discussing them at conferences and in journals; and with the advent of "suicidology" those preconceptions formed the core of what, even today, are offered as the reasons people kill themselves. In the next chapters we will selectively review the application of these answers to *why indigenous individuals* end their own lives, but it is important to understand at the outset that there was a comprehensive bias built in to these answers: Native suicide could be reduced to the same system of mechanics and dynamics being developed with respect to non-Native suicide. In other words, it has been assumed all along that Indians commit suicide for the same reasons everyone else did, only all the more so.

To be sure, we have a certain amount of sympathy for this viewpoint. After all, we Native people are *people*, too, first and foremost.

To presume that something entirely different was going on with us (causing us to commit suicide for different reasons and in different ways from the rest of humanity) would not just be a form of mystical racism. It would also call into question the capacity of suicidology to investigate the phenomenon, since it would, of necessity, be outside their experience and their forms of investigation (sort of like asking a plumber to fix your television...).

On the other hand, as we shall show the presumption that modern suicidology has everything well in hand (especially about people with whom they have no real connection) is in keeping with that sort of western intellectual imperialism that has not just entirely misrepresented and misunderstood Native peoples, it has invited and coerced us into misunderstanding ourselves. "In keeping" is the important qualification; does acceptance of a specific useful technology ("suicide science" in this example) commit one to adopt the entire program of intellectual imperialism? At issue is the status of the answers provided by suicidology: are they *science* — like gravity or temperature or atom bombs are science — or just the current fashion, like with hair-dos and drinks?

The Broken Indian

Science or not, suicidology has chosen to reformulate the question: "Why are Indians killing themselves at such high rates?" as "What's wrong with Indians that makes them want to kill themselves at such high rates?" When placed side-by-side these are obviously very different questions, and we can already hear the objections from various researchers that they do no such thing. We beg to differ, and we will make our case in time. Objections notwithstanding, the tendency to cast the "Indian suicide problem" as some function of our own peculiarities is so common (we are tempted to characterize it as *universal*) that here we will call it the **Broken Indian Model**. Simply, the model presumes that deficiencies or defects or shortcomings *in us* are responsible for our acts of suicide. The basic task of "suicide science," then, is to discover the responsible defect(s). Once that's done, discussions can be held to decide, first, whether there is anything that *can* be done about it and second, whether *real* Canadians should *bother doing it*.

The next chapters will, after raising background issues of which we should all be aware (Chapter 2), be spent first examining a representative selection of Broken Indian explanations for our levels of suicide (Chapter 3) and then having a long hard look at what is often taken as the most likely explanation (Chapter 4) before we detail our own thinking in Chapter 5 and Chapter 6. But, since we've seen fit to preview (and even call into question) much of what already has been written about Native suicide, we see no reason to avoid making our own position known at the outset.

In fact this is easy to do, since the lead author made it public at a suicidology conference over 20 years ago now. The current co-authors share and endorse that position, and the present work in many ways merely elaborates and restates it. Its appearance in the lead author's previous book on Indian residential schooling makes no difference, since nobody paid any attention to it then, either. But, *plus ça change*. What follows is a slightly revised version of the original statement:

> While there had been more than moderate awareness for some time, suicide in North American indigenous communities began to gain attention in higher governmental and policy making circles in the early 1980's (Syer-Solursh, 1987). In recent years, aboriginal suicide has been the specific subject of a number of investigations; the sheer volume of these and other relevant works makes their close analysis the task for another venue. Here we will look at a relatively concentrated statement we consider problematic *and* typical, taken from the ***Focus Group on Suicide*** of the Native Psychologists in Canada. We should point out that selections from many similar works could have been used instead.
>
> The underlying **Philosophy** guiding their work appears on page 3 of the collected presentations. Suicide is "the final self-destructive act of despair, committed while in a state of hopelessness and depression." Young Aboriginal men are "unable to find meaning in their lives," "feel abandoned by their culture," "ease their pain and frustration" with drugs and alcohol, and end up worsening "their mental state." The immediate disruption suicide causes in Aboriginal communities should be treated by "qualified individuals," while long-term solutions must "break the cycle of abuse, denial, and despair." Programs

directed at heading off "crisis situations," preventing "substance abuse and neglect of children," and improving "recreational activities" are necessary, and school-based interventions teaching "confidence, self-worth, and coping skills" are indicated. All-in-all, the fundamental underlying assumptions of the Native Psychologists do not differ in any significant way from earlier, more generic summaries of the underlying bases of Indian suicide: Indians suffer from low self-esteem, are depressed and hopeless, drink too much, seem unable to adapt to the institutions (like education) of mainstream society, feel alienated from society at large, come from unstable home environments, and suffer from personal financial difficulties. In combination, these factors have helped to bring about a suicide rate for indigenous peoples that has been and (for nobody knows how long) remains at least four or five times the national average, at least for some age groups.

What's wrong with this picture? To get a simple and direct overview of the difficulties, allow us to take you back 70-80 years in time and jump to another continent. During the Nightmare Years (1933 to 1945), the suicide rate of German Jews is conservatively estimated to have been at least two or three times higher than the rate for German citizens in general, and during the years of intensive removal to concentration camps (1943 to 1945) it was at least **50** times the rate for non-Jewish Germans (Hilberg, 1992). As appalling as these figures are, we don't consider that they tax the limits of human understanding. "Yes, the facts are horrifying," we say, "but completely understandable given what was going on." Another group that wasn't surprised was the Nazi government, which was embarrassed by the information, tried to suppress it nationally and internationally, and who embarked upon a campaign of having Jewish religious leaders extol their congregations to "tough it out." *Not one* social scientific study was designed or conducted to establish why the Jews were behaving in such a fashion, nor was there any apparent urge to uncover the "inner dynamics" of Jewish suicide.

Now suppose that one of today's Nazi rehabilitationists undertook to account for this particular historical "embarrassment" by arguing that Jews in Nazi Germany suffered from (1) personal financial problems; (2) fear of going outside; (3) anxiety about being identified with their ethnic group; (4) low self-esteem; (5) feelings of alienation from their mainstream society; and (6) unstable family lives. Would any but the already-perverted entertain even for a moment these proposals? Even at the time of this outrage, the Nazis didn't have the gall to retreat into such explanations, which, in 1944, would have had the additional "advantage" of being complementary to an already prevalent dogma of Jewish racial inferiority.

How easy it has become for the social scientists of today to do what even the Nazis couldn't bring themselves to do. In truth, does not the history of Jewish suicide during the holocaust, like the histories of suicide in the Arawaks, the Home Children, and the Marshallese Islanders, and countless other oppressed groups, teach us that suicide is in part a *normal human reaction to conditions of prolonged, ruthless domination*? The predominant depiction of suicide in Aboriginal Peoples inhabiting Canada rhetorically neglects these parallels, biasing those trying to come to grips with the phenomenon away from the readily apparent and into esoteric realms. "Models" of Indian suicide are individualistic, relying on supposed internal characteristics instead of looking at the inverted pyramid of social, economic, and political forces impinging upon Aboriginal Peoples. Existing explanations blame the victim, finding that they suffer from personal adjustment problems or emotional deficiencies like "low self-esteem" and "depression." None of the existing Just-So Stories alleviate the situation by acting or suggesting action against the forces of oppression; they don't even recognize them. The cost-effectiveness of the government's providing perfunctory, end-of-pipe social intervention programs instead of meeting their contractual treaty obligations doesn't surface as an issue. And the people charged with "doing something" about Aboriginal suicide accept this limited frame of reference and repeat the irrelevancies of their masters. In total, the "search" for the "individual differences" that differentiate suicide attempters and succeeders from those who are neither is morally comparable to the social scientist who looks for the "individual differences" that predict length of survival in a concentration camp. "Treatment" within such a model is convincing the inmates to accept their situations.

However, in the real world, the "proper treatment" for the "Jewish Suicide Problem" wasn't to send cheerleaders into what remained of their communities; it was the elimination of the system of unspeakable cruelty that destroyed their lives. And the "proper treatment" for the "Indian Suicide Problem" isn't to send cheerleaders into *our* communities; it is the elimination of the system that is destroying *our* lives.

We shall have occasion throughout this book to return to this statement, since it does a good job of summarizing the issues we think most important while it provides a context for understanding Native suicide that isn't reflected in the work that's out there. The fact that we now feel compelled to write an entire book spelling out in excruciating detail something already done sufficiently (in our opinion) says something, we feel, about the ideological clash that is reflected in Native suicidology. But for now, the two sides of the issue at least have been identified.

DYING TO PLEASE YOU:

INDIGENOUS SUICIDE IN CONTEMPORARY CANADA

Chapter 2, The Devil in the Details:
Preliminary Considerations

Cleaning Up Beforehand

We sympathise with those who want to get to the substance of our work as quickly as possible, which is why in the introductory chapter we sketched out our position as well as that of mainstream suicidology. Clearly, these thumbnails were not intended to do justice either to our approach or to those we wish to challenge. To be fair to everyone, however, and provide characterizations with even a little depth, either a certain amount of background information has to be taken for granted (which we think would be overly presumptuous of us) or it must be provided (which would require the investment of time and effort). In the present chapter we begin the latter process. A fair presentation of the mainstream theories, and an appreciation of our objections to them, requires familiarity with topics like background assumptions, specialized vocabulary, and so on. In the larger sense these are comparatively minor points, but they are pressing enough to be given the better part of this chapter and the next.

We grant that some may find this tiresome; most people we envision as being our audience are probably eager to "get on with it" and have us start elaborating our own position. We think this is entirely the wrong attitude. First, unless we eliminate whatever lurking (and unrecognized) commitments people may have to the previous positions we think it would be harder for them to accept something entirely different. All things considered, it's better to move the old couch out of the living room than to straightaway try to get the new one in. Second, we are, after all, writing about *suicide*, and, ultimately, it is our aim to contribute (as far as we possibly can) to its *eradication*. We think that it is worth every effort there is to make this happen, regardless of how difficult it may be for all involved. We don't doubt that even the people who take positions in opposition to ours would prefer followers with a critical, thoughtful allegiance rather than blind obedience to some obscure doctrine.

And maybe we should take a moment to remind everyone that the two of us are in no position whatsoever to do anything with our critique: we can't advertise it, issue directives, outlaw other viewpoints, implement programs consistent with our thinking, etc. This also describes many if not most (or even all) of the suicidologists we will review; any influence they have or may have had concerning the creation of programs of intervention in Native suicide is likely to have been *advisory*. This is but to say that researchers, in any field, only make recommendations; political and economic institutions (which we are not) implement policies and programs, and those policies and programs may or may not be consistent with recommendations they may either entertain or ignore.

All this is but to say: *the difference between our approaches and those we will review (and reject) is not a popularity contest.* If our thinking is correct and we fail to convince our readers of this, *people will die, needlessly and prematurely.* If our thinking is wrong and we succeed in convincing our readers anyway, *people will die, needlessly and prematurely...* and so on (we hope you're following our drift). If we're wrong we do not wish to convert you to our point of view; and we have *no doubt whatsoever* that the suicide theorists we review have an identical commitment.

It is you, our reader, who is in a position different from mainstream suicidologists and the two of us: you are in the position to do something about Native suicide, even if (may gods forefend) it is limited to just your own. So let's do it the hard way. We pray that you adopt the care and seriousness assumed by those of us who write about suicide; that you bring all your powers of evaluation to bear on reaching correct conclusions about why indigenous peoples are killing themselves and what should be done to stop it.

People will still die; that is, after all, the nature of life. But we won't die needlessly and prematurely.

What Is Suicide?

Recognizing suicide. "Suicide" is one of those words thrown around as if everyone knows what it refers to — you know, straightforward dictionary definitions like "killing yourself" — but which gets more complicated the longer you think about it. For example, many people can kill themselves in ways not considered suicide (as in car accidents), so "something else" must be at work that makes a death a *suicide*. Killing yourself with the *intention* to kill yourself is often proposed as the key, but that is its own can of worms: no one, and we mean no one, has ever seen an intention or ever will. Even in the strictest circumstances, intentions must be inferred; that is, deduced from facts and circumstances that *can* be observed (as when judges or juries determine whether there was an *intention to kill* in deciding whether a death was manslaughter or murder). Proper facts and circumstances are not always available (and particularly not in *suicide*, when the prime witness is deceased) and are themselves open to contradictory interpretations (e.g., did he *know* the gun was loaded?). And, anyway, who would argue that "intentionally" jumping out of a burning building to escape fire and smoke and subsequently falling to one's death qualifies as a death by suicide? Or that an "intention to die" isn't at least partly at work when someone jumps off a bridge after taking out a multi-million dollar life insurance policy?

In real life, the average person is never responsible for concluding that a particular death is suicide; so when confronted by these and similar complexities we're usually content to "leave it to the experts." But the experts are neither omniscient nor unbiased in their conclusions. Deciding that a death was or was not "suicide" has always had *religious* (e.g., denying ceremonial and/or burial rights to individuals so designated), *legal* (in England, until 1961, people unsuccessful in suicide were criminally prosecuted and even sentenced to death), *probative* (insurance premiums may be invalidated), or *familial* ("the gun went off accidentally" has comforted more than one family) consequences, and more (Szasz, 1999). If that were not enough, consider that the finding "death by suicide" frequently has been abused, as in an uncountable number of cases of murder by lynching, police brutality/neglect, political upheaval, and numerous other occasions of the convenient deaths of dismissible persons. And finally, consider that disguising a murder to look like a suicide is not just a plot device in mystery stories.

The average person has the impression that identifying suicides is similar to identifying constellations: something easy enough to do with guidelines and practice. This is far from the case. There is no "touchstone" which experts use to distinguish suicides from other kinds of deaths, which is one reason we advised against taking the DIAND graph in Chapter 1 at face value. In fact, we think all such graphs and the statistics they're drawn from must be viewed with scepticism, as they necessarily incorporate a certain amount of noise (as we will continue to demonstrate here).

"Suicide" is a concept, not an object with observable characteristics (Smith and Chrisjohn, 2002/2017, *infra*). We must see that it is a word *we, the living* use to make sense of the circumstances we encounter. As such, we can be biased, misled, inept, misinformed, distracted, and, yes, even occasionally correct in its application.

Defining suicide. Suicidologists at the beginning of their expositions often undertake to *define* what it is they will henceforth call "a suicide." Previously proposed definitions might be examined, found inadequate, and thus provide a rationale for a new and improved definition. Or, a contorted set of circumstances may be imagined and the failure of existing definitions to say whether the death in that situation is "really" a suicide forms the basis for proposing an improvement. We consider the "champion" of such contorted circumstances currently to be: someone with suicidal intent places a time-delayed bomb in his house to explode in a month, then leaves his residence only to receive a head injury in a car accident which induces amnesia; and, upon returning to his premises semi-recovered, is blown up in the explosion he no longer anticipates or desires (Anderberg, 1989). Would that be a suicide??

Resolution of such concerns are well beyond our interests. Some Native suicides could conceivably be that obscure, but their clarification might at best influence one or two suicides per year, and we've already made it clear we don't consider the pursuit of precise suicide rates a proper use of our time. As well, we think the quest for "definitional purity" misunderstands the actual purpose of a definition: it is to specify as clearly as possible what one is, and is not, going to *consider* to be "a suicide" for the purposes of the inquiry being made. Some theorists, we will find, are perfectly willing to leave the problem of definition to others and will base their analyses on what other individuals have defined as suicide, accurately or not. And others will work to include finer and more obscure distinctions, as above. It gets worse.

The word *suicide* is itself a relatively recent (circa 1651) word, one not available to Shakespeare, for instance, or he well might have used it in *Hamlet, Julius Caesar*, and several other pieces. It is considered a rather clumsy attempt at making up a *Latinized* expression for the behavior of self-terminating Europeans of that time, in that the Romans themselves never even had a word for it (Daube, 1977) nor even anything like the modern world's conception of suicide (for example, financially desperate people could and did sell stones in public areas for people to throw at them to stone them to death, so they could provide for their heirs with the proceeds; no part of this was either unusual or considered illegal). If told that suicide is a "natural phenomenon," you should consider no one in human history seems to have noticed it for quite a long time or thought it important enough to give it a name.

For a modern concept, "suicide" carries an enormous amount of baggage along with it. For example, it has often been spoken of as the most personal act one can perform, but a survey of its employment shows that suicide is something, apparently, that can be committed by an entire country; a political party; an entire religion; a human racial (sic) group; one's brain; multinational corporations; shoes; military squads; various types of animals and insects; "the intellect;" cultures; professions; and other entities. You might object that at least some of these "suicide performers" are only *metaphorically* on this list. But that merely reaffirms the definitional problems that arise in trying to draw a line demarcating "real suicides" from "bogus, non-suicides."

Suicide is a *pejorative* term, in spite of all attempts to naturalize (if not normalize) it. This has been traced (Szasz, 1999 & 2011) to ecclesiastical influences after the fall of Rome, when church doctrine stipulated that one's life belonged to god and that taking it was therefore a kind of murderous theft. *Self-murder* consequently became established (and has afterward remained) as another synonym for suicide. It was doubtless religious authority that induced laws such as those in England (already mentioned), where attempted suicide was criminalized to the extent of carrying with it the death penalty. Eventually, the only way to avoid this punishment was to establish (claim?) that the perpetrator was *deranged*, not in his/her "right mind," and therefore not criminally responsible for his/her actions (Marsh, 2010). This defense enabled the replacement of religious adjudication of the miscreant as "selfish," "weak-willed," "irresponsible," or "heretical" with psychiatry's bestowal of "crazy," though of course both these retained aspects of moral judgments. This can most easily be seen in the still-current appraisal of suicide as "the coward's way out."

The "psychiatrization" of suicide was at best a mixed blessing. It is hard to see how stigmatizing suicidal individuals as "crazy" rather than "sinful" was an advance, as, despite all efforts to the contrary, people who are or who have been under psychiatric care, or medication, or incarceration, are still widely held to be abnormal, dangerous, "mentally sick," etc., and to be treated with suspicion. The move from religious to psychiatric dominance was, most assuredly, *not* accomplished because of scientific discoveries or advancements in knowledge, but by the well-established, old-fashioned methods of blather, bombast, and empty rhetoric (Marsh, 2010); in effect, early psychiatry *bullied its way* into predominance over religion rather than earning its position.

One of the clearest ways to see how moral judgment and insanity continues to inhere in the term is in how western media have employed the concepts of "kamikaze" or "suicide" pilots in WWII and "suicide bombers" in the modern Near East. Clearly, the term is meant to suggest that only crazed fanatics — a variety of insanely irrational individuals — could have been responsible for the action being reported. The possibility that there are groups of people in the world who have grievances sufficiently deeply abiding to warrant (to them, anyway) such action never arises as a possibility. This requires an intense and excessive absence of the knowledge of history… which, thankfully, the same media helpfully supplies. But the abject, wholesale dismissal of these inconceivable actions — unless done by a selfless GI undertaking a "suicide mission" or brave Israelites resisting the evil Roman Empire — could not be accomplished without the slur attached to the word "suicide" in the first place.

Then what is it? We are still not clear of the word's encumbrances. We have already noted that there are in common use synonyms and synonymic phrases for suicide, "self-murder" and "the coward's way out" being just two. A look at suicidology texts and articles produces more than a few additional phrases, such as "self-destructive behavior," "self-harm," "self-injury," and "self-accomplished death." A look at the content of the literature with these newer formulations reveals that they address not just what we would, ordinarily and naïvely, consider suicide (death after a person's actions or inactions), but behaviors that depart considerably from that yardstick, such as: self-mutilation, failure to take prescribed medication, drug and alcohol use, prostitution, smoking, failure to exercise, and adopting "lifestyle choices" deemed (by the author of whatever particular piece) "unhealthy in the long term." What is going on here?

Well, to our mind, at least some of this expansion is warranted. The concept of *parasuicide* has not only been around for some time, it makes a great deal of sense. It is the notion that it's possible to commit suicide in "slow motion," so to speak, by engaging in behavior (like smoking) that even a reclusive optimist must by now realize leads inevitably to slow, lingering death. Tobacco use (particularly factory-farmed, pesticide-soaked tobacco) does everything that cigarette packages tell you it will do. Alcohol use, dubious under even the best of circumstances (we lose perhaps thousands of central nervous system cells every day by natural processes; a good drinking binge can multiply that by 100 times over), amounts to self-destruction when practiced with a diagnosed cirrhotic liver, or diabetes, or a pancreatic ulcer, or many other conditions. And limiting your exercise program to the continuous stuffing of your festering gob with empty, salt-and-sugar-laden calories is well known to be dangerous (as is the practice of throwing it all up later).

But, while the argument that some behaviors amount to "killing oneself in slow motion" has merit, it is impossible in practice to take such deaths into account *as* suicides. This is because the ways of dying from "slow suicide" behaviors are indistinguishable from *just dying* (via heart attacks, perforated ulcers, cirrhotic livers, and a thousand other ways). The DIAND graph given in the first chapter, then, has to be "wrong" in an absolute sense, since at least some people alive in those days (both Native and non-Native) must have died slow, lingering, self-inflicted deaths, but weren't listed as "suicides" anywhere. (Here's another reason to take such data as "informative" rather than "definitive.")

While we lament the difficulties of broadening the notion of suicide for some cases, other cases we're not so sure about. Take "self-mutilation" as an example. "Death by one's own hand" necessarily involves inflicting injury to the natural form and function of the body, some of these injuries (say, from hanging or self-laceration) being more obvious than others.

Now, some people attempting to end her/his life have been interrupted in their actions — these are known as *attempted* suicides. Further, it is strongly held by suicidologists that some of these attempts at suicide were disingenuous in some sense, such as: the person realized he/she would be interrupted before the act was completed. These are known as suicide *gestures*. Finally, consider that it is possible that specific actions are known to be sub-lethal... insufficient to actually cause death, at least in the immediate term... and that someone could knowingly adopt a sub-lethal method of self-harm as a gesture, rather than a "genuine" attempt at suicide. So, someone who intentionally inflicts a slight, non-lethal laceration wound should be considered a kind of failed-attempted-parasuicide, which in fact is a suicide.

In the space of one short paragraph we've become as convoluted as the amnesic self-bomber at the beginning of the previous section. Including self-mutilations, forgetting to take one's meds, renting out one's body, and similar actions as kinds of parasuicide has stretched the category we're hoping to address out of all recognition. Are we to think that anyone who doesn't strictly follow the prescribed regimen for maximum longevity should be included in the category of "deaths by suicide" after they die? Are people with tattoos and piercings, or who don't jog for 45 minutes every morning, or who enjoy an occasional glass of wine at a meal with friends (where they put *butter* or *sour cream* on their baked potatoes!) just kinds of low-level slow suicides? Asserting some kind of underlying connection between behaviors that, descriptively, are readily distinguishable is a kind of metaphysics (that is, an assertion of knowledge of something that *cannot* be known, like what god's nickname is, or whether you have to pay for parking in heaven) called "contempt for the individual" case by Wittgenstein (1951/2009). Such assertions are merely that: groundless blather, an attempt to insinuate a point of view without being able to provide evidence for it.

Of course, some of this *has to be granted!* We can follow the logic that, someone who is seriously suicidal may for various reasons be incapable of "doing it right the first time," and may end up with the consequences (both physical and psychic) of the unsuccessful attempt. We are also well aware of circumstances where people, returning from alcohol-buying trips to town, have perished in car crashes due to driving recklessly along universally-acknowledged perilous roads, where afterwards their deaths become recorded as "automobile accidents." The principle that some actions, dancing on the wrong side of the line between life and death, end up recorded in the wrong statistical column isn't that difficult to grasp.

We sincerely hope such individuals will be identified before meeting their ultimate fate and be given, with respect and diligence, whatever help she/he wants and needs. But working backwards from that scenario is simply unjustifiable; a person who obsessively slits his/her own forearms, for example, isn't necessarily "an incipient case" of someone who must eventually slash his/her own wrists, nor must there be there the embryonic nugget of later self-destruction buried somewhere in his/her psyche. To believe this, and worse, to insinuate that there is an underlying unity by the artifice of debasing already difficult distinctions, are ideological presumptions that reflect the way suicide is understood by modern suicidology. We shall clarify, extend, and justify this judgment at length later in this work. But for now, please hold in mind the points we've tried to make thus far about the definition of suicide:

> 1) suicide isn't an object with identifiable characteristics: it is a concept, that is, a word or phrase *each of us* uses or applies to try to make some sense of our experience;

> 2) the concept of suicide, which is comparatively modern, carries moral ("sinful") and ideological ("insane") associations that must be recognized as such and not treated as if scientific facts;

> 3) the definition of suicide can be made so broad and all-inclusive ("self-harm") that it ceases to exist as a useful concept, or at the very least, obscures the actions we wish to address.

Formal Definitions of Suicide

We are not going to make any attempt to survey comprehensively the existing definitions of suicide; for one thing, as Wekstein (1979), Shneidman (1985), and others have noted, there are a lot of them. For another, definitions overlap as different suicidologists accept and reject various proposals among themselves. Our aim here is, at best, to give a representative sampling of definitions of suicide from some of the theoretical orientations in current use.

At the risk of exhausting whatever good will our reader still has, we must point out two more refinements. Once again, no suicidologist undertakes to explain *all* suicides. As we've noted previously, definitions of suicide are the specifications of exactly what type of deaths one is presuming to explain, which means that, because they're working with (perhaps slightly, perhaps enormously) different definitions, any two suicidologists won't necessarily be trying to explain the same kinds of deaths or explain them in the same way. Instead, it is largely agreed that *suicides come in different kinds. Suicide typologies,* or compilations of its presumed different kinds, are the offspring of the interaction between (1) *defining the act of suicide* and (2) *expounding a theory of suicide.* Typologies are, as we shall see, quite common.

Second, no suicidologist undertakes to explain *all* suicides. This sounds like what we just said, but this time we want to emphasize that no suicidologist is so deluded as to believe she/he can explain everything. (This will include us.) If nothing else will do it, a stiff belt of reality will induce humility in even the most autocratic researcher.

What all our warnings and asides will eventually come down to is this: what has suicidology actually worked out about why indigenous peoples commit suicide? Before looking at that in greater detail, however, we will have a look at what suicidologists *say* they're explaining.

Durkheim's Approach. Durkheim (1897/1966), a founder of the field of sociology and the author of an early monograph about suicide, exemplifies the points we just made. Being more concerned with establishing sociology as an academic discipline separate from others (such as psychology), his definition of suicide both demarcated a limited field of the phenomenon and established a corresponding typology.

It was his contention that, although "mental flaws" (as studied by psychologists) might well describe and account for individual cases of suicide, national rates of suicide — which tended to be stable over long periods of time, but which varied from nation to nation and within nation during periods of certain kinds of turmoil — suggested that other forces, *social facts* in his terminology, had a kind of persistent, background influence (like the connection between environmental pollutants and ill-health). Mental flaws, whatever they were, were, according to him, not the subject matter of sociology, and so his definition explicitly tried to eliminate reference to possible psychological aspects of suicide:

> We [sic] may say conclusively [sic]: the term *suicide is applied to all cases of death resulting directly or indirectly from a positive or negative act of the victim himself* [sic], *which he* [sic] *knows will produce this result.* An attempt is an act thus defined but falling short of actual death (Durkheim, 1897/1966, p. 44).

We will merely note at this point the *failure* of Durkheim to avoid any psychological aspects, since this definition refers to *knowledge* the successful suicidal person has, something Durkheim — and nobody else, for that matter — can possibly access (especially after the person is dead).

In addition, Durkheim proposes the first suicide typology; that is, his position that social forces (or social facts) can account for the historical and contemporary rates of suicide suggested to him that these social forces subtended different forms of suicidal acts. Since we are sympathetic to the general notion that social factors are most important in explaining Native suicide, we will return to Durkheim's approach in Chapter 4. Here we will give only the briefest outline of his position.

The social forces he nominated for influencing nations' suicide rates were *regulation* and *integration*, and these forces gave rise to *egoistic, altruistic, and anomic* types of suicide. A fourth type, *fatalistic*, was deemed insignificant and banished to a single footnote. Durkheim and his modern followers only make use of the first three forms (van Hooff, 2000; Wekstein, 1979).

Shneidman's Work. Shneidman was "present at creation" of the discipline of suicidology in 1968, and if the word/conception wasn't his own creation, he was well-placed to put a stop to it if he was so inclined. In contrast to Durkheim, Shneidman's approach to understanding suicide was explicitly and overwhelmingly psychological: "Even though I know that each suicidal death is a multifaceted event... I retain the belief that, in the proper distillation of the event, its essential nature is *psychological* (Shneidman, 1996, p. 5)."

> Currently in the Western world [sic] suicide is a conscious act of self-induced annihilation [sic], best understood as a multidimensional malaise [sic] in a needful individual who defines an issue for which suicide is perceived as the best solution (Shneidman, 1985, p. 203).

He also asserts:

> Anguish or disturbance or perturbation is caused by pain, sometimes physical pain, but more often psychological pain. Psychological pain is the basic ingredient of suicide. (But there's a lot more.) Suicide is never born out of exaltation or joy; it is a child of the negative emotions. But in order to begin to understand *suicide*, we need to think about what anguish means, as well as why people entertain thoughts of death, especially death as

a way of stopping unbearable misery. Suicidal death, in other words, as an escape from pain. Perturbation and lethality are the bad parents of human self-destruction (Shneidman, 1996, p. 6 - 7).

There is more from the same source, but this plane has already departed from the Land of Clarity. We don't blame you if you're confused here. Is he talking about an interrelated set of phenomena, a family tree, or baking a cake... or is he just babbling? Never mind. He probably was very tired.

Characteristic of psychological approaches is his assertion that personal, internal, individual, AND INVISIBLE *gremlins* of the mind are responsible for the behavior of interest. That is, the same self-assurance evident in the examples abstracted from the Focus Group of Native Psychologists (Chapter 1) is at play here. This is in sharp contrast to the kinds of things Durkheim emphasized in his approach; it may be difficult to pinpoint a start time to wars, economic downturns, and the like, but they're fairly obvious once they're in operation.

Szasz's Position. Thomas Szasz, a psychiatrist, was an outspoken critic of psychiatry (charging, for example, that it misrepresented moral and ethical issues as if they were scientific ones), discerning long before Marsh (2010) that the move from ecclesiastical to psychological and medical metaphors ("mental illness") was accomplished through bad logic and without the benefit of any evidence (Szasz, 1961; 1970). He wrote two books in his lifetime specifically on the subject of suicide (Szasz, 1999 & 2011), although it came up as a subsidiary issue in many other of his works.

Szasz defined suicide with admirable clarity:

> I use the word "suicide" to refer to taking one's own life voluntarily and deliberately, either by killing oneself directly or by abstaining from a directly life-saving act; in other words, I regard any behavior motivated by a preference for death over life that leads directly (perhaps only after a lapse of several days) to the cessation of one's life as suicide (Szasz, 1999, p. 2).

An important feature of his approach to suicide was his opinion that *suicide is a human right*, and that interference with its successful completion — say, by diagnosing a person as insane and depriving him/her of the capacity to carry out the deed by incarceration or by the administration of drugs — was an unwarranted intrusion into personal liberty. This is an important and unique perspective, in that (1) it provides a political perspective on what is ordinarily taken as a purely individual and mental one, and (2) it takes a diametrically opposed position from existing ones on the desirability of suicide intervention. We will look at his position again in the last chapter of this work.

Suicide Epidemiology. An important treatment of the issue, "what is a suicide," is to leave its resolution to others and go forward with whatever it was you were doing. The epidemiological approach to suicide makes use of governmental records or other archival materials to analyze relations between deaths (suicidal and otherwise) and other pieces of information that have been compiled. Epidemiologists are not coroners, juries, or philosophers (though of course they can be philosophically inclined). In the data they employ, usually *someone else*, somewhere along the line of recording information, has made the decision that a particular death was or was not a suicide, quite possibly by a formal (e.g., coroner's jury) or informal (family pleading with the doctor making out a death certificate) process not available to the scrutiny of the epidemiologist, even if she/he would be interested in it. Thus, the epidemiological definition of suicide is a completely pragmatic one: suicide is whatever someone else has already pronounced to be a suicide.

As Douglas (1966; 1967) has pointed out, this makes the correspondence between suicide theory and research nebulous, at best. Epidemiologists represent the extreme "positivist" pole of suicide research, which believes it can investigate the why's and wherefore's of suicide by gathering and analyzing relations in data — that is, suicidology is seen as a branch of empirical science, wherein the nature of suicide will be revealed by objective scientific methodology.

But there are others (which include all the current authors) who reject this formulation. Szasz, for one, as pointed out above, sees moralizing where others claim science, and even those who don't endorse Szasz's politicizing see the kind of un-clarity we've documented here as making it difficult (if not impossible) to regard statistically-based findings as conclusive.

Our own position, developed more fully later, is that a positivist approach is too limiting and misdirected. We've emphasized that *suicide is not an object*, and we consequently believe *treating it as one operationally* subjects the phenomenon to systematic misunderstanding, in general but more especially in the case of indigenous suicide. This will all become clearer, we hope. For now, however, we must recognize that there are research traditions that don't fully engage with the problem of saying what a suicide is.

Suicide Typologies

Again, since no one suggests that suicidal acts are all identical to each other, and because no theorist (so far, anyway) makes any claim to explaining all suicidal acts, the phenomenon of suicide is frequently expressed as occurring in different forms or specific types — as typologies. Some typologies are merely descriptive of different actions that are, or have been called, suicide; others arise from theoretical presumptions that require that there be people who kill themselves for particular reasons. We'll have a look at both types.

Durkheim's Typology. We have already seen this but mention it here for completeness. Durkheim proposes that societies differ in the amount of *regulation* and *integration* they possess (neither of which is adequately defined within his theory, but this does not concern us here). Excessively integrated societies give rise to *altruistic* suicides; inadequately integrated ones to *egoistic* suicides; and inadequately regulated societies give rise to *anomic* suicides in their peoples. We will have a more detailed look at this approach in Chapter 4.

It is important to note that Durkheim is not trying to answer the question: "Why did X commit suicide?" with, for example, an answer of the form: "Because, living in an excessively integrated society, X did it to help his fellow citizens." He was trying not to give personal, individual answers to why specific people killed themselves; he was saying that structures of different societies gave rise to different *types* of suicide. However, as we shall see in Chapter 4, he was not entirely successful in maintaining his position.

Fairbairn's List. Fairbairn (1995) provides a useful list of actions that, in one context or another, have been termed suicide. In contrast to Durkheim, these actions are not connected to any particular theoretical orientation. The elements of his list are:

No Hope Suicide — the person committing suicide does so because his/her life is unhappy and unfulfilling in the extreme without hope of change for the better in the future. Fairbairn considers this the most common form of suicide in western societies.

Existential Suicide — the "suiciding person" holds the opinion that life, for one reason or another, is not worth the trouble (we all die eventually, anyhow). But see Baechler's typology, below.

Dutiful Suicide — the notion that taking one's own life is expected, normative behavior in some cultures (seppuku in Japan or suttee in India; although the latter sounds to us much more like murder).

Altruistic Suicide — similar to Durkheim's element, but with an additional philanthropic undercurrent, such as making one's organs available for transplants or setting oneself afire to avow one's faith.

Revenge Suicide — killing yourself to get back at another, as a way of punishing or hurting them.

Political or Ideological Suicide — done when killing yourself has the specific aim of making a political or ideological point. Fairbairn considers kamikaze pilots and terrorists to be in this category, as well as monks who set themselves ablaze to protest political oppression in Vietnam in the '60's.

Judicial Suicide — Fairbairn considers that some people may kill themselves because they consider the sentence they've received in trials may have been insufficient for their offense (and so, for example, they may impose the death sentence on themselves).

Other-Driven Suicide — the situation in which a person is coerced into killing themselves by another (or others). Socrates' death (after an Athenian court ordered him to kill himself) is considered to be in this category.

Multiple Suicide and Mass Suicide — multiple suicides are considered by Fairbairn to arise from suicide pacts.

Mass suicides is a jumble of different actions, including such things as the Jonestown incident (which to us sound, again, like murder) or mass deaths that arose in the depopulating of the Americas (again, murder, not suicide).

And, as long as we're making lists, we should include a suggestion made by students of our Native Suicidology seminar:

> *Suicide by Cop* — much more common today than when Fairbairn made his list, in this scenario someone publicly brandishes a dangerous weapon (with or without a hostage) and is subsequently terminated by a fusillade of police bullets.

Fairbairn may seem to be operating as if there is some underlying unity to these deaths... that the person dying wants to die (for whatever reason)... but in fact he is simply listing those actions that, in some publication at some time or other, someone has called a "suicide." Hence he provides a set of actions that any specific suicidologist may designate as *the form of suicide she/he wishes to address* in their research or analysis. As we've already noted, this is extremely useful, since every suicidologist, directly or indirectly, establishes such a limit.

Baechler's Typology. Baechler's (1979) enumeration of types of suicide, like Durkheim's, arises from his particular theoretical approach to the phenomenon. But whereas Durkheim's theory and typology took a common-sense definition of suicide as its starting point, Baechler sees suicide differently from most modern suicidologists: his definition of the act more or less presupposes the typology he produces. In addition, where Durkheim is focused on social forces Baechler is personal and individual.

Baechler's (1979) definition of suicide is: "*Suicide denotes all behavior that seeks and finds the solution to an existential problem by making an attempt on the life of the subject* (p. 11; italics in original)." Smith and Bloom (1985) state: "For Baechler, suicide is a positive act of a relatively normal individual committed to solve a problem of living." We are in general sympathy with the move to un-demonize people who commit suicide, but also agree with the old saying that "suicide is a permanent solution to a temporary problem."

It is in elaborating the problems suicide attempts aim to solve that Baechler develops his typology.

Problems of Escape
1. *Flight*: escape from an intolerable situation
2. *Grief*: loss of a central element of one's way of life
3. *Punishment*: elimination of a fault, real or imagined

Problems of Aggression
4. *Vengeance*: inflict remorse on another or condemnation
5. *Crime*: see "Suicide by Cop," above
6. *Blackmail*: withholding of something dear to another
7. *Appeal*: suicide as an alarm signal to others

Oblative Problems (Religious/Ethical Commitment)
8. *Sacrifice*: greater good over personal welfare
9. *Transfiguration*: hastening heavenly reward

Ludic Problems (Playfulness)
10. *Ordeal*: proving oneself to oneself and others by risky actions

As can be seen, despite his rather idiosyncratic definition of suicide, Baechler suggests categories of suicide not greatly different from those already mentioned. However, it is a more nuanced list, with distinctions being made that others gloss over (e.g., distinguishing self-sacrifice from the attractions the Pearly Gates may hold).

Summary

Although it wasn't our intention to sew confusion, the complexities of the behaviors called "suicide" in contemporary Canada should be obvious by now. The people who have tried to pin it down by elaborating its varieties, hypothesizing internal and external components and influences, and speculating about "what is related to what and why" have performed a necessary part of our specific inquiry. To be more to the point, in this work the two of us will not be concerned with whether Indians have died in order to prove themselves, or to give off an alarm, or because they felt they owed it to someone — although we have no difficulty seeing that such things in all probability have happened. We're even willing to entertain Durkheim's notion of killing yourself from just plain "having the crazies" (since a case of "having the crazies" is cheap and as available as one's local drug pusher).

But the problems we're attempting to deal with aren't resolved by the simple act of focusing attention on a limited subset of actions. Suicidologists haven't claimed to have come to grips with the phenomenon of Native suicide merely by defining with greater clarity what "true" suicide is. Rather, they have undertaken to connect up those definitions with hypothetical biological, psychological, and sociological factors, singly and in combination, that they suppose provide us an understanding of the mechanisms that produce individual suicidal actions.

In the next chapter we will look at why, according to modern suicidology, indigenous peoples in Canada commit suicide at such disproportionate rates. However, just as the outcome — suicide — was in need of clarification, the direct and indirect influences need, at the very least, to be conceptualized before we can make sense of their explanations.

DYING TO PLEASE YOU:

INDIGENOUS SUICIDE IN CONTEMPORARY CANADA

Chapter 3, Double, Double, Toilet Trouble: Research,
Theory, and Practice in Indigenous Suicide

Suicide Research

Even before suicidology "took off" as a speciality Douglas (1966; 1967) questioned the possibility of it researching its own declared phenomena of interest. In this work we've already hinted at some of the difficulties from time-to-time; over all, the problems come down to the gap between what officially gets called "suicide" and what suicidologists consider to be the causal forces that may or may not influence personal acts of suicide. Even more importantly, few appreciate the conceptual problems suicidology skates past (Maraun, 2014) or the relation between those unresolved but fundamental difficulties and establishing empirical results.

But why should such details concern us here? If we're against indigenous individuals killing themselves, shouldn't we just get on with stopping them, rather than worrying about how coroners conduct their inquiries or where psychologists get their ideas about what goes on in the minds of people who kill themselves? Or, to put it another way, isn't "suicide research" *someone else's* job (*our* job being to stop Natives in our communities from actually killing themselves)?

Uses of Research. Again, wrong attitude. Let's start with the graph we reproduced back in Chapter 1. For all its limitations (real and imagined), it was used originally not just to establish that Native suicide was a problem, but also as a rationale to galvanize someone into doing something about it. If everyone had left things at "Gee, I seem to recall that a lot of Indians have killed themselves these last few years" it's more or less certain that today there would be nothing specifically in place anywhere targeting indigenous suicide. "Native Suicide" has been an area of research that funding institutions have accorded priority status for decades now, a status it would never have achieved except that that 1978 graph was based on research — flawed, questionable, and necessarily wrong, to some unknown degree — which strongly suggested that there was a "problem."

Furthermore, we must understand the (complex) connection between the research that occurs (that is, the research supported by those funding institutions) and whatever specific suicide intervention programs eventually appear on reserves or in communities. Let's be clear: there is no direct *correspondence* between research findings and intervention programs. The intervention programs that are endorsed and implemented (anywhere in Canada) will depend on what programs will be funded; "what programs will be funded" is an institutional policy decision; and policy decision-makers are very poor researchers (if you can even consider them "researchers" in any sense). That is, decision-makers usually lack the technical expertise to evaluate options; instead, they will cherry-pick research findings that confirm their presumptions and inclinations (much like the Nixon administration cherry-picked Jensen's own cherry-picked research summary to "justify" eliminating Head Start in the US in the late '60's and early '70's). The programs that eventually receive funding meet financial criteria (e.g. "cost-effectiveness"); or optical criteria (e.g., it "looks" like the government is "doing something"); or strike the decision-maker in a personal way ("Oh, that was on Dr. Phil last week!"); or reinforces the existing racial biases; or will be made on other grounds that are never shared with the people who are left to implement them.

What we're saying is: policy initiatives (e.g., funding a particular Native suicide intervention program) will have *some* research-based justification, even if it is a bad one. So... if there's a program in your community that purports to address a local suicide issue, then at some (possibly remote) level, someone's research, somewhere, suggested to at least one bureaucrat that the program, on some ground or other, was a reasonable idea. We think it would be better if all of us knew, beginning to end, just what line of reasoning (including the research grounds) led to programmatic decisions. But if we don't have sufficient research sophistication, we will end up getting someone else's idea of "what should be done" about deaths in our communities.

We'll go you one better: suppose your reserve is running a suicide intervention program (say, a telephone hot-line). Is it working? That is, is it preventing local people from killing themselves? Should your reserve continue operating it, or should you end it and put another, superior program in place? How would you decide that a new and different program was better than the one you already have? Is it possible that the program in place is actually *making things worse* in some way? If a stranger shows up, tells you that your program isn't working, and offers to provide a different service that will work better, how do you evaluate the pitch? Is it science, or snake oil?

These are all research issues. For better or worse it is woven into the fabric of how we think about and how we react to the issues of suicide in our communities. Without an understanding of the origins, assumptions, and results of research inquiries, we are excluded from all decision processes and limited to implementing what someone else tells us to do.

"Research," in Brief. So far we've thrown this term around without saying what it means. The danger is that most people will associate "research" with what it was they did in school for a paper or presentation: look up (in books or magazines or on the internet) *what someone else has already found to be the case* with respect to some topic or other. But in reality that isn't what research is. Research is an active process of generating new information: it is collecting original data and analyzing it so as to *establish or find out what is the case*. Research is an act of creation, not one of looking up.

Now, we will grant that, often, conducting your own research involves and benefits from looking up what people who have worked on the problem currently think is the case. But that is, at best, a point of departure for authentic research. Authentic research is an attempt to improve upon, refine, or even refute what is already considered to be the case. Reading that, for example, many suicidologists *believe* that hot-lines "really work" is no guarantee they're working on your reserve. (As a matter of fact, it isn't a guarantee that hot-lines work for *anyone*.) "Research" would be the effort to show that it does or does not, in fact, "really work" on your reserve.

We also grant that establishing your own local program of research is *largely beside the point of stopping local suicides*. Carrying out a research study is a lot of work, most of it not bearing on (and perhaps even hindering) an existing on-the-ground program of intervention. So we're not actually advocating that indigenous peoples run their own "authentic research programs" (although we're certainly not against that). Instead, we believe that we have to become, more broadly, sophisticated enough with respect to research, *in order to evaluate the claims of competing possible programs*. Only then do we have even the possibility of being informed consumers of programs that may be offered to us.

Research Fraud. We hope we're not giving the impression that we're high on research. We just think our general lack of knowledge here is being used against us. It's bad enough that it's reduced us to being consumers of services *someone else* thinks is good for us, but the problem is even bigger than that. We can think of several examples, but one should be sufficient to make our point.

In truth, if there is a suicide prevention program in your community, it's most likely there because (1) your community has experienced suicides in recent years; (2) the government announced an initiative that would fund a program that does whatever it is that your community is now doing (hot lines, drop-in centers, mentoring, etc.); and (3) someone in the band office filled out (or hired someone to fill out) the necessary paperwork. In this process there was no engagement with evaluating the program's efficiency claims, research results, theoretic orientations, or anything else... at either the governmental or the band level.

Lack of sophistication in research has permitted what we consider to be a particularly malevolent kind of "suicide consultant" to milk Native communities for some time now. They arrive shortly after a rash of suicides have occurred, promising to implement a program that not only will reduce the suicide rate: it will supposedly do so with the sensitivity of "authentic Native" therapeutic techniques. The consultant likely knows the ins and outs of prospective funding agencies and undertakes to run the necessary interference with outside bureaucracies. Lo and behold, they get a grant, they set up a program, and... the suicide rate declines! The consultant then trains some local people to keep his/her program in operation; and then he/she leaves because she/he is "needed so badly elsewhere."

And then the suicide rate goes up again.

Panic time! "What are we doing wrong!" "Whose fault is this?" "We've been letting things slide!" "Can we get the consultant back?!" "We need more training!"

The lead author remembers hearing all this from David Streiner, an epidemiologist, at Toronto East General Grand Rounds over 30 years ago. Suicide rates *cannot* remain constant, because after a rash of suicides, there are necessarily fewer people to commit suicide. That means that *the suicide rate MUST go down until the population has had a chance to build up again*: from the bottom up, as young people get older and move into more "dangerous" age groups. He suggested that it would take about 3 to 5 years for age groups usually targeted by suicide intervention programs to rebuild their numbers. Then, barring any substantive change in the conditions that had given rise to suicide in the first place, the rate will go back up once the critical age group(s) has had the chance to re-populate themselves. This up-and-down rhythm to suicide rates (which we think should be called the Streiner Curve in his honor) is not just something seen in Native communities; it's a statistical necessity and thus describes the fluctuation in suicide rates for any sub-population of individuals.

So: if you're a flim-flam suicide consultant, make sure to show up as soon as you can after a cluster of suicides; institute some kind of intervention program (what kind doesn't matter — have everyone eat more cheese, for example); take credit when the rate necessarily goes down; then get out of town before people start killing themselves again. Sound familiar?

People who work for a particular program swear by it. They say they *know* it works because they *see* it work, but when pressed they're sketchy on details. For a variety of reasons, nobody is actually doing research; they're just running a program. (We've already noted that conducting research can easily get in the way of delivering a service.) Belief that the program works is just that: an act of faith. As Upton Sinclair[2] once noted: "It is difficult to get a man to understand something when his salary depends upon his not understanding it."

All-in-all, disconnection from the demands of research makes us patsies for both legitimate and illegitimate purveyors of programs.

Conclusions. We've dragged on this part of our presentation far too long. Maybe we just should have said "Hey, be careful about research," and let it go at that. But not only is ignorance of the technology of research an enormous problem, so is its worship and mystification.

Our genuine attitude is much more complicated. We used the oldest graphical representation of indigenous suicide we could find not just to point out that this is a long-recognized problem; and not just to identify it as the starting point for modern suicidology's interest in Indians; and not just to argue it's 5 percentage points off here or 12 percentage points off there. Ultimately, we used it as a way of saying *we don't care* about what the suicide rate was or is... but about what it someday *will be. Even one* suicide was excessive, in our opinion: *one more* will be one too many.

At times there seems to us a kind of "suicide sweepstakes" running in the background and which surfaces for a brief moment each year. One year it's the Guarani peoples of South America leading the world in

2   Thank you, Bruce!

suicidal deaths; the next it's the Innu and Inuit of Labrador, or the Oji-Cree of Northern Ontario; or it's factory workers in China, small land-holding farmers in India, etc., etc. There's a kind of voyeurism behind all of this that we find morally objectionable. Does research provide large monetary rewards (to a small number of people), help people get university degrees and well-paid jobs, elevate people (again, a very small number of them) to professional notoriety and status in the field, while it makes them feel really good about themselves? Definitely. Does research really indicate what the issues are that surround indigenous suicide and what could and should be done to alleviate the problem? *Only* maybe... if a lot of things change.

Suicide Theory

At least part of what is known as suicidology theory is implicit in definitions we're already looked at, but it's important to get a sense of the different frames of reference adhered to by practitioners. In the soft disciplines (psychology, sociology, etc.; we will not refer to them as "sciences") "theory" is often treated as a second-class citizen in comparison with pragmatically-oriented research. It is passed over as cowardly "armchair speculation" when what's needed is blood-and-guts formulations for boots-on-the-ground programs on the front line. These war metaphor comparisons may be effective fund-raising gimmicks but to the extent they reflect a sincere belief that theory and practice can (and should) be divorced, those holding that belief need a strong dose of reality. Suicide research, pragmatic or otherwise, can't do anything until it clarifies what constitutes "a suicide" or any other concept in its supposed range of interest (Baker and Hacker, 1982). Further, at least some suicidologists (e.g., Rogers, 2001) have noticed that a 50-year domination by pragmatic and technological investigations (rather than theory-referenced ones) hasn't led to any reduction in suicide rates (and that is for *any* population, not just Indians).

But then, one of the problems facing suicide theorizing is what is accepted as theory. Nothing we've seen even remotely approximates what is typical for the genuine sciences; instead, we find off-the-cuff opinions ("Well, my theory is..."), vague formulations, and antiquated, tottering generalizations being offered as if functioning modern theories. A position often considered the very first comprehensive theory of suicide, that of Durkheim (1897/1966; to which we've already referred), is still taken as at least the starting point for disputes and innovations, if not as the basic formulation to be followed.

That being the case, our review of suicide theory will be as uneven as the situation demands. Rather than lump in here every "theory" of suicide we can find and then provide our evaluation, we will sketch out the three types suicidologists agree upon. After all, *every* specific theory of suicide has not seriously been entertained with respect to Native peoples.

Suicide theories come in three forms: biological, psychological, and sociological. In practice, particular suicidologists emphasize one of these approaches while paying at least lip-service to the importance of the others. What that means is that (again, in practice) most suicidologists are bio-psycho-social theorists, or psycho-socio-biological theorists, or some combination or permutation of the three. The situation is well-represented in the diagram below, borrowed from Fusé's (1997) work (originally it was his Figure 9). What we see is a kind of "kitchen sink" approach to suicide. The picture is a frank expression of the general (but mistaken) notion that, if you mention all three possibilities, your theory of suicide can't be wrong (since you've covered all the possible bases). Implicit in formulations conforming to Fusé's diagram — which is every theory of suicide we've been able to locate — is the solicitation to view suicide in causal mechanistic terms; that is, it is seen to arise individually in the internal workings of the person committing suicide. Speculation about the mechanism *creating* suicide leads (*naturally*, it is assumed) to speculation about how to *interfere* with that mechanism; where appropriate, we will make those connection explicit.

Once we've seen what kinds of suicide theories there are, the last part of this chapter will be devoted to looking at what we consider to be the more important attempts of modern suicidology to understand indigenous suicide.

Biological Theories. We shall not inspect biological theories of suicide so much as make fun of them; in this, we follow a venerable tradition begun by Durkheim 120 years ago. Even though some of his criticism was unconvincing (if not premature), the situation has not improved in the intervening years.

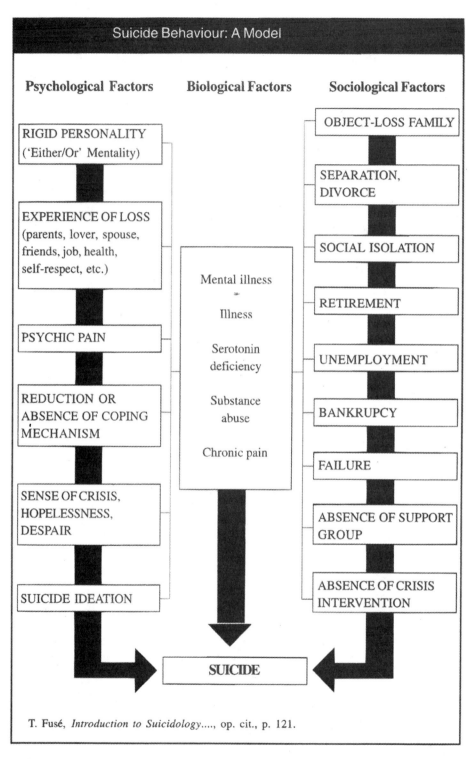

Figure 2. Fusé's (1997) Figure 9, an original diagrammatic summary of suicide theory.

These days a great deal of trouble has been taken to convince everyone that the ultimate explanation for every human issue will be found in our biology. As recently as 2000, the National Post ran a front-page story (Evenson, 2000) announcing that some Canadian researchers had "discovered a gene" "contributing" to "the tendency" of "some people" to "attempt" to kill themselves (this is, of course, a classic example of the "picture of a painting of a shadow of a statue of a man" regression; you don't realize how far you are from the phenomenon you're really interested in until you've taken a few steps back).

Although the article was couched in appropriately probabilistic, rather than deterministic language, and although it was (at the insistence of the researchers who supposedly made the discovery) retracted soon afterwards (but, this time, most definitely *not* in large letters on the front page), the damage (intended or not) had already been done. Today, we regularly encounter individuals who, when acquainted with our work on Native suicide, remark "Oh, yes... it's genetic, isn't it?" without batting an eye. They seem to think that this blatantly racist falsehood — that our widely-publicized higher suicide rate is nothing more than another aspect of our general sub-humanity — is an established fact; one that, if the two of us are any good at what we do, we should know about and share.

The campaign to substitute scientific-sounding mumbo-jumbo in the place of *actual* theories of human dynamics — that is, theories which might either prove true or false, but which could be tested to find out what, in fact, is the case — may be as old as language itself. Who knows? But in the realm of Indian/non-Indian relations it goes back to 1492, a coincidence we will explore in greater detail in our next book on racism. Here we will call it what it is: a purely political move riding on the coattails of a pseudoscience that a systemically mis-educated mainstream population is no longer sophisticated enough to detect.

Have a look at the Biological Factors column in Fusé's (1997) figure just cited. "Mental illness" is listed as one of them, without any indication that this is pure mythology. More than 50 years ago Szasz (1961) argued the position that problems in living were metaphorically, not literally, "illnesses" (a position he continued to defend prolifically and proficiently for the rest of his life; e. g., Szasz, 1987; 2002; 2007), and that, when *real* brain diseases are detected (e.g., tuberculosis of the central nervous system, or secondary or tertiary syphilis), *real* doctors treat them with *real* medicines and *real* medical interventions. His thesis has been evaded and ignored by "the mainstream," but never convincingly answered. Today, despite the widespread *belief* that "mental illnesses" are "illnesses just like other illnesses," there remains no evidence whatsoever that any purely psychiatric (and not demonstrably physical) disorder (like suicide) has an underlying biological disease mechanism (Ross and Pam, 1995; Valenstein, 2002; Caplan and Cosgrove, 2004).

Or take "Serotonin deficiency" under the same heading. Review after review has failed to substantiate any connection between too much or too little of this particular neurotransmitter and depression; or suicide; or "mental illness." Mercola (2011) and Levine (2016) are readable and recent restatements of this circumstance. But on television we've all seen the Bouncing Brain Chemical Ball that goes flat when it's "depressed" (it stops smiling, anyway) while the voice-over says this "*may be due* [inserted only because of the threat of legal action for false advertising] to a chemical imbalance in the brain" (which of course is exactly the same thing as saying it MAY NOT be due to any such imbalance). We are then all encouraged to ask our doctors about getting some other, *different* chemicals for ourselves... so that we won't have deflated chemical balls moping about in *our* heads. Is the *cartoon* such a convincing argument — compared to the universal inability to detect such an impact in impartial scientific studies — that we're forced to believe the assertion is true?

The entire area of reasoning about mind, body, chemistry, genes, and behavior is a conceptual and practical mish-mash that, if you know where to look (for example, Lewontin, Rose, and Kamin, 1984; Bennett and Hacker, 2003; Noe, 2009; Krimsky and Gruber, 2013; Maraun, 2014), you can get a clear understanding of what's wrong with attempts to reduce human behavior to the biology that underlies it. But it *is* work, and it's work we're all discouraged from doing by those who benefit from transporting human actions, human decisions, and human thoughts into the esoteric realms of genes, chemicals, and overstretched metaphors.

People are going to tell you that we have gone too far in this dismissal; that we don't know what we're talking about; that we're completely wrong. We're going to make this as simple as possible: have a look back at the excerpt with which we ended Chapter 1. Would *anyone* but a frothing neo-Nazi lunatic be willing to argue that the

Jews were collectively suffering from a serotonin deficiency from 1933 until May of 1945? Or that a "suicide gene" knew to turn itself on after the Law for the Restoration of the Professional Civil Service was passed and then turn itself off after Zhukov's army captured Berlin? Or that, had Prozac been available for the Nazis to administer to Jews awaiting their transportation orders, or living crammed into ghettos, or being remorselessly brutalized in concentration camps, everything would have been just fine?

Biological "explanations" deserve none of our time; we'll give them no further attention here.

Psychological Models. If for no other reason, the popularity and availability of psychological models of suicide demand our attention. But this may mean that they are cheap and superficially satisfying rather than that they're accurate and scientifically respectable. We advise caution.

A psychological model is invoked whenever the explanation of behavior is proposed to include one or more unobservable characteristic which theoretically varies from person to person. A good, short example of the psychological modeling of suicide is the summary from the Focus Group on Native suicide, which we abstracted in Chapter 1. In the space of less than two pages — their "underlying philosophy" — one can find the following assertions made: Natives who commit suicide are depressed, hopeless, frustrated, and in a state of despair, feel detached from their culture and life itself, are likely to be high and/ or drunk, are in denial (about something), don't like themselves very much, can't cope, and have too much time on their hands. Finally, they are in need of professional help.

This is an impressive display. These people have, literally, *incredible* insight into the mental condition of people immediately before those people killed themselves. But, given that the people about whom they are speaking were *dead* at the time of these assessments, we're entitled to ask what kind of virtuosity is being displayed here. Was it empirical data acquisition and analysis? (That is, did they interrupt Natives in the process of committing suicide, ask them if they were willing to participate in a research study, get them to fill out questionnaires, interview them, have them sign a release so that their medical histories could be accessed, etc., and then watch them slowly die as they entered the information into lap-tops and ran statistical analyses?) Was it psychic powers? Or some kind of special psychological spontaneous intuition (concerning people they never interacted with or even met)? Or what?

One can find out by reading the actual individual reports upon which the "Philosophical Summary" was based: it was what the forum participants all had heard from here and there. None of the focus group members were psychologists (at least, at the time the reports were done), so none of them had access to the secret mind-reading techniques for which psychologists are famous (watch any TV crime show that has a psychologist as a regular character to see what we mean). No one had run a study or collected data or analyzed it or presented it... not even other peoples' work. So: no research of any kind was involved beyond the occasional rehashing of what was available already; their "data" were just whatever the forum members had read about, heard about, or thought up themselves in scintillating moments of insight.

In fairness we must stress that in doing this the participants were no worse (nor any better) than the rest of us. We have all learned to speak and think of ourselves (and each other) as if we are containers filled with various gremlins, and that these gremlins, singly or in various confederations, command the mechanical control of our bodies and manage our moment-to-moment activities. In explaining suicides — those of Native people or anyone else — the gremlins have been given the names "depression," "despair," "hopelessness," "helplessness," and so on... and which gremlins are proposed for the more prominent roles vary slightly from one suicidologist to another. So, when the participants in the focus group asserted a role for one gremlin or another, they were doing little more than repeating wisdom received from other people, *experienced gremlinologists* (better known as "psychologists"), who had been able in previous research studies (or so they assure us) to locate, capture, and identify these mental vermin. What's more, some gremlinologists claim to know how to feed them, train them, and even how to kill them.

We can make this formulation more concrete. Below, we introduce our own graphical representation of the *psychological* approach to suicide: Bobbi/Bob. We will encounter Bobbi/Bob again later in this book, since, not only is s/he popular, s/he is indispensable to this entire line of thought. Bobbi/Bob is of no particular race, age, or sex (we will vary his/her/its name from time-to-time). This is the depiction of the psychological interpretation of Bobbi's actions, whatever they are, including committing suicide: *they are postulated to be some complex function of her personal, individual, and internal characteristics.*

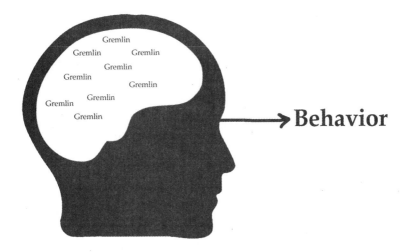

Figure 3. The psychological model of human behavior, with the help of Bobbi/Bob.

The lead author discussed at length this conceptualization of human action in a previous book (Chrisjohn and Young, 1997) so here we will merely hit some high (or low) points of the model as it conceptualizes suicide.

The origin of the internal gremlins is not necessarily specified: they may arise from direct or indirect (social) learning, they may have their origin in a genetic, biological process, or may be some combination of nature and nurture (biopsychology is considered by some to be a not totally reprehensible sub-discipline of psychology). For any particular Bobbi, their presence or absence, strength, history, alliances, etc., in her head (we locate it in the head, but there's no particular reason to put the gremlins there apart from psychology's tendency to equate "mind" with "brain") may be reportable by Bobbi and/or people who know her (in which case, interviews, questionnaires, rating scales, and autobiographies can supply data); but some psychologists hold that Bobbi has no necessary insight into her mental content, which can only be discerned by indirect assessments or by eminently insightful listeners. Whatever.

It is through the development of statistical associations (or sometimes simply narrative assertions) between these invisible (to everyone but The Initiated), putative causes and their observable (e.g., death by suicide) effects that different psychological models of suicide have been developed and modified. Theoretically, we should have said "developed, modified, and refuted," since psychology pretends to be a science; but no less an *über*-psychologist than Paul Meehl (1973) himself noticed that psychological theories don't die, but just sort of lose their following and peter out after a while.

The "modified" part of our characterization is important, too, in that, as evidence *against* a particular psychological theory accumulates (by psychology's rules of evaluation), theories don't disappear as much as they become more obscure. Thus, Beck's (1967) rather simple initial model of suicide:

Figure 4. Depression and suicide in the early days.

became something like:

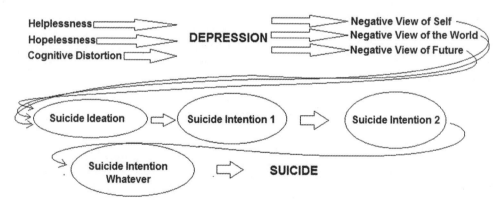

Figure 5. Depression and suicide: a clarification?

in a little over a decade, without any corresponding increase in strength of prediction. For all we know, things are even worse now. (Be assured, we're not particularly trying to pick on Beck; the point is that there is nothing to prevent this kind of proliferation when the variables of interest are unobservable and hypothetical.)

Further, the notion of "explanatory internal gremlins" (which creatures being central to psychological modelling) is questionable. Asserting that "there is an invisible gremlin inside us which does that 'thing' which we are trying to explain" is not an explanation; for example, asserting that people have "memory" because there's a gremlin in our head that remembers things doesn't explain what *memory* is. All too often, psychological models are little more than "Just-So" stories that serve to hide the fact that the "theory" is a disguised restatement of the conclusion its proponents want to reach.

Thus, the supposed strengths of psychological models of suicide — an appeal to "common sense" explanations which sound like the things we say to explain our own behavior and that of the people around us — are in fact its weaknesses — an easy proliferation of invisible gremlins detectable only by abstruse and dubious technologies. Whether any particular theory "really" is an explanation or assists us in understanding indigenous suicide requires that we be alert to the possibility that we are simply being told that suicide happens because our internal gremlin wants it to happen. We commit suicide because our gremlin is depressed... but then, how did *it* get depressed... is there a depressed gremlin inside *its* head? And how did *that* gremlin get depressed... is there a depressed gremlin in *its* head? ... *and are you starting to see a pattern forming here?*

Sociological Models. Speculation about why people commit suicide probably goes back to the time of whoever was the first person to kill her/himself, but credit for the first *formal* models is usually given to sociologists. Sociological models have the same fundamental causal structure as psychological ones; for example:

Figure 6. A sociological model of suicide.

Notice that here the explanatory variable is defensibly more public and visible than in the psychological model. Although there can still be considerable controversy about which name would be most appropriate (hiccup, readjustment, recession, depression, meltdown, etc.), consensus that *some* kind of an "economic downturn" had occurred would likely be apparent. Still, for some of the factors sociologists consider important (e.g., socio-economic status; social class; institutional racism), measurement problems can be as convoluted and unconvincing as they are for "intelligence," "depression," "need for achievement," or any other conventionally psychological factor. On balance, however, the question of whether a postulated cause is in reality some academic hallucination is less pressing in sociology than it is in psychology.

Notice also that the effect is indexed with respect to "rates" of suicide, not any particular suicide one may wish to account for. Collective and social, and not personal, indicators register the impact of social causes. How "a downturn in the economy" might bring about "Bob's suicide" is not spelled out (although some people, e.g. Baechler (1979), insists it *should* be); but often it's easy enough to construct hypothetical sequences if need arises (e.g., "Bob lost his job *because* of the economic downturn and killed himself *because* he worried about providing for his family). Still, those sequences *are* hypothetical, and the same social factor can purportedly produce contrary outcomes (e.g., a childhood in the slums might lead to a life of crime or a persistent drive to scholarly excellence); hence, Baechler's insistence on providing a complete causal sequence from social factor to personal outcome.

Nevertheless... or perhaps consequently... social forces are often couched in personal terminology. If we look back once again at Fusé's (1997) figure, under "Sociological Factors" we find that many of the entries seem to be of that nature: "bankruptcy," "unemployment," "retirement," "separation/divorce," "failure," and perhaps even "object-loss family," "absence of support groups," and "absence of crisis intervention" can be seen as direct personal instantiations of variation in any number of possible social factors. That is, saying, e.g., "bankruptcy occurs" can only mean individual people must become unable to handle their debts; and so on through the list. The factor "social isolation" is more even entangled between the individual and social levels, since social forces obviously are involved in the construction of living space; but, equally, Bob could "feel" alone in a Japanese shopping mall. There is thus a tension between which level (social or personal) is appropriate for expressing the effect of large-scale social factors.

Finally, we want to point out the obviously contingent status of what are taken as the causal, explanatory variables. For example, "bankruptcy," "unemployment," and the like presume something like western capitalism as the functioning economic system, just as "retirement" presupposes a world in which older people will be deprived of their jobs (and even the concept of "jobs" is itself obviously contingent). Thus, which social variables are likely to be important in suicide depends in complex ways on the features of the social world people inhabit.

(We have to point out that this is *also the case for psychological variables*. They have no more claim to universality than any social force anyone might care to mention (e.g., Cole, 1999; Ratner, 2012; Racine and Slaney, 2014; Vygotsky, 1986). The variables of cognition and orexis (temperament) are treated as static features of the human psyche only because of the (deliberate?) confusion of physical traits with supposed mental ones; it is an act of ideology and faith, not of science.)

Durkheim (1897/1966) is easily the most famous of sociological theorists of suicide, but he is far from the only representative even from his own time period. Tarde (Kral, 1994), a contemporary of Durkheim, put forward an account of suicide in terms of what today would likely be called social learning theory. In any event, Durkheim's continued popularity is evidenced by the frequent adoption of his sociological model in explaining, for example, Native suicide.

However, like psychological theories of suicide, sociological ones need not set out to achieve comprehensiveness, and can instead focus on one or two social factors deemed important, neglected, essential, misunderstood, or otherwise improperly treated by research. Thus, individual studies of suicide have made mention of all the social factors listed in Fuse's (1997) diagram, and more. With respect to indigenous suicide, our presumed marginalization in a larger Canadian society has attuned suicidologists to the possibility that unique causal factors (couched in appropriately personal terminology, of course) may arise in our various Nations, and may account for our relatively elevated suicide rate.

Suicide Practice

Our discussions of suicide research and suicide theory have been a prelude to looking at what suicidologists have actually proposed as explanations for our elevated suicide rates. As we've already noted, there is a considerable and growing literature on this subject to be found in books, academic journal articles, journalistic accounts, and biographies, much of it done by suicidologists who have allotted a significant portion of their career specifically to this issue. The discussion thus far in this chapter has been intended to prepare us all to work our way through this literature.

If what follows is in any kind of order it's an order neither of us have been able to discern. The papers and books were sorted into piles based on principal authors, whose names provided the heading titles (we hope we didn't get any of the principal authors wrong, and apologize in advance if we did). The two of us tackled whichever pile grabbed our attention first, for whatever reason. The draft summaries were then discussed between us before they were put into the final form given here.

We make no claim to comprehensiveness; there are doubtless many people who have attacked the problem of indigenous suicide who, for one reason or another, we didn't include here. In general, that won't be because we hadn't heard of it, but more likely because the approach and conclusions were already well-represented in the work of another program. It may seem to some that several comparatively minor efforts have been included; this is likely because they presented a viewpoint it was important to note, whether or not we found merit in it. After all, who knows through what door wisdom will walk?

Clare Brant. Brant's (1993) contribution to indigenous suicidology was a submission to a round table organized by the Royal Commission on Aboriginal Peoples. It was a selective review of previous research rather than a report of new work.

To be right up front, Brant's submission was flawed in a number of ways. For one thing, it treats results for different (e.g., Alaskan Natives, MicMacs, and Oji-Crees) First Nations as more or less interchangeable; this Pan-Indianism is not warranted by any fact of national similarity, nor does he supply any argument in its favor. In his defense, however, we must point out the comparative absence of hard data on the possible causes of Native suicide at the time his report was written may well have forced this policy upon him.

A second problem is Brant's tendency to go well beyond what his evidence will support. For example, we are told we must "see" how the change in economic circumstance leads to self-esteem "eroding" (as social problems erode, too; this, however, is likely due to undue haste in composition and editing). While the two of us support this conjecture, there is nothing *obvious* about it, and pains must be taken to clarify the connection. In fact, immediately before urging the clarity of the connection upon us, he writes: "This author has never heard a satisfactory explanation of why lower classes in an upwardly mobile capitalist democracy frequently engage not only in self destructive behaviour but in substance abuse." We agree: such connections are *not* clear.

The epidemiological information he quotes is of no particular use, either then or now. For one thing, such details change within a very sort time period and are sample-specific; for another, they're dependent on the nebulous details of designating deaths "suicides" or not, as already discussed.

Potentially more useful is the list of personal characteristics of Native suicides which he develops within the first half of the paper. The specific characteristics are not, in fact, supported by the original research of the papers he cites, but the low research quality of his sources is *not* Dr. Brant's fault. In no particular order of importance, Brant offers the following features of Native suicides: *low* or *corrupted self-esteem*; *identity issues*; *powerlessness*; *anomie* (citing Durkheim, but somewhat "off" in his interpretation of Durkheim's variable); *poverty*; and *stress*.

As is evident from this list, the "causes of Native suicide" are seen as a mixture of psychological and sociological factors as we have defined them here. The sociological variables (at least, powerlessness and poverty, if not anomie) are easier to defend as palpable; the psychological ones considerably less so. However, emphasis and priority is given to psychological factors.

Some may disagree with our assessment that Brant passes over social factors, but consider: "stress," which people might generally consider a psychological factor, is supported with a long list of objective characteristics of the on-reserve living conditions (then as now) of Native peoples (e.g., inadequate housing, lack of employment, disorganized band administration, restricted means of transportation). These characteristics all have strong factual support. But rather than leave his analysis at the point of describing the 3rd-World living conditions of many Indians, he chooses to "congeal" them into a psychological gremlin, *stress*. The why and how of the centrality of *stress* — that is, by what process these conditions are turned into "stress" (and *not* into anger, unrest, determination, protest, fear, depression, altruism... whatever) — is not a process Brant shares with us. But by similar mysterious processes, *colonialism* turns into *powerlessness*, (and not *resistance*), *marginalization* becomes *low self-esteem* (and not *self-assertion*), and even *societal breakdown* becomes *anomie*, conceptualized as a personally felt experience (rather than *revitalization* conceived as communal growth).

Brant's (1993) paper conforms to a pattern we will see again and again as we review studies: *social, political, economic, and legal factors (which, in general, are all easier to substantiate via hard evidence) are conceived as acting by way of their transformation (via non-specified processes) into psychological factors.* Given his background in psychoanalytically-based psychiatry, Brant's commitment to the psychological model is unsurprising. Nevertheless, the move from the readily demonstrable (manifest social circumstances) to the chronically unclear (presumed internal gremlins) stands greatly in need of justification.

For Brant, then, indigenous suicide, arises out of a Broken Indian. But, that commitment aside, ultimately he gives us his clear realization that the Broken Indian wasn't that way to begin with.

Al Evans. Evans' (2004) work is a combination of autobiography, biography (of Ojibway artist Benjamin Chee Chee), and rambling advertisement for the Broken Indian model described in Chapter 1. In many ways it is a band-camp sort of a book: all the instruments are there (plus a few nobody anticipated), but they don't harmonize. The result is, well, *noise*; and that's a pity, since endurable music might have resulted.

The central pillar of Evans' presentation is the suicide of Benjamin Chee Chee in 1977. Or is it? Even the description Evans (a former RCMP officer) provides is dubious on the face of it; it would easily be considered a "suspicious death while in police custody" by anyone unwilling to swallow whole the police account as given. We learn, for instance, that Chee Chee had been beaten up by police on more than a few occasions during his life, one time after having been tied up by five officers (to even up the odds, we presume). But, we are assured, "...any time the police beat Benny, he asked for it (Evans, 2004, p. 19)."

That aside, the specifics of Chee Chee's life and art (as interesting as they were and are) here can be pertinent only insofar as they help inform why indigenous people commit suicide. To this end, Benjamin Chee Chee was, well, *one Broken Indian*. Pathological family dynamics, institutionalization at a young age, interpersonal difficulties, rage, alcohol... you name it, he had it. But Evans makes no claim of having a personal or therapeutic basis for his conclusions concerning Chee Chee's descent into suicide (if that's what it was); all his information was second-hand, at best. (We say "at best" because some of his conclusions were formed by looking at his art as if it was a series of projective tests — psychological tests of known negligible scientific value — that opened his inner self to scrutiny by people like Evans. Indeed, several of Evans' informants, none of them with the fig-leaf of formal psychological training to provide cover, draw projective/psychological conclusions about Chee Chee by looking at his art, too. Chee Chee continually denied the validity of any such projections, but, hey, who's the Indian here and who are the White Knights?)

Thus it is clear: Evans' work is of no *empirical* value whatsoever. The content of his book is either hearsay and second-hand reporting, or the replaying of what is the prefabricated "wisdom" of standard modern suicidology. As we've seen earlier from the Focus Group on Native Suicide: suicidal indigenous individuals (include Benjamin Chee Chee, we are led to believe) suffer from Durkheim-style anomie (transformed, as it was in Brant's work, into a personal, internal, individual gremlin), low self-esteem and/or poor self-image, alcoholism, inability to relate to others, loss (see below) of cultural identity, depression, helplessness, hopeless, and more. Again: there is no data to evaluate, no argument to analyze. That's the way it is because other people have told Evans that that's the way it is... he's just passing along the information. We won't repeat the myriads of objections any real scientist would have to the way in which these conclusions have been reached. But to summarize: here, again, the Broken Indian is simply being asserted, not proven as an entity.

This is a grim picture indeed; were this all there was to Evans' (2004) work it would have been better to spare all of us the trouble of acknowledging it. However, he is, quite obviously, an intelligent and curious individual, and Indians are something he desperately wants to understand. The clumsiness with which he undertakes this task is almost endearing (as when after the sharing out of his pack of store-bought, factory-farmed cigarettes among a group of men who have wordlessly gathered with him to watch over the body of a young woman who has killed herself (as they await the arrival of the coroner), he intra-psychically turns the whole episode into a symbolic "peace-pipe ritual"). But then again he can readily display a basic ineptness with real issues that cancels any sympathy he may have built up (as when: he continually refers to things that have been stolen and/ or targeted for destruction as "lost" (e.g., *lost* culture, *lost* identity, *lost* language); or when he justifies the "warrior" attitude of Ojibways by noting they were creative and pantheistic, too... never mentioning the fact that *their country was being invaded!* How "war-like" would *you* be, we would like to ask him, if someone started setting up house in *your* living room?).

As ham-handed and ill-conceived as all this is, however, one realization abides: that the gremlins driving Native people to suicide are there as a result of the economic, political, social, and legal machinations of mainstream Canada. Evans is aware that residential/ industrial schools weren't a good thing (that is, he is aware that the teachers had no qualifications and no "education" took place in them and that abuses, sexual and otherwise, were legion; but then joins in the defamation of those who survived the experience and endorses the deliberately misdirecting canard that "residential school syndrome" resulted; see Chrisjohn & Young, 1997). He can see that European imperialism, and the Canadian colonialism that formed out of it, were destructive and dismissive of indigenous cultures (but doesn't really understand why; *paternalism, good intentions gone bad,* "vague feelings of egalitarianism," and the "desire to assimilate" Indians into the Canadian mainstream are the best suggestions he can come up with). And he quite correctly rejects the blatantly racist but widely held mainstream notion that Indian problems are "all in the genes" (even as he conjures up that Nazi reprobate, Carl Jung, as endorsing Evans' staid and irrelevant therapeutic agenda). It is as if some of the band is unpacking or still tuning up, while other members have marched off in various directions several hours ago.

In short, Evans (2004) is the picture of the average Canadian the lead author thought (hoped?) he might reach in his earlier book on Indian residential schooling: an intelligent and open-minded individual who would be willing to entertain leaving the Dark Side if someone else provided a flashlight. And, as central as the Broken Indian is to his notion of why Indians commit suicide (and what should be done about it), clearly he is developing his own doubts about where the gremlins of the suicidal Indian's mind come from. We must congratulate even the baby-step he has been able to take, as documented in his work; for, in our experience, it has been far too giant a leap for most.

Laurence Kirmayer. Laurence Kirmayer is a psychiatrist at McGill University with long involvement both with cross-cultural issues in general and Native peoples in particular. Unlike the researchers examined so far, he has numerous publications presenting his own original empirical work in Native suicide. This means that his surveys of existing work in indigenous suicide (e. g., Kirmayer, 1993; Kirmayer, Brass, Holton, Paul, Simpson, & Tait, 2007) do not merely report the findings of others but critically engage them, providing an appropriate methodological context for their evaluation. In every way, Kirmayer's publications in indigenous suicide in Canada represent the best of what has been done and the cutting edge of what might be done.

Nevertheless, we have difficulties with both his approach and his findings, some of them deep enough to preclude resolution within these pages. We think it better to make our differences clear before undertaking a review of his publications; otherwise, it might seem we are nit-picking and fault-finding our way through what is, indeed, an impressive body of serious work. Readers are likely to be unaware of the extent to which fundamental issues are controversial, even in a field which, like suicidology, claims the trappings of real science.

We mentioned in our review of Brant (above) that he had a tendency toward Pan-Indianism; that is, treating the results for one Native nation as bearing upon other Native nations. This is like treating France as a part of England (or vice versa), although not really, because France and England have much greater similarity, we would argue, than Oneidas and Mi'kmaqs. Kirmayer has the same tendency toward Pan-Indianism and is up-front about it, arguing that the relative unavailability of statistics for individual First Nations (although he is able to produce an amazing variety of them) forces it upon him. True. Still, within the empiricist methodological framework he adopts, these are logically indefensible apples - oranges comparisons which establish nothing. So then, why make them? It merely creates the impression that some empirical fact has been discovered when, later, these kinds of comparisons are nevertheless made long after the warnings about them have been forgotten.

This contrast between methodological purity at the outset and empirical pragmatism in the body of results is characteristic of Kirmayer's work. He is quite correctly concerned about how alteration in research instrumentation conceptually muddies any comparisons being made (2007, p. 6), but only to the point of advising "caution."

In reality, incomparable instrumentation categorically rules out such comparisons (Chrisjohn, Pace, Young, & Mrochuk, 1997; Maraun, 1998). Unless measurement instruments can be shown to meet the logical and philosophical demands of construct validity — that instruments measure the same "thing," in the same units, with the same degree of precision (Cronbach, 1971) — no scientific conclusion is warranted. The import of this is inescapable: since, in fact, no "instrument" (which includes rating scales, checklists, questionnaires, self-reports, educational and psychological tests, structured and unstructured interviews, etc.) has even remotely approached this minimal standard, their use with First Nations populations is not just unethical, it is of *no scientific value*. Kirmayer recognizes this: "When survey questionnaires have not been culturally adapted and validated, and when individuals are unsure about how the data collected will be used, the accuracy of the information may be compromised (2007, p. 6)." Agreed: except, replace "any purported measurement instrument" for "survey questionnaires;" acknowledge that no instrument has even been so adapted and so validated; recognize that "how the data collected will be used" is *always* a worry when non-Indians study Indians; and change "may be" to "necessarily is;" and we have a match.

These problems (Pan-Indianism and irresolute methodological purity) are indicative of an impasse, one in which indigenous peoples will suffer and die unless some accommodation can be reached. But in reality this goes far beyond treating different First Nations as interchangeable or pointing out the failure of social disciplines to adhere to their own logic of research inference. Kirmayer's employment of the medicalized version of the psychological model (evident in the way the reified "mental health" metaphor is regarded as fact) arises from an ideological position which is so widespread it is thought by many just to be true. Critics of this belief system (Szasz we have already mentioned; the work of Vygotsky and his followers on *cultural* psychology instead of the *cross-cultural* psychology Kirmayer practices must be included; and Wittgenstein's (1951/2009) dismantling of positivist, empiricist philosophy is central to the development of a coherent alternative) get little or no hearing in the circles in which Kirmayer moves.

We will postpone for now engaging these issues any further. Later, when we will be forced to address them more specifically, we will not resolve them; after all, why should anyone listen to our concerns? But we will do what we can, since we are of the opinion that continuing along the path marked by the kind of research Kirmayer does so well will ultimately *not* moderate the indigenous suicide epidemic. So, until then, even given the shortcomings of his work (which Kirmayer himself acknowledges), we will take his results as is. We think they still have considerable value.

Kirmayer makes the by-now standard divisions into psychological and sociological antecedents, and biological ones are woven into the findings by the device of presuming a biological basis for at least some of them (e.g., depression). Taking the psychological variables first, Kirmayer et al. (2007, p. 53) provide a summary diagram of their review (their Figure 3 - 1). (This particular report is widely available at no cost on the internet and so will not be included here.) Although given in the general form of a structural equation or causal modeling diagram, no presumed strengths of effect are included.

This omission warrants an extended discussion. From their box, "Risk Factors," we can see that Kirmayer et al. (2007) consider the empirical research strong enough to say that individual standing with respect to *depression, substance abuse, diagnosed personality disorder, hopelessness, abuse/neglect, school achievement, social isolation,* and *exposure to suicide* all influence the likelihood that an indigenous person will him/herself commit suicide. This list is substantially similar to what others have already offered, except that in this instance an empirical basis exists for making the association. However, Kirmayer et al. do not give any indication of how strong, individually or collectively, these factors are in bringing about the result (suicide). Statistical significance testing, which is used to make the kind of finding Kirmayer et al. report, is *not* an indication of strength of association. When strength indicators *are* calculated for results such as these (which *should be done*, standardly and typically; Rogers & Lester, 2010), and which should be easy to do, since these are all organismic variables, and not experimentally manipulated ones, the uniform finding in other published research has been that the predictors (depression, substance abuse, etc.) account for the criterion (death by suicide or not) to an *embarrassingly slight degree,* a situation which *worsens* when cross-validation (that is, the replication of the study and its resulting coefficients of effect) is attempted.

So: once again we are told that depression, substance abuse, etc. are the reasons Indians kill themselves. Unlike the work we've looked at so far, Kirmayer et al. (2007) have either examined real data that support these generalizations or have generated the data themselves.

But *how much* these factors contribute to the result either can't be deduced from the results reviewed or are too ephemeral to carry much weight.

"Risk Factors" are not the only box of personal influences on suicide. Another box contains what can be considered precipitating contributions (an acute crisis; the suicide of friends or family members; the break-up of a relationship; school failure; and trouble with the law); and yet another, immediate precursors (intoxication; availability of means to commit suicide; and lack of rescue). The first of these are not, of course, characteristics of individuals, but rather are things that can happen to people to impel them in the direction of choosing suicide. The second are even more immediate and situational specific ("availability of means," for example, is one of the Big Three Questions crisis intervention workers are taught in making a determination of immediate suicide risk); that is, "red flags" for suicide rather than mere "influences." The succinct and direct manner in which Kirmayer et al. (2007) present this important information is to be applauded.

A fourth box, "Protective Factors," lists personal individual characteristics that are considered to act as sorts of internal counter-gremlins to the ones given in the "Risk Factors" box. We postpone our discussion of these hypothetical internal characteristics until Chapter 6, when (1) we have formulated our own position with much greater detail, and (2) we will present a more elaborate statement of Native suicide resiliency. Here we note that the idea of personal protective factors in suicide has been around for a long time, but that it recently is receiving comparatively much more attention. In any event, we consider the existence of "protective" gremlins as likely (or not) as the existence of the "mean" ones.

The arrangement of boxes and the code system used to describe the linkages, again, mimics to a great extent that of a structural equation model. But, again, no attempt is made to quantify the degree of "causal power" involved in increasing or decreasing suicide. Presumably, the available data don't warrant any attempt at estimation.

Of course, we could pick nits if we wanted to. (The kids said "bored," not "depressed," and asserting that boredom *is* depression for adolescents is changing the definition of the construct and putting words into the mouths of their respondents.) But if there is a case for the empirical verification of the role of gremlins of the mind in Native suicide, Kirmayer et al. (2007) make it.

Moving along to social factors, our general sense is that Kirmayer et al.'s (2007) handling of social factors is not that dissimilar from that proposed by Brant, Evans, or even Fusé; even Durkheim is given his customary due consideration. Kirmayer et al. (2007) give similar attention to the problems of finances, reserve living, education, opportunity, and so on, one large difference being, again, that they supply reference to empirical research studies in support of the social factors given. There are notable additions to the list of social factors, too, sometimes developed through their willingness to elaborate more detail than other writers in their analyses: incarceration, forced assimilation, traditionalism, acculturation, modernization, residential school (and sexual abuses therein suffered), intergenerational effects of residential schooling, and the 60's and 70's scoop are examples of social factors receiving enhanced, systematic, balanced, and creditable treatment in their work.

This is not to say there are not, once again, nits to pick if we so chose. These are, however, less with the finding than they are with the relatively flat reporting of the interpretations of the findings. As we've already strongly indicated, we find sociological facts to be the most convincing answers to the question: why do indigenous peoples in contemporary Canada have such a high comparative suicide rate? Since we are on the point of making our own case, what we find inexact in the works cited by Kirmayer et al. (2007) will soon be clear enough.

Finally, although they provide as good an empirical case as can be made for the impact of social factors on suicide, the data Kirmayer et al. (2007) generate and cite are insufficient to make any estimate of degree of influence. What is both desirable and theoretically possible in Native suicidology continues to be practically unattainable or unavailable.

Nishnawbe Aski Nation Youth Forum on Suicide. In contrast to the high-powered, technologically-sophisticated approach represented by the work of Kirmayer and his colleagues, in 1996 the Nishnawbe Aski Youth undertook to research for themselves the causes of Native suicide. There are 49 separate Nishnawbe communities within this region, and the nation's Youth Forum undertook to visit each one to ask face-to-face: why are our young people killing themselves? It was not an interest in objective science that occasioned this work: in the decade running up to undertaking their report, more than 130 Nishnawbe youth had committed suicide.

The Nishnawbe Aski Nation is an extremely large area of Ontario (plus a sliver of Quebec), covering Treaty 5 and Treaty 9 areas, mostly north of the CNR rail line, abutting both James and Hudson Bay and adjoining Manitoba in the west. The Forum operated from a budget of slightly more than $300,000, which sounds like a lot until you understand that transportation (of necessity by air) ate up well over 90% of it. Forum delegates traveled to every national location at least once, where at least a full day was made available for presentations to be made and discussions to be held. Although young people were given priority in assembly, no one who wished to contribute was deprived of the opportunity. The Elderly were especially honoured for their wisdom in the matter and their assistance in assembling information.

What did the Nishnawbe Aski Youth find out?

Their nearly 400-page final report spells out their findings in detail: they found, more or less, what everyone else we've been reviewing found. Depression, hopelessness, sadness, identity problems, boredom, lack of facilities, lack of opportunities, absence of a future, poverty, abuse, alcohol, drugs... it is all here.

How are we to understand this?

To us, something seems drastically amiss when what was (quite literally) a shoe-string operation can produce the same results as, well, adequately-financed and well-staffed teams of multiply-lettered research directors employing squads of functionaries working with world-class analytic capacities. The Nishnawbe Aski didn't produce measures of the strength of impact of the causes they identified, but then neither did "the Experts." All-in-all it seems reasonable to say "Well done!" to the shoe-stringers, and wonder why it took a nuclear weapon to swat a fly when "the Experts" undertook to do it.

But then, this denigrates "the Experts" unfairly and unnecessarily. Even a cursory look at, for example, Kirmayer et al. (2007) is enough to convince *anyone*, we assert, that a serious effort of scholarship was there undertaken and achieved. Nishnawbe Aski can declare their *belief* that depression, hopelessness, etc., are, each of them, important; but Kirmayer et al. can declare a *finding*, based on palpable evidence (which any interested reader can check for her/himself by reading the list of references), that depression, hopelessness, etc. are the important factors.

After all, ultimately, where did the participants in the Youth Forum on Suicide obtain their information? Research laboratories or think tanks were no part of their available resources at the time their commission operated. It's possible, even likely, that their informants had talked to people or had heard of people or read something or intuited something of importance; but, in all fairness, none of this information can compare to what programs like Kirmayer's have produced.

We have to face a simple fact: participants in the Nishnawbe Aski Youth Forum on Suicide were, most likely, *repeating what they'd already heard or already been told* were the important causes of indigenous suicide. Some of it might well include the research findings available in the early 90's, and to that extent, it might have value in developing local initiatives against suicide. But, to the extent the findings and suggestions they obtained departed from replicable findings of academic researchers, the Nishnawbe Aski Nation was neither in any position to implement those alternatives nor to evaluate their value.

We must ask, then, what was the point of conducting this Forum? We twisted and turned on this point ourselves, trying to avoid what we see as the only answer: it was a public relations ploy. By whom, we have no idea, but we suspect that a search for the source of funding would help. Let's go through it again: in the previous decade, almost 140 aboriginal youth were dead by their own hands in Nishnawbe Aski territory. The demand for "something to be done" wouldn't have had to have been vocalized for it to be the common currency of the Nishnawbe Aski people. Three hundred thousand dollars sounds like a lot of money, but, in reality, it is a pittance, given the area, the population, and the extremity of the emergency. When you factor in, as we've said, that most of it went for transportation, then in reality what you have to say is this: "The $300,000 went to the airlines involved, *NOT* to ameliorate the suicide crisis."

The Nishnawbe Aski Nation was obviously desperate to do something about a crisis of, to all of us on the outside of it, unimaginable proportions. They were offered a straw to clutch at and they took it, because, in reality, nothing else was being offered. They were told that traveling around and talking it out amongst themselves constituted research (it does not: Sokal and Bricmont, 1998; Ross, 1996; they were either lied to or trusted a fool), and that doing this would locate the problem(s) (it did not and it could not, we will argue).

If we knew exactly at whom to point a finger, we would say: "Shame!"

Conclusions

In our examination of the literature there are doubtless a number of other researchers who have made important contributions to indigenous suicidology. We break off our review at this point, however, knowing, first, that the work they had done will come up in due course later, and second, that the results are starting to repeat themselves: that the work we're skipping past contributes nothing new at this point, and that, frankly, it's getting a little boring. It's probable that anyone interested enough in this topic to pick up this book could have produced much the same "master list" as could be distilled from the work cited here, and we see no point in harping any further on this.

We don't know about you but the two of us were hoping for more than this when we began accumulating the literature, years ago now. We're disturbed that there is such a correspondence between lay and professional opinion, especially when "professional opinion" has so little empirically to support it. To us this doesn't sound like the average indigenous person has assiduously been reading a lot of the available suicidology literature: it sounds more like the drumbeats of a PR bandwagon, like Native people are being recruited to a mainstream viewpoint rather than being convinced with real data; with all parties repeating a mantra over and over again until they parrot it without any real understanding. Have Native suicide rates improved in recent years? No one makes this claim, and we found no evidence that this is so. And yet it would seem that all the research that needs to be done has been done now; we supposedly know with confidence which factors, psychological and social (and even biological), are doing the damage, so we can start blocking or eliminating their influence with various interventions. It will all just take more money (for the experts) and some time...

And shouldn't we now ask: what was the point of the care with which the pioneer suicidologists set out definitions, clarified concepts, or developed typologies? Native suicidology didn't need them to discover the forces underlying it's phenomenon of interest! With the exception of Kirmayer (who falls back word-for-word on Durkheim's 120-year-old proposal), nobody cited here bothered either to define the term or limit their inquiries to a specific subset of "death by one's own hand" events. So, even more to the point, was research really necessary, or at least, as much of it as has occurred?

Such pessimism is warranted only if you're willing to believe that, in the time period initiated by the DIAND graph in 1978 and running up to now, a great deal has been learned about indigenous suicide. We don't think so. Suicide researchers of long standing, James Rogers and David Lester, in the subtitle of their 2010 book (*Understanding Suicide: Why We Don't and How We Might*), weren't lamenting any personal shortcomings on their part; they were expressing concern that *mainstream suicidology itself* didn't know as much as it believed itself to know.

And, in a real sense, indigenous suicidology is frankly a backwater of mainstream suicidology. It has to be understood: there is no way things can be "fine" in indigenous suicidology if the mainstream has hit a wall.

This is the position the lead author took when he stopped providing direct service a long time ago. There was no shaking the feeling that what the system was willing and able to provide was inconsistent with what was really needed by the Native people who came to the clinic seeking help. It has taken from that point until now to develop our statement of what the mainstream has failed to see about Indians and about itself, what the "Native suicide crisis" really is, and what really needs to happen.

The real book begins now.

DYING TO PLEASE YOU:

INDIGENOUS SUICIDE IN CONTEMPORARY CANADA

Chapter 4, Toward an Historical and Materialist Approach to
Indigenous Suicide: Background

Special Contributions by:
Rachael Lynne Arsenault
Carolyne May Shaw
Teresa McGee
Kem Harris-Ajig
Stacey Frances Dawe
Heather Moffatt
Jenny Atwin
Miranda Davenport

Preliminaries

Many of the conclusions we have reached thus far are likely so removed from the reader's mind that we feel we should summarize them at least briefly before going any further. First: the concept of suicide itself is far from clear. It is, for instance, used to refer to a host of actions, occurrences, and behaviors that bear no discernible relationships to one another. As well, its various theoretical formulations depend on putative insubstantial entities ("gremlins of the mind") that, rather than being "evident" or factual, are ideological necessities. And the word "suicide" itself is tarnished with a long history of use, misuse, and abuse that it carries with it to this day.

Second, although the full range of "social scientific" explanatory theories of suicide has been applied at one time or another to the problem of indigenous suicide, we find all of them unsatisfactory... this, likely, in opposition to those experts (still extant) who put forward the explanations in the first place. Our difficulty is that, in terms of their own criterion for what would constitute a successful account of indigenous suicide — predictive success of their models — mainstream theorists have no supporting evidence to offer; or, if they do, they haven't bothered to share it; or, if they do offer it, it is insufficient support for the conclusions drawn. Further, mainstream thinking about suicide is simply *applied* to us as if in the belief that it *must be* correct. The possibility that mainstream models and approaches misconceive "indigenous suicide" doesn't arise.

The common theme of ideology — "belief system," to put it simply — runs through our critique of the issue of the understanding of indigenous suicide. The real problems of belief systems are not that people have them, but that people do not recognize them as such: that people confound beliefs with facts; that people impose (sometimes thoughtlessly, sometimes maliciously) their beliefs upon other people; and that people — even when pretending to roles of "dispassionate, objective scientists" — take criticism of their belief systems as an attack upon themselves. This last point (that attacks on belief systems can in some cases be attacks on the people holding them) may indeed be true; but, in any event, what are the *facts* must first be separated out from *ideological presumptions*. Then, and only then, can the spirit of the objections made by those outside a particular ideological system be properly understood.

However, whether or not our readers share our skepticism regarding the adequacy of existing formalizations of indigenous suicide, a proof of the insufficiency of existing accounts is not a necessary precondition for proposing alternative formulations: one may *prefer* to approach even a conventionally widely-accepted explanation from a different perspective; and *de gustibus non disputandum est* (there is no arguing about tastes).

Neither is one necessarily committed to producing new empirical results which, somehow, "disprove" the older, inadequate theories. Regardless of how non-existent, limited, ambiguous, inappropriate, or self-contradictory have been the attempts to evaluate theories, producing new and superior formal empirical data is itself only important when data address an empirical issue. When the issue is conceptual, data are not pertinent and do not help (Wittgenstein, 1951/2009). An (admittedly immodest) example of this is the work of Einstein (1922) on relativity. Einstein was no laboratory scientist and produced no additional experimental results as grounds for his theorizing, but merely took already agreed-upon results and expressed them from a perspective different from that which was taken for granted by the scientists of the day. That is, he didn't consider the problem of early 20th-century physics to be an absence of facts or information, but as having an improper conceptual framework with which to understand the facts it already had. Submitting Einstein's theory to predictive empirical test came some time *after* he argued that the known facts "made better sense" when viewed from the novel perspective he proposed.

In the present case the only "known" fact we have to concern ourselves with is the one we began with: everyone agrees (within the limits established in our earlier review) that indigenous individuals living in Canada are proportionally more likely to commit suicide than are non-indigenous individuals. The analytical quality of what has been presented as "findings" on Native suicide is not sufficient, we have argued, to demand its incorporation into any "new" approach (the way, for example, Einstein worked to incorporate the results of the Michelson–Morley experiment). We start our exposition, therefore, with an almost entirely clean slate.

Sociological Models of Indigenous Suicide

As we showed in the previous chapter, there have been numerous attempts to conceptualize indigenous suicide in sociological terms, the most popular (but certainly not the only) version being that of Durkheim (1897/1966). Recognizably "sociological" explanations are embraced by specialist and layman, native and non-native alike. To us, this preference for sociological explanations likely arises from the commonplace and uncontroversial understanding that (for whatever reasons) indigenous peoples have a "pretty tough time" in Canadian society. When observed at all, we are seen as un/under-employed, un/under-educated, (comparatively) un-healthy, etc., etc., etc. It is a small step from these assumptions to concluding that our elevated rate of suicide arises thereby from some combination of the social forces under which we live and the unhealthy life-choices we sometimes make.

Conservatism and Liberalism. The ostensible uniformity of this line of reasoning masks what we shall call *liberal* and *conservative* (not Liberal and Conservative) background narratives. The liberal positions holds that the conditions of life for indigenous peoples — that is, as members of a marginalized sub-culture of Canadian society — are typically stressful; which status produces depression and other "mental states" that precede suicide; which states are (perhaps) fortified by bad lifestyle habits like alcohol abuse, drug use, and concomitant depravities; which, in combination, bring about the entity we are calling the Broken Indian; which, after sufficient decay, then commits suicide.

The conservative view is that, in a very real sense, the Broken Indian is pre-existing condition. Depending on which specific conservative is doing the talking, conservative opinion conceives of indigenous individuals variously endowed with weak wills, bad genes, character flaws, and other innate defects that are the particular personal burdens of all of us Native individuals. Because of these flaws we are thought often to make lifestyle choices that aggravate, perhaps even *produce*, the admittedly-degrading conditions under which we live. These conditions foster a host of negative mental states, at least some of which (like hopelessness and depression) are precursors to the sequence of mental events that end in suicide (following the hypothetical sequence of events as already identified and detailed in the liberal narrative, above).

Selected Social Forces. Thus, there is at least a nod to a litany of social forces — employment conditions, job opportunities, educational failure, family breakdown, substance abuse, and the like — which give rise to suicide in indigenous peoples, regardless of where in the mainstream Canadian political spectrum you reside. We find (see below) this acknowledgement of the potential influence more important than the nuances of difference between liberal and conservative positions. But another interesting feature of the correspondence between what many regard as antithetical positions is the limited range of social forces that are deemed worthy of inclusion into the supposed causal sequence. We can illustrate this point with a personal anecdote.

Nearly 30 years ago, the lead author was asked to comment on a draft version of a report on suicide in Canada. Specifically, the report's author had included some discussion of Native suicide and wanted feedback on the quality of the job done. Although the report was well-executed overall, in its initial discussion of Native suicide it had by-and-large simply repeated the roster of social factors we have already noted here. Asked to clarify his remarks, RDC noted the *absence* of the acknowledgement of (such obviously *social*) factors as racism, marginalization, condescension, infantilization, disparagement, and (unidirectional) cultural ignorance; social factors which (then as now) were the universal, near-daily experience of indigenous peoples in Canada. The response of the author to this suggestion has injured ever since: "Do you really think those things are important?"

Yes, we did, and we still do, think they are important... so much so that we will repeat here, at the outset of our own analysis, our bias:

> *Something akin to the sociological model of suicide must be correct.*

Our point, however, is that the lay public as well as authoritative suicidologists, though willing to include, even highlight social factors into their understanding of why indigenous people commit suicide, are prepared only to admit *certain* social factors into their considerations, and — as we shall see — only in a curious and bizarre manner.

Indigenous Suicide in Durkheim's Terms

The recognition of social forces, as well as the limited range they assume in modern suicide theory, was influenced by Durkheim's

(1897/1966) pioneering work. Often considered (incorrectly) to be the first formal work done on the topic of suicide, more than 100 years after its original publication arguably it has not been supplanted as a fundamental analytic text (Lester, 1994; Plaut, 1999; Pickering and Walford, 2000). In the previous chapter we reviewed several studies where, explicitly or implicitly, Durkheim's thinking had been used as the framework for understanding indigenous suicide. Here we will have a longer look at one such application, that of Davenport and Davenport (1987). We will take Durkheim's position *as is*: for present purposes its status (in terms of coherence and empirical support) is not at issue; rather, we follow Davenport and Davenport in treating it as a kind of lens through which to view Native suicide.

Davenport and Davenport (1987, p. 533) state that Durkheim identified "three major forms or types of suicide: egoistic, altruistic, and anomic (p. 533)." They then go on to evaluate the conceptual fit between their understanding of Indian suicide and Durkheim's forms. While each type is found to have at least some limited degree of relevance, it is Durkheim's *anomic* form that they conclude is most descriptive of Indian suicide. That is, they argue that Durkheim's description of his anomic form of suicide — "*Whenever serious readjustments take place in the social order, whether or not due to a sudden growth or to an unexpected catastrophe, men are more inclined to self-destruction* (Durkheim, 1897/1966, p. 246)" — is the most important explanatory variable in understanding indigenous suicide.

The dictionary definition of "anomie," the word that is the basis for the descriptive form ("anomic") originally advanced by Durkheim, refers to both a social condition — *social instability that originates in the collapse of norms and values* — and a personal one — *feelings of personal consternation and alienation that comes from purposelessness and an absence of values*. Davenport and Davenport (1987) predication of Indian suicide on anomie thus asserts both aspects and insinuates a causal linkage between the two. A fair formulation would be something like this:

> *Native individuals are susceptible to committing suicide because of the social instability which arose from the post-Columbian collapse of Native norms and values, which brought about personal, individual feelings of confusion, purposelessness, and estrangement.*

These "feelings" are the initial mental precursors of the sequence of events hypothesized by the sociological model; ultimately, they lead to suicide of the Broken Indian as agreed by both liberal and conservative, Native and non-Native, professional and lay-person alike.

Should anyone think we are putting words into anyone's mouth, we invite them to review the literature we cited earlier. With or without reference to Durkheim, time and again the breakdown of indigenous society is portrayed as leading to the "mental stressors" that are principally responsible for individual Natives killing themselves. If anything, Davenport and Davenport (1987) are being more clear and thorough than others who have made similar suggestions; that is, Davenport and Davenport take care to ground their evaluations in well-established suicidological theory. And, as a consequence, with their work the popularity of sociological explanations of Native suicide is given the blessing of formal social science.

A Curious, Bizarre Application of Durkheim

Nevertheless, there are problems in Davenport and Davenport's (1987) exposition. For Durkheim (1897/1966), anomic suicide is a formal scientific term, overlapping (of course) with common usage but given a specific meaning within the limited context of his proposed theory of suicide. It is potentially as wrong-headed to confuse Durkheim's *anomie* with the dictionary definition as it is to confuse Newton's *force* with everyday usage.

What does Durkheim mean by *anomie*, then? Durkheim's theory of suicide is that societies can be characterized by, among other things, the degree to which their citizens are *regulated* and the degree to which they are *integrated*. Both terms are more characterized than defined in Durkheim's work, but, as we have stated, we are not evaluating Durkheim's theory here. It is fair, however, to point out that precisely what he means by these two terms is controversial in the extreme: Pope (1976), for example, maintains they are not distinguishable.

Regardless of their adequacy as distinct concepts, Durkheim (1897/1966) uses them as the formalism standing behind his suicide typology. Two types of suicide, *altruistic* and *egoistic*, are proposed as arising, respectively, in excessively and insufficiently *integrated* societies. *Anomic* suicide is proposed to come about in societies that are insufficiently *regulated*. We repeat: Durkheim gave a general characterization of regulation as follows: "Whenever serious readjustments take place in the social order, whether or not due to a sudden growth or to an unexpected catastrophe, men are more inclined to self-destruction (Durkheim, 1897/1966, p. 246)."

Thus, if we are to take seriously Davenport and Davenport's conclusions (that *anomic suicide* best describes the phenomenon of indigenous self-destruction), we must accept that our societies became (at some point) *insufficiently regulative* of its citizenry, and that it was this lack of regulation — normlessness, rootlessness, the collapse of values — that initiated (among other things) the elevation of our suicide rates to the levels we continue to endure today.

Well: when and how did this happen? Recalling that they are focused on what became the United States (and *not* Canada), Davenport and Davenport's (1987) list of upheavals includes military defeat, loss of the buffalo, loss of identity, and loss of existing political, religious, linguistic, and related cultural structures. The instability, lawlessness, normlessness, and personal insecurity which arose as a result was, upon their reading of Durkheim (and their understanding of history), the individual provenience of the greater part of modern indigenous suicide.

Historical Suppression. However, this familiar story, like far too many of the fairy-tales told about the indigenous peoples of North America, is a purely ideologically-based departure from reality, dripping in ignorance and frosted with Eurocentrism. While Davenport and Davenport's (1987) characterization of Indian life is, at numerous times, patronizing and offensive (for example, their remarks that continued commitment to treaties may be "clouding the issue" is simply none of their business), this might most simply be chalked up to plain ignorance. When making the case for *anomie as the source of our tendency to commit suicide*, however, they must be held to account.

Consistent with their use of the evasive and euphemistic phrase "military defeat" to characterize the outcomes of manufactured pretexts for the slaughter of various stone-aged peoples by a modern industrial society, Davenport and Davenport employ the insipid and misleading word *"loss"* for things that were *not "lost" in any sense of the word*: the buffalo was *deliberately slaughtered* by Euros for the express purpose of denying indigenous peoples their food source ("Better kill buffalo than have him feed the Sioux;" General Philip Sheridan — also famed for his succinct defense of the slaughter of Native children, "Nits make lice"); and language, religion, political sovereignty, etc. were all *expressly targeted for destruction* by the dominant European-based society in Canada and the United States alike.

Complicity. In their mischaracterization of the "deregulation upheavals" experienced by the indigenous peoples of the Americas, Davenport and Davenport treat the outrages visited upon us are as if they were simply "events," or things that "just sort-of happened," rather than as what they were: *deliberate, calculated attempts to obliterate us*. Whether by their own intentional suppression of facts or by the omission of facts arising out of their ignorance, time and again Davenport and Davenport (1987) systematically mischaracterize the source of Native peoples' destruction; *and in doing so,* leave out the agent of indigenous misery: *Davenport and Davenport's own dominant society*. In other words, Davenport and Davenport (1987) *blame the victim* with a vengeance.

To suggest that the victims of this conspiracy "felt estranged" from the people trying to murder them is heroic mis/understatement, like Al Evans' calling Ojibways "warlike" when they were *fighting for their homes and lives*. To characterize indigenous peoples as "normless" when their norms have been destroyed, "rootless" when their lives have been uprooted, "valueless" when their values have been despised and mocked — and then to hide the purveyor of all these barbarities from any consideration — takes an ideological devotion or informational deficiency, along with an intellectual license, that flouts description.

In casting about for a "social force" to explain indigenous suicide, is "insufficiency of regulation" (that is, something that is *our own fault,* since our societies weren't strong enough to regulate us) the best modern suicidology is able to come up with? At the very least, this omits a host of "social forces" that are neither as vacuous nor as detached from reality: how about "genocide" as a social force?; or mass-murder?; or institutionalized theft, incarceration, and expropriation?; or wholesale dehumanization? Need we go on?

Exactly how did such obvious social forces escape Davenport and Davenport's (1987) notice (or their comment)? Actually, the fault is arguably not entirely theirs.

Durkheim's Model as Ideology

As we have noted, Davenport and Davenport begin their exposition by asserting that Durkheim proposed "three major forms or types of suicide," but is must be obvious to anyone paying attention that something has been left out. This is evident from a glance at Figure 7, which is a graphical representation of Durkheim's (1897/1966) proposals. If the theoretical problems slipped past your notice in the strictly textual presentation, they cannot when viewing the graph: should there not be a "type" of suicide associated with *too much regulation?*

In fact, Durkheim (1897/1966) *does* propose a fourth type. However, he gives it such short shrift that Davenport and Davenport (1987) can be forgiven for not considering it a *major* form or type of suicide. In his 405-page book Durkheim considers it in a *single paragraph relegated to a footnote!* His entire discussion bears repeating here:

> The above considerations show that there is a type of suicide the opposite of anomic suicide, just as egoistic and altruistic suicides are opposites. It is the suicide deriving from excessive regulation, that of persons with futures pitilessly blocked and passions violently choked by oppressive discipline. It is the suicide of very young husbands, or the married woman who is childless. So, for completeness' sake, we should set up a fourth suicidal type. But it has so little contemporary importance and examples are so hard to find aside from the cases just mentioned that is seems useless to dwell upon it. However, it might be said to have historical interest. Do not the suicides of slaves, said to be frequent under certain conditions... belong to this type, or all suicides attributable to excessive physical or moral despotism? To bring out the ineluctible and inflexible nature of a rule against which there is no appeal, and in contrast with the expression "anomy" which has just been used, we might call it *fatalistic suicide* (Durkheim, 1897/ 1966; p. 276).

We can now supply a name for the end of the pole opposite anomie: it is *fatalistic suicide.*

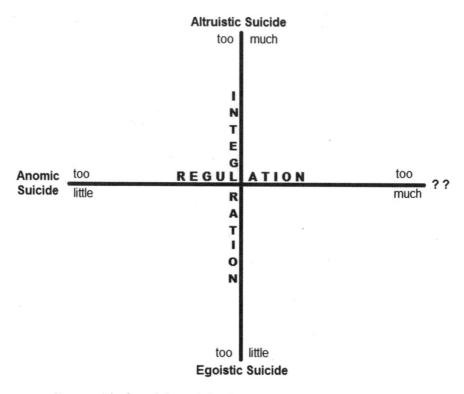

Figure 7. The formal theory behind Durkheim's typology of suicide.

We can with fairness draw two conclusions: first, that Durkheim was cognizant of the fact that *people might be driven to suicide by tyranny and oppression*; and second, that, in his opinion, tyranny and oppression in his world and time was reserved for newly-married husbands and childless wives.[3]

Durkheim was, of course, writing in 1897, and not in some far-flung future utopian society capable of transmitting his work backwards to our time. He was, in fact, living in what is now recognized as the period of greatest imperialist expansion in French history (Conklin, 1997; Conklin, Fishman, & Zaretsky, 2011; Aldrich, 1996). Given this, he was either blissfully ignorant of or consciously suppressing what his own country *had done* in China, Cochinchina, Martinique,

---

3   Kirmayer et al. (2007) is among the few that recognize that Durkheim noted a fourth type of suicide arising from oppressive treatment. Unaccountably, however, the brief discussion that arises thereafter traces the problem back to band council policies rather than following the trail to the Canadian colonialism that created reserve politics to begin with and now maintains them.

Haiti, Algiers, Tunisia, Madagascar, French Guiana, etc., along with being similarly vacated with respect to what his compatriots *currently were doing* in Cochinchina, Senegal, Central Africa, Chad, etc. What neighbouring England, Spain, Holland, Germany, and even Belgium had done and were doing to the people of the other 98% of the world's land mass seems to have escaped his notice, too. Finally, in the world he cannot pretend absolute detachment from — his own society, which in 1897 included women (?!), Jews, Roma, ex-Communards (4,000 of whom were simply banished to North Africa), and at least seventy other internal linguistic/cultural/ethnic minorities — Durkheim is unable to identify anything remotely approaching what you or we might regard as truly oppressive.

Durkheim, having sufficient insight to conclude that *individual members of oppressed peoples sometimes commit suicide because of that oppression*, now can find no place for it on his Panglossian planet. And, far from being Durkheim's special infirmity, we have been unable to locate a single instance in a large literature critical of Durkheim's work that mentions this particular deficiency on his part. If Durkheim was wrapped in the cocoon of unquestioned western European superiority (physical *and* moral), it was a cocoon which accommodates every other suicidologist we have been able to locate, too. The description itself is striking (even if at times fatuous): "persons with futures pitilessly blocked and passions violently choked by oppressive discipline... suicides attributable to excessive physical or moral despotism [there are *proper amounts* of these kinds of *despotism*?]... the ineluctible and inflexible nature of a rule against which there is no appeal..." We find it astounding that Durkheim, his followers, and even his detractors could not locate this elephant in the room, particularly when they were all working with such an excellent description of it.[4]

---

4   Here and afterwards we will adopt Durkheim's terminology ("fatalistic suicide") when we can't otherwise avoid it. As we will develop later in this work, the imputation of "fatalism" to oppressed peoples as the proximal cause of their "suicides" is another unsubstantiated rhetorical act of victim-blaming. By characterizing the issue as one of personally experienced emotion, i.e., "feeling fatalistic," Durkheim's formulation expands into: oppression "causes fatalism" in the oppressed, which then "causes depression" or some other such symptom in them, which then "causes them to commit suicide." The entire hypothesized series is unwarranted and beyond substantiation. No: it is sufficient to affirm the existence of oppression and condemn the injustice and outrageousness of it.

Durkheim's Follies

Still and all, the only novelty that can be laid at Durkheim's door is his insistence on social forces as explanations of suicide; but even here we will find his legacy equivocal at best. He was, in fact, less interested in suicide per se than in promoting sociology as a separate academic discipline. Having just finished The Rules of Sociological Method (1895/1982) two years earlier, he selected the phenomenon of suicide to demonstrate that his sociological approach could produce insights impossible to obtain otherwise. It is sometimes thought he rejected psychological insights, but he stipulated that "mental flaws" accounted for some substantial but unnamed fraction of the cases of suicide. Instead, what he aimed to show was that (with all due respect to mental flaws) there were demonstrable variations in the features of different societies and within the same society over time; and, that changes in suicide rates corresponded to some degree to those demonstrable societal variations.

Durkheim's selections for *the* social forces influencing suicide (integration and regulation) were, as we've noted, not only nebulously defined and questionably operationalized, they were really nothing more than the forces he thought to be dominating the France of his time — *regulation:* secular; *integration:* religious — and thus have little application to other times and other places (how *integrated* or *regulated* is current Canadian society? Would those two adjectives (or their opposites) be the first that sprang to mind if asked to characterize it? How would we investigate or substantiate our judgment?). A consequence of this is that Durkheim's supposedly objective, positivist empiricism cannot be regarded as any such thing, but only as axe-grinding once again posing as science.

Fatalistic suicide, in particular, was no *deduction* from *objectively-discovered forms of society*, but rather, a topic of embarrassment, to be dropped as quickly and as quietly as possible. Having elevated France's own internal conflicts between secular and religious authority as the most important social forces general enough to explain suicides not caused by mental flaws, and then applying the Goldilocks Principle (too much, too little, *just right*), Durkheim was placed to assert the "discovery" that secular government was capable of driving people to suicide. But with the Paris Commune, the Dreyfus Affair, etc. abiding in Frances's all-too-recent past, there were numerous controversies which Durkheim was likely disinclined to assert a radical, critical, and potentially anti-governmental position; hence its reduction to a few ridiculous exemplars in a spare, forlorn footnote. Durkheim also considered altruistic suicide outdated and rare, but managed nonetheless to write 27 pages about it.

No, rather than a deduction from an objective scientific finding, fatalistic suicide was a pompous name for something no one with an ounce of humanity could doubt: *that oppression kills people*. And the proof that this was nothing out of the ordinary was the work of a real innovator in suicide: Karl Marx. Marx's contributions to suicidology was until recently almost entirely unknown (*Marx on Suicide* (*MOS*); Plaut and Anderson, 1999) but deserves our recognition and appreciation.

Durkheim's Vardøger

In 1845, Marx, slowly starving in Belgium after having been chased out of France (after having been chased out of Germany), was commissioned to produce a German translation of a book by one Jacques Peuchet, a French bureaucrat who had died in 1830 but who had left a mémoire. Peuchet had lived in interesting times (sometimes coming close to death as a result of the positions he had held in various governments), but had eventually ended up in charge of the bureau in Paris responsible for pulling the bodies of suicides out of the Seine. One aspect of Peuchet's job was to interview neighbours, friends, and surviving family members of the deceased and write what today would be called a psychological autopsy: a short summary of what had caused each individual to commit suicide (as far as it could be determined). Published in numerous volumes, much of the content of his memoir consisted of little more than the summaries his bureaucracy had produced. However, Peuchet had permitted himself the latitude to moralize here and there as well as speculate on the why's and wherefore's of suicide. Marx's job was not only to translate, but to edit down and focus the memoir so that it would fit, physically and editorially, into a small socialist journal called *Gesellschaftsspiegel* (*Mirror of Society*).

It is as important to situate Marx's translation in his time and circumstances as it is to situate Durkheim's book in Durkheim's period. A year earlier Marx had written what has come down to us as *The Economic and Philosophic Manuscripts of 1844* (*EPM*; Marx, 1844/1988), a compendium of speculative thoughts and notes to himself never meant for publication. Marx often wrote notebooks to himself that presaged later publication on similar topics. *EPM* is important because it contained his only extended discussion of *alienation*, an analysis that signalled his intellectual distancing of himself from Hegel and that, arguably, became a unifying, underlying humanistic theme for all, or nearly all, of his work that came after.

MOS — Marx's translation of Peuchet — was, at crucial points, less a rendering of Peuchet's words or expressions than they were expressions of Marx's own thinking on the topic of suicide, infused with the spirit of his "Paris" writings. Specific word translations are "bent" in directions hardly intended by Peuchet's original words, and entire phrases and sentences necessarily reflecting Marx's own thoughts (since Peuchet had quite literally written nothing) are introduced. Peuchet, indeed, did not take the then-common, strictly moralist position on suicide; but neither did he adopt anything like a psychological position, writing:

> Above all, it is absurd to claim that an act, which occurs so often, is an unnatural act. Suicide is in no way unnatural, as we witness it daily. What is contrary to nature does not occur. It lies, on the contrary, *in the nature of our society* to cause so many suicides... (Plaut and Anderson, 1999, p. 47 - 48; italics indicate an "enhancement" by Marx).

But it is in the editorial hands of Marx that Peuchet's words become more than mere liberal reproach for so many needless deaths:

> One condemns suicide with foregone conclusions. But, the very existence of suicide is an open protest against these unsophisticated conclusions... (p. 48).
> How is it that people commit suicide, despite such great anathema against it? The blood of the despairing does not flow through the same arteries as that of those cold beings who have the leisure to debate such fruitless questions. Man is a mystery to man; one knows only how to blame him, but does not know him... (p. 48).
> It has been believed that suicide could be prevented by abusive punishments and by branding with infamy the memory of the guilty one. What can one say about the indignity of such branding, hurled at people who are no

longer there to plead their case? The unfortunate rarely bother themselves with all this. And, if the act of suicide accuses someone, it is usually those remaining behind, because in this crowd there was not one person for whom it was worth staying alive... (p. 49 - 50).

To one who wishes to flee this world, how do the insults that the world promises to heap on his corpse matter? He see therein only another act of cowardice on the part of the living. In fact, what kind of society is it wherein one finds the most profound loneliness in the midst of millions of people, a society where one can be overwhelmed by an uncontrollable urge to kill oneself without anyone suspecting it? This society is no society, but, as Rousseau said, a desert populated by wild animals... (p. 50).

It is apparent (and from far more of *MOS* than we can cite) that Durkheim was anticipated in crucial ways by Peuchet/Marx; first in downplaying the role of personal, individual causes in the explanation of suicide, and second in emphasizing social ones. Marx's candidate for the social force responsible: *oppression*. Thus, as Plaut and Anderson (1999) note, the four cases Marx abstracts from perhaps thousands he could have chosen from Peuchet's mémoire are all arguably instances of what would (later) be classified as *fatalistic suicide* by Durkheim. Marx, in *EPM*, even provided a genealogy for oppression: it arose from *alienation*, which he defined as nothing less than *the human condition under capitalism*. Finally, Peuchet/Marx anticipate a substantive point we have already condemned in Durkheim: victim-blaming and the researching of causes of suicide is an evasion of what is perfectly obvious. That is, the data necessary to the understanding of suicide was already (in 1845) at hand; what was needed for understanding was a better way to organize it.

It is going too far to suggest that Peuchet/Marx constitutes the first formal "theory" of suicide; the work is far too narrow and unsystematic for that claim to be made or maintained. But that does not detract in any way from the fact that, at the very beginning of Marx's thinking on "materialism of an historical kind," he was able to find in Peuchet the inspiration to do important and original work. Moreover, there even are grounds to speculate that Marx's translation of Peuchet inspired Durkheim's bourgeois efforts (much of Peuchet's original work was destroyed during the Paris Commune, so Marx's translation was possibly the only version available to Durkheim); although Durkheim suppressed the connection if it existed.

Even if Marx, with the insights and intellectual tools he developed in his early writings, failed to develop a "theory" of suicide — one which we could then apply to the problem of understanding indigenous suicide — there is nothing to stop us from doing so now. There is no direct route from *MOS* and *EPM* to this; after all, in his own way, the Marx of 1844/45 was as ignorant of indigenous peoples and our issues as Davenport and Davenport of 1987. But it is at the very least a simple matter of courtesy to acknowledge his priority and his contribution to the description we develop here.

Help Wanted

However that may be, we contend that in Marx's early writings, first, that there is a clear, succinct, sufficient, although not necessary account of why people commit suicide, and second, that this account, when appropriately enlarged upon, is an accurate description of why indigenous peoples in contemporary Canada are committing suicide. We will deal with the latter contention in the next chapter and expand on the first part in the remainder of this one.

Again, following Plaut and Anderson (1999), *MOS* and *EPM* will be taken as mutually informative with respect to Marx's description of the phenomenon of suicide. We see three interrelated propositions as centrally important to our task here: (1) the practical grounds for the explication of human behavior is historical and material; (2) defining "alienation" following Marx (1844/1988), alienation is oppression; (3) oppression instantiates suicide describable as Durkheim's fatalistic type.

Oppression is the precursor of fatalistic suicide. The third proposition need not consume a great deal of our time or effort here, since neither Marx nor Durkheim had any trouble making the connection, and, on his own, even Chrisjohn, in the vignette with which we ended Chapter 1, saw the linkage without any prompting from anyone. The only confusion we can see is whether one wants a radical, liberal, or "common sense" conception standing behind the linkage. Here, for completeness' sake, we point out that in our discussion of Davenport and Davenport (1987) we made an informal case that the liberal conception is at best mistaken or misleading, and at worst disingenuous. In other words, we think it is either common sense or are willing to grant Marx - Peuchet pride of place. We will explain more completely by the end of this chapter.

Alienation <=> Oppression. Much more central to this entire discussion is Marx's concept of *alienation*. The same commonsensical approach taken in the previous section is helpful: the capitalism of the Marx of 1844 was, beyond a doubt, oppressive. Men worked 12-hour days or longer (until electric lighting could extend the length of the working day and eventually help create shift work) in order to eke out a bare existence; women and children were, if anything, even more ruthlessly exploited; no provision was made for work safety, interruptions of work periods, family needs, health benefits, or any sort of indulgence; and worse. (Marx's first volume of *Capital* (1867/1977) continues to be an important source of information about this period.) In short, under the capitalism of Marx's time people led lives "piteously blocked by oppressive discipline" and existed under "an inflexible rule against which there was no appeal." Is this sounding familiar?

But in *EPM* Marx was trying to go past the obvious abuses attending capitalism. In trying to capture capitalism's essence, he does not settle for obvious targets (maximizing profits; eliminating competition; etc.) but argues that, under capitalism, *workmanship* — that is, labour — *is separated from ownership*. Simply put: workers do not own what they make, and owners do not make what they own. For Marx, this feature of capitalism distinguishes it from all other forms of organizing the productive capacity of societies. For various reasons Marx names this separation — which is objectively true and obvious (just try to go home with a car after working on an assembly line all day at the factory) but nowadays is just taken as the natural order of things — *alienation*.

There is no particular need, nor do we wish, to detour at this point into an elaborate discussion of Marx's early works (see Schaff, 1980; Wallimann, 1981). But it is worth noting that, in equating alienation with an objective circumstance (the division of productive forces into workmanship and ownership) Marx departs from Hegel's notion of alienated labour as essentially anthropological and mystical — a nebulous spiritual force which is collectively characteristic of humanity — and designates it as a *social force* rather than an *individual characteristic*. For Marx, alienation is not a feeling or an experience or an emotion or anything like the gremlins-in-the-mind we have been studying; it is not consciously, unconsciously, or subconsciously held. It is a *social fact* of capitalism, *whether or not you're aware of it*. That is, it is entirely a *material* phenomenon, one that is directly manifest, and not an *idealistic* one (such as Hegel's idea of an injured personal soul distanced from a universal World Spirit).

Thus Marx's objections to capitalism, even in 1844/1988, weren't limited to the kinds of depredations given slight mention at the outset of this section. Since, for Marx, our natural state was for our labour and its outcome to form an essential unity, their separation was itself oppressive in and of itself. By virtue of its very existence capitalism was oppressive, according to Marx, even if its victims weren't individually or collectively aware of it.

We must interject here, Marx wasn't arguing that capitalism and *only* capitalism was oppressive. Slavery was oppressive (as even Durkheim seemed to agree), feudalism was oppressive, and individual circumstances in any society might be arranged such that a person or persons, individually or collectively, were subjected to oppression. Capitalism itself was eventually forced to moderate its early excesses, so that the average Canadian today may find the demands of a job to be something of a nuisance, but doesn't think of it as oppressive.

If you're keeping score, this completes what we undertook to show at the beginning of the last major heading. In Marx's early works, there is a clear, succinct, although insufficient account of why people commit suicide: capitalism is alienation; alienation is oppression; oppression causes suicide. Other things can be oppressive; and people may kill themselves for reasons other than that they are oppressed. This means that Marx's "theory" of suicide is *sufficient* to produce them, but *unnecessary* since there are other ways for suicides to happen.

The Practical Grounds for the Explication of Behavior. And yet we have one more self-appointed task to undertake before moving on. Since it does not form an essential part of our demonstration you can wonder just what it's doing here. But we wish to assert that the practical grounds for the explication of human behavior falls within the realm of what is historical and material, and not what is necessarily intangible. To do this we will need the assistance of an old friend, Bobbi/Bob.

In the next chapter we will have more to say about this picture. For now just consider the following: assume the behavior of interest is suicide; assume that Bobbi/Bob lived in a capitalist society; and assume that the intrinsic oppression of alienation was a causal factor in her/his death. Where was alienation, inside Bobbi/Bob, and how did it get in there? Alienation isn't a feature of individuals, but rather a feature of the society in which Bobbi/Bob resided. To demand that it must somehow, in some manner, have also become an *internal resident* of Bobbi/Bob is pure presumption, as would be any hypothesized process by which this transference supposedly took place.

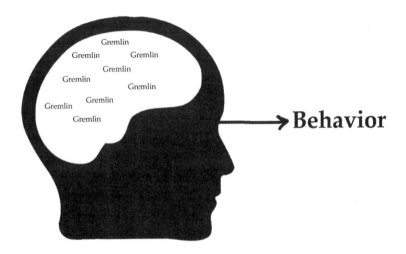

Figure 8. The return of Bobbi/Bob

Consider the issue this way: *must* a fish have some internal conception of *water*, and is it this *conception* (resident somewhere within its conscious or unconscious mind), rather than *water itself*, the thing that somehow constrains and directs its actions? Or can it just get on with its life without confronting the "big fish questions" of why there's water some places and not others, who put it there, and what's it all for? In considering this, recall that human beings — perhaps even more inquisitive creatures than fish — didn't know about *air* (and its relation to oxygen, blood circulation, breathing, and heartbeat) until well into the 17th century, although, of course, we had noted that people who stopped breathing were less likely to come to dinner.

To accord alienation not just internal and invisible existence, but *agentive power* as well (sufficient to get Bobbi/Bob to *kill* him-

or herself) is nothing more than a dogmatic devotion to the belief that behavior must be reduced to invisible (but presumed) internal mechanics. It has long been recognized that dogmatic thinking can readily produce abracadabra-style "solutions" to any conundrum; what it can't produce is empirical science. And, people: empirical science is what modern suicidology pretends to be.

Our insistence on historical and material grounds for explicating human behavior is based on the fact that, by so insisting, we won't be led astray chasing will-o-the-wisps that end up explaining nothing. By *history*, we mean that, in principle, the sequence of concrete actions that give rise to the final action can be documented; by *material*, that it is open to investigation and inspection. Later we will review the inherent weakness of the personal, internal, individual gremlins theory of mind, and will even give our readers an idea of what brought it into existence in the first place. For now, notice what our description of Marx's statement on suicide gives us: a coherent account of the phenomenon based in material reality.

As for the "lurking gremlins" theory of behavior, we share Shakespeare's skepticism. Certainly, there are many who insist that they can call such spirits from the vasty deep. But do the spirits actually come when they are called?

DYING TO PLEASE YOU:

INDIGENOUS SUICIDE IN CONTEMPORARY CANADA

Chapter 5, Not to Be...

Introduction

For as many people as have asked us: "Why do so many Indians commit suicide?," we hope we've made it abundantly clear: there's no big mystery here. The lead author gave a sufficient, if somewhat terse account (summarized at the beginning of this book) over 20 years ago now. That explanation was (and is) in complete accord both with informal, gut-level speculation and with subsequent academic theorizing (since, in fact, nothing has been put forward that substantiates any other suggestion and no hard findings exist that are in disagreement with the alienation-oppression-suicide model we've attribute to the early Marx). If the search continues for an "answer" it can only be because people don't like the one we've already given them.

Or maybe we haven't been as clear as we've thought we've been. Since we haven't run out of things to say, that possibility grants us leave to try another tack. The freedom of not being tied to the preconception that Indians *broken in some way* are the ones that commit suicide opens up all kinds of possibilities.

Back to Broken Indian Mountain

Surfacing from time-to-time in our narrative is someone/thing we've called the Broken Indian Model of indigenous suicide, which is, in simple terms, the Blame-the-Victim (Ryan, 1971; 1981) idea that we're committing suicide because we have some inherent (possibly even racial) defect that predisposes us to suicide. If we've painted it as a wallflower, in reality the Broken Indian Model is the life of the party; as we show in Table 1, there's virtually no Native place in the institutional world of Canada it does not hold pride of place.

We make no claim that Table 1 is comprehensive, only that it's an instructive overview. Taken as a whole, we would argue, it is pure fiction (there is no such thing as "residential school syndrome," for example; Chrisjohn & Young, 1997). In the "Disorder" column "school failure" appears quite a few times because, well, we've been "failing" for quite some time now, so much so that the baloney explanations have proliferated there like mushrooms in manure. But it is in fact the "Explanation" column where the heart of the Broken Indian model lies. These all share two important features: first, as already noted, that they blame the victim and, second, that there is no scientific evidence

Table 1

The BROKEN INDIAN: Indians As Poly-Pathogenic People

Disorder	Explanation	Recommended Intervention
diabetes	"thrifty gene"	drugs
tuberculosis	inherent respiratory insufficiency	let them die
alcohol/drug use/abuse	alcoholism gene	counselling/drugs
residential school syndrome	attending residential school	counselling/drugs
child behavioural problems	bad parenting skills	counselling/drugs & apprehension
family violence	bad parenting skills	counselling/drugs & apprehension
school failure	genetic stupidity	shovels & brooms
school failure	left-brainedness	modify curriculum & expectations
school failure	FASD	snakes & ladders
school failure	ADHD	drugs/expulsion
school failure	visual learning style	modify curriculum & expectations
school failure	ego-dystonic personality disorder	snakes & ladders
criminality	bad impulse control	prison & tough love
elder abuse	bad life skills	life-skills training
AIDS/STD's	bad parenting skills	let them die
un/underemployment	lazy; Indian-time	tough love
high infant mortality rate	bad parenting skills; alcoholism gene	apprehension
suicide	suicide gene; anomic suicide	counselling/drugs

Note: specialists called for are psychologists, social workers, and various neo-tech pseudo-specialists.

for any of them (that's right, none; we know they're popular, but its popularity has nothing to do with whether or not something is true). "Interventions" appear to be diverse, but in reality they devolve into three categories: (1) let nature take its course, (2) suppress the unwanted behavior with drugs, or (3) Missionary Work (which is our phrase for the collection of non-chemically-based interventions used on indigenous peoples; we'll explain later). Regardless of which intervention is chosen for a particular case, mainstream interveners when-and-if it ends badly are ready with the response, "We did everything we could" (which, we think, is likely to have been the case, but in a perverse way). And, at the very last line of the table we've placed the subject of this particular inquiry, indigenous suicide.

We think, first of all, that this is the way all the disorders of the poly-pathogenic indigenous peoples are seen and understood by the non-poly-pathogenic Canadians. This is the list of characteristic defects of creatures that are the unusual and unique burdens of authentic (that is, non-Indian) Canadians (*suicide* being just another member of this list). On its own, suicidology is seen as an arcane specialization beyond the ken of the riff-raff; considered by itself, it garners its own headlines, generates its own literature, has its own funding arrangements, runs its own programs, etc. But seen as just another element on a long list of indigenous defects, suicide is almost overwhelmed by the immensity and range of the events within which it is submerged.

Taking all the elements together at one time (and recall that our list isn't complete) presents us with a new problem: what the dickens is going on here, that there are people walking around (and many, many buried) in Canada, today, looking like, well, fugitives from a train-wreck? We can see only two explanations (though some variations on those two give the false appearance of being another option). One: *that these are the most inferior, dismal, twisted, third-rate, pathetic excuses for human beings ever to be seen or likely ever to have been seen.* Or two: *someone put these people on a train and then drove them over a cliff.* As the Explanations column of Table 1 shows, we think the average non-poly-pathogenic Canadian, liberal or conservative, has chosen the Option One.

The first explanation *blames the victim,* the second *demands we look for the perpetrator or perpetrators;* the first explanation *sees it arising from a fickle, irreversible, Mother Nature,* the second *demands deeper explanations to develop real interventions;* the first explanation is *mystical and unscientific*, the second *historical and material*; the first explanation is *racist*, the second *human*; the first explanation *encourages the status quo*, the second *demands radical activity*; the first explanation *paves over problems with prison and drugs and false consciousness*, the second option... does what?

The Broken Indian list, left to stand, is offered and taken as proof of our sub-human status; it provides the mainstream with the justification for our marginalized political, social, legal, historical, and economic positions within the society of "real" Canadian; it is the paternalistic grounds for "gradualism" in self-*governance* (but not *government*), and every other purported "reclamation effort" made by a benevolent and long-suffering mainstream; and it's a demonstration of why we Native peoples need to depend on the charity and the kindness of people who are our betters.

A Myth of Our Own

But the Broken Indian Model is false. If held by the average non-poly-pathogenic Canadian, he or she is either ignorantly wrong, complicit in promoting the model, or both. If held by the average poly-pathogenic indigenous person, he or she is ignorantly wrong, complicit in promoting it, or both. Shorn of all its pseudoscientific blather, the Broken Indian is the unadulterated plutonium of racism. There can be no holier-than-thou neutrality with respect to this issue, as we shall prove in our next book on the topic of the Canadian form of racism.

But as for now: there is an entirely different story to be told, and indeed, bits and pieces of if have come out from time-to-time. But these are in so many fragments and they arise across such a range of specific, seemingly unrelated topics of concern that, at this point, the alternative to unadulterated racism lacks the simplistic, brutal harmony of the idea that "Indians aren't really people; so, no wonder they're so screwed up" as a common ideology. We're going to have to start from an entirely different point.

A man walking through a huge, almost empty parking lot observes another man standing at the end of an enormous flatbed truck, upon which are placed hundreds of pottery vases. The man next to the truck is picking up a vase and smashing it on the asphalt around him, over and over again; the shards of broken pottery are everywhere. The man passing through asks the man what he's doing, and the man breaking the pottery says that he's furnishing his new house, selecting vases now, and will only include goods of highest quality and durability. The vases that can withstand the treatment, which are being put aside, will be accepted and used, he says. The man nods in agreement and continues on his way; the new homeowner continues his selection process.

Think whatever you like of our fairy-tale, our conclusions are: the man smashing the vases is demented; the man walking past is complicit in the useless destruction of perfectly good vases; and, if this story is set in Canada, soon another man will show up and invent "Vaseology," the science of why some vases break one way while other vases break another.

And we're the vases. And our myth is true. This is how we see it:

What were treated as "Disorders" in Table 1 should, in our opinion, be identified as **Reaction**s or **Responses** … the different ways in which *any* object may come apart when mistreated. That is, nothing on this list, suicide included, should be seen as it own separate thing: when "stressed" in an inappropriate, unjustifiable way, some Native people "come apart" by committing suicide, some by failing academically, some by becoming chronically unemployed, and so on. (We are aware that what we are calling "Reactions" interact with one another in complicated ways, but we are not modeling that here.) The way these were presented in Table 1, as we've said, was as if these were independent diseases, events, problems, and other conditions that JUST HAPPEN TO PEOPLE FOR SOME REASON (and to Indian people more often). But in Table 2, they arise as effects of a common cause, OPPRESSION. The circular reasoning inherent in the gremlin model (more formally known as the homunculus fallacy; Kenny, 1971), where causes are vapid Just-So stories ("Indians drink because they have an invisible gremlin inside them that's an alcoholic; Indians commit suicide because there's an invisible gremlin inside of them that wants them to kill themselves; etc."), is obliterated. To situate our analysis properly we have placed new entries at the start and end of the disorders/reactions column; here we will comment on the first one and leave the last to later, when we consider our therapeutic recommendations.

Submission, which now tops our chart, is, of course, ***the point of oppression***. That is, the oppressor's program is to intrude into the lives of the oppressed and impose compliance to an alternative order (Bauman, 1989); to force (through punishment, credible threat, legislation, or

Table 2

The TYRRANIZED INDIAN: The Historical and Material Picture

Reaction	Explanation	Is There A Cure?
submission	being broken	no, you're already dead
diabetes	being broken	activism
tuberculosis	being broken	activism
alcohol/drug use/abuse	being broken	activism
residential school syndrome	being broken	activism
child behavioural problems	being broken	activism
family violence	being broken	activism
school failure	being broken	activism
criminality	being broken	activism
elder abuse	being broken	activism
AIDS/STD's	being broken	activism
un/underemployment	being broken	activism
high infant mortality rate	being broken	activism
suicide	being broken	activism
informed resistance	refusal	no, you're not broken

OPPRESSION

whatever assures compliance) the oppressed to do the oppressor's bidding, whether that's digging ditches, picking cotton, or anything else. One's culture, one's *form of life* (to use Wittgenstein's (1951/2009) more accurate terminology) is a *praxis*, an *engagement*, a *doing*, and in surrendering to the demands of the oppressor, the oppressed necessarily *cease to do as they wish, cease engaging in the praxis that constitutes their form of life*. Submission to the will of the oppressor is a manifestation of being **broken**. Rather than uniformly ridiculing those who have been broken, societies historically have worked to solidify the oppression they have achieved by the creation of various mythologies, expressed in a variety of ways: as in the myths that certain colors of skin instantiate superiority (racism), certain genitalia confer predominance (sexism), certain advantageous positions indicate nobility (classism), or even, certain metals in the soul (gold, silver, bronze) denote competence.

Often, selected members of the oppressed (*compradors*) are praised for their success in emulating their oppressors and are held out as "role models," the pusillanimity of whom being the goal to which the oppressed all should aspire. Those who betray their people are even rewarded by the oppressor with a measure of relative prosperity, not just in the hope of making other members of the oppressed envious of their achievement (and thereby making submission to the will of the oppressor more tempting), but in an attempt to forestall rebellion and resistance in the greater number of the oppressed (e.g., as indirect controls) and secure the assistance of the comprador in additional acts of suppression (e.g., providing a veneer of "due process" to further depredations).

At the beginning of our inquiry suicide was a solitary, mysterious event that, for some reason, had chosen to invade our worlds and spread its destruction among our nations. But now, placed within its proper context, its unmasking has enabled us to break through the fog and allowed us to see what is really going on within this lingering crisis: that some individuals members of oppressed peoples kill themselves. As we shall see, suicide is more than just one more entry on the list of outcomes of our oppression; it is also the key to understanding *informed resistance*, the only reaction to oppression that is not, ultimately, self-destructive of our forms of life.

Oppression. Of course, we have yet to address the engine that powers the reformulation we are proposing. We will find this to be a tricky business, first, because we think it *obvious* and its discussion to be largely unnecessary; and second because we think it *obvious* and its discussion to be *insulting* to our prime readership. In both instances, however, we consider there are enough loose ends that it's worth time making good the connections.

Oppression, Obvious and Unnecessary. The sequence we postulate as applying to the suicide of indigenous peoples is the one we credited to Marx in the previous chapter: *capitalism is alienation; alienation is oppression; oppression causes suicide.* Are Native peoples in Canada alienated? Obviously, yes. But once again we must belabour the obvious to avoid being glib.

For years now we have had any number of occasions to point out an obvious truth: *whatever the indigenous nations (of what was later to become Canada) were at time of contact, we were not capitalists.* Capitalism itself is now recognized as being post-Columbian,[5] so it would have been odd if our nations (even with our extensive pre-Columbian networks of trade, the story of which has been largely expunged by mainstream historians: Jennings, 1994; Mann, 2006) had somehow invented capitalism before the soon-to-be arch-capitalists.

Because we were not capitalists, we were not (indeed, *could not have been*) alienated in Marx's (1844/1988) sense *until European colonizing nations undertook to destroy our Native economies and force our peoples to operate within the European economic system.* Indeed, initially England and France were perfectly happy reaping the benefits of our early trade with them, when it took 16 beaver pelts to purchase one rifle on this side of the Atlantic while one pelt purchased 16 rifles on the European side (a 256% mark-up, not counting transportation expenses; impressive even by today's 3rd-world sweatshop standards). But, once the commodification of the land itself became an important consideration,[6] Native peoples increasingly were faced with the

---

5   Blaut, 1993; although certain important features of capitalist political economies were present in Europe before 1492, these were insufficient for formally defined capitalism to have come into being until European nations had the incentive to mass reproduce the means (e.g., weapons and ships) of dispossessing indigenous American nations.

6   ...for England; France was for the most part content to exploit trade relations rather than, as England, dispossess Indians so as to acquire cheap land to sell. With little territory and many fugitive populations to accommodate (Huguenots, Catholics, Irish, Scots, and more), some of their own making, land dispossession became an English obsession, one which the indigenous nations of the early colonial period realized the importance of when choosing sides in the wars of European colonization.

demand to either submit to the hegemony of English settlers or go off somewhere and die.

We repeat: Native peoples are, first and foremost, *peoples*, and as such were no less affected by, nor any more cognizant of, the consequences of life in a world where the fruits of one's labour were supposedly owned by someone who hadn't done the work. The coercion to abandon our own economic practices and either adapt to life on the margins of the transplanted European mainstream (as no more than exploited labour, since the real work of the fur trade was done by indigenous peoples; the much-vaunted voyageurs were merely the 17th and 18th century equivalents of truck drivers) or shoulder the burdens attending a move away to an increasingly small but unaffected area (and try to maintain traditional tribal forms of life) was (and still is) oppression unimaginable.

So, for various reasons capitalism and the alienation synonymous with its imposition did not infest indigenous nations in one go, any more than capitalism was a light-switch that instantly went from off to on. Even, or perhaps we should say especially, in Europe, the transition to this new economic system was achieved only through prolonged, bloody struggle (Perelman, 2000), an imposition incomplete even in non-nominally communistic countries until well into the 20th century. The widespread opposition to capitalism, largely unknown even to the descendants of the peoples of Europe who resisted, now are events consigned to the dustbins of inconvenient history. But *these* were the peoples of whom Marx wrote when he proclaimed that *oppression kills*.

Oppression, Obvious and Insulting. Recall our earlier discussion of liberal and conservative opinion on indigenous suicide: we argued that they differed in the story as to how "the Indian" became sick enough to commit suicide and how much, in principle, intervention could be expect to change our rates. But they agreed that the locus of the problem (and thus the locus of intervention) was indigenous peoples and their communities, leading to near universal acceptance of "social forces" models of indigenous suicide.

The blindness we spoke of at that point — the willingness to see some social factors but the inability to comprehend social factors originating in the mainstream oppression of indigenous people — necessitates we make the point here that it is not just the oppression of capitalism's split between workmanship and ownership that constitutes the oppression Native peoples endure on a daily basis. But it is intellectually embarrassing to have to make it: to indigenous people because, as we say, it's *part of our daily experience*; and to mainstream Canadians because it indicates a lack of personal and collective insight that is as appalling as it is astonishing. So we say to our sisters and brothers reading this: by all means, skip past this section if you find it too insulting to your intelligence. To everyone else we say: remove all your rhetorical appeals to the munificent motives behind the actions and policies of the mainstream with respect to Native peoples, and *look at what has happened and is happening.*

In Table 3 we compress a long, disturbing history leading up to the point Canada's policy of oppressing Native peoples can be treated as "its own" (even though there has always been, and continues to be cross-fertilization of ideas between the WIMPs — Western Imperial Malevolent Powers — when it comes to the elimination of their "indigenous problems"). Some of this is available in standard histories,[7] although we must insist that empty speculation about the motives of historical figures be replaced with material facts (for example, England abandons Canada after the American Civil War because of the projected cost of protecting it from what was then the largest and best equipped army on Earth, not because of any collective desire on the part of Canadian settler society for freedom and independence). To us it is clear that, from the time it achieved "independent" WIMP status, Canada took the eventual *elimination* of indigenous peoples, their ownerships, and their rights as *fundamental* to what the founders wished Canada to become. The myth of the "Vanishing Indian" became the continental slogan rationalizing Manifest Destiny, and "helping Mother Nature get to where she was headed anyway" was cemented into policy.

In the United States this additionally took the form of physical slaughter (toned down somewhat in recent decades), but Canada could not emulate this: the BNA Act and treaties already in place in 1867 legally required at least the appearance of fair dealings with Native nations. Nevertheless, in order to bring about Canada as it exists today,

---

7   In addition to the forthcoming Chrisjohn & McKay, 2018, we recommend the following list of references for people who wish to come to reasonable understanding of modern indigenous issues: Davis & Zannis, 1973; Shewell, 2004; Lux, 2001; Kulchyski, 1994; Thatcher, 2004; Chrisjohn & Young, 1997; Robinson & Quinney, 1985; and Titley, 1986.

Table 3

Historical and Material Origins of Oppression of Indigenous Peoples in Canada

1	2	3	4
Europeans encounter North, Central & South America and begin showing up in force and with regularity. They become WIMPs -- Western Imperial Malevolent Powers -- and attack any indigenous population that cannot defend themselves.	The ideology of racism is created by WIMPs to disqualify us as human beings to which moral and legal considerations apply.	Racism becomes the ideological and moral evasion of charges of murder, theft, and enslavement in interaction with American and African indigenous peoples, since, e.g., killing a beast may not be nice, but it isn't murder; neither can you steal from one.	Racism in its extreme form proves untenable: "nonhuman" is dialled down to "subhuman."

5	6	7	8
Indians save Canada for English (1812) and are thought useful as a buffer-state to the USA. For this, Indians are accorded status as allies (until it becomes convenient for England to discard them).	England fears the cost of protecting Canada from USA (1867) & cuts itself loose politically while maintaining its economic grasp. Canadian Settler WIMPs love the thought of reaping larger, local economic benefits, but are saddled with terms of the BNA Act, which technically enjoins them from slaughtering Indians in order extinguish title issues (as the USA has undertaken).	However, Canada, like Settler WIMPs in other lands, retains the need to evade aboriginal title in a manner consistent with Western legal principles.	Canadian WIMPs learn how Euro-Tasmanian WIMPs eliminated their aboriginal people: by encouraging "assimilation" by penalizing every aspect of indigenous forms of life, making traditional means of survival impossible, and permitting mitigation of misery only upon signing a legal declaration that they are no longer indigenous people. First Indian Act is created (1876) & "enfranchisement," or Canadian bureaucratic genocide, becomes official.

OPPRESSION BECOMES POLICY

105

successive federal governments and the Canadian legal system has had to deal with the continuing problem of aboriginal title and rights. At the time of this writing, the thorny problem of how to appropriate indigenous land and property without paying for it persists; the possibility that indigenous nations maintain their ownership while being compensated for previous outright robberies is not allowed to be raised as an issue.

But it was the success of the bureaucratic genocide in Tasmania (after the failure of the physical version) that inspired imitation on Canada's part. Starting from the First Indian Act in 1876 and continuing to the version currently in force, Canada has maintained a carrot-and-stick approach to "encourage" the legal termination of Native peoples; and, in so doing, they hope to create *Terra Nullius* after the fact, thus ending in one fell stroke all Western legal doubts concerning title. The policy is, simply: on the "stick" side, to outlaw and punish any attempt to live "like an Indian" while destroying the possibility of maintaining one's own indigenous form of life;[8] and on the "carrot" side, impose on Native peoples constraints on the exercise of full freedoms enjoyed by "real" Canadians, as well as access to "real" Canadian's services and opportunities: that is, limit them to those indigenous individuals who sign a paper affirming they are no longer indigenous. (Native women who married non-Natives were tossed off band lists automatically until the mid-1980's, when the sexism was so plain even conservatives could no longer defend it. Now Native women and, more importantly, their children lose their status more slowly.) This has been known all along as *enfranchisement*, since for a long time the most obvious change was being allowed to vote in Canadian elections. But enfranchisement effectively terminates (as Canada sees it) any legal obligation on the part of Canada to consider someone who signs such a declaration as "aboriginal (sic)."

To put it simply, when we're all gone, Canada's title extinguishment problems, past and present, are all gone, too.

This is not intended to be, nor is it offered as, a primer on the institutionalized oppression of indigenous peoples in Canada. If this is all news to you, then *do the work* entailed in reading some of the

8   And, for the 1,000,000[th] time, we do not mean "living in tipis and eating badgers." We mean, to exist within authentically indigenous ethical, political, moral, and material systems which accommodate as far as is considered prudent commensurate changes in living conditions. That is, to exist precisely as European settler populations have since 1607.

titles we listed earlier and then dig deeper on your own. The truth is, citizens have a responsibility to know what their governments are up to, and if this deliberate, long-standing policy of coercing termination has somehow slipped past you, dig into its history (unless you're happy with what's being achieved in all this, which means you can stop reading now).

It matters not at all which specific policy you examine: residential school, the 60's and 70's scoop, housing policy, reserve sanitation, violence against Native women... the list seems endless at times. None of these policy initiatives "make sense" in terms of the stated public motives; yet all of them can be understood in terms of making life as an Indian (on or off a reserve) unendurable. Take Indian Residential Schooling as a single example (Chrisjohn & Young, 1997). Ostensibly "a fulfilment" of treaty obligations to provide education to First Nations, it was obviously a cost-effective abrogation of that responsibility, since the "teachers" were no such thing, the "schools" were prisons, and the "curriculum" non-existent. The churches saw it as an opportunity for unbounded and unsupervised proselytizing, until shortfalls in government funding required replacing the staff with the children themselves. Rampant abuses (sexual, physical, psychological) and massive numbers of deaths have led to no charges sticking against anyone involved, even though the entire exercise *obviously conformed to the international law on genocide.*[9]

Canada has called this a policy of "assimilation." The correct word, as we've just employed it, is "genocide." For those of you who don't know what the word means, go to the United Nations web site and look at it. It will do no good to look at Canadian sources; Canada undertook to mangle international law and world opinion when it came to implementing the Genocide Convention in this country, and so the average Canadian believes erroneously that genocide requires killing (the Canadian Criminal Code leaves out 60% of the offenses as detailed in international law; Chrisjohn, et al., 2002).

Recall that, for example, Evans (2004) was reduced to postulating "vague feelings of egalitarianism," the "desire to assimilate," and such when trying to account for the actions of his people with respect to we

9   ...which Canada took a leading role in writing in 1948, and then suppressing in successive versions of Canada's criminal code. Chrisjohn & Young pointed all this out in 1994/1997; however, now that non-Indians are beginning to make the same point, in recent years it has become acceptable (for everyone but politicians, that is) to say that Canada committed the non-genocide form of genocide, *cultural genocide.*

of indigenous nations. It is a telling expedient: The Bobbi/Bob Model is invoked, with two brand new, spur-of-the-moment resident gremlins, "Desire to Assimilate" and "Feeling of Egalitarianism (Half-Baked Version)" rattling around in the heads of hypothetical Canadians in power, causing them to rape indigenous children and starve them into submission while using them as medical guinea pigs. Ah, yes, it's oh so clear now! The good-old Desire to Assimilate gremlin and his/her buddy, Vague Feeling of Egalitarianism! They explain everything!

It would be pathetic if it were not so obviously intellectually dishonest. The material grounds behind the dispossession of indigenous people, historically and into the present day, requires no such mental gymnastics to account for a completely consistent predisposition on the part of "Canada" and her officials to oppress and suppress its true owners. It only requires capitalism.

The Importance of Alienation

In order to place "oppression" at the leading edge of the process that, among other things, drives us indigenous peoples to suicide, we have shown that: (1) since Native peoples were not capitalists, the imposition of a capitalist economy was, by definition, oppressive (as it was for Europeans themselves when capitalism first came into being), since *capitalism is alienating*, and *alienation is oppression* (and *oppression causes fatalistic suicide*), and (2) the policies of successive Canadian governments and their institutions specifically have attempted to coerce Native peoples either to accept the mainstream political economy or live... and die... miserably. In our opinion the direct attack on indigenous forms of life constitute oppression *over and above* what Europeans themselves experienced during their own eras of transition to capitalism. And it is an ongoing attack, termed "assimilation" by governments and their apologists, and "genocide" by people who don't fall for elementary rhetorical tricks.

But we find it necessary at this point to return to Marx's concept of alienation, which we ran past quickly at several points in the previous chapter. To review, Marx (1844/1988) applied the term "alienation" to the separation of workmanship from ownership that he argued was the thematic heart of capitalism. As "the human condition under capitalism," alienation merely described how things ran, not what was going on in people's heads ("psychology" would not be invented for another 30 years or so). So, for Marx, it was not a "felt experience," but simply a way Europeans had hit upon to increase productivity. The dehumanization inherent in capitalism (which is the oppression inherent in it) arose from its elimination of what until then had been an inviolable tenet of human existence: an intimate connection between "doing work in your mind" and "doing work in the outside world."

Since this glimpse of alienation was sufficient for us to make our point we were content to leave it at that... until now, where we hope to show that the ongoing coercion to assimilate indigenous peoples works more hardship on us than it did during the fight in Europe to implement capitalism as the economic system. Indeed, it makes much more sense to consider the duress Canada imposes upon indigenous people to be a *double dose* of alienation.

Rather than simply assert that separating workmanship from ownership was dehumanizing because human beings had never worked that way before, Marx (1844/1988) made what was in fact an airtight argument. He began by arguing that it was human nature to work "in the mind" before working "in the world," and that two-sided aspect to human praxis constituted the difference between people and non-people. Animals work "in the world," too, but they give less an indication of working "in the mind." For instance, a spider builds the same web each time, or a bird builds the same nest. Human beings, by contrast, constantly change (improve?) their work "in the world," learning by experience and from interacting with the forces around them.

However, under capitalism, Marx notes, people no longer reflect that intricate interplay of work in the mind and in the world that is our unique heritage. Rather, we do as we're told (that is, under orders, we do someone else's work in the mind) or we lose our jobs.

This is an important argument on Marx's part, but it turns on one's willingness to accept his account of what human nature is. The track record of "human nature statements" is none too good, with all too often those kinds of statements being used to avoid serious thinking by making a metaphysical statement ("Its human nature that there are rich people and poor people;" "Some people are just smarter than others... it's human nature") which (as we argued earlier) are beyond proving or disproving (does god play badminton, and is he/she/it left-handed or right?). Although the world of philosophy seems to be on the verge of a breakthrough that may soon actually allow an evaluation of Marx's theory (Hacker, 2007 & 2013; Cuneo & Woudenberg, 2004) these developments were not far enough advanced to be included here.

So, whether or not you agree that capitalism is dehumanizing because alienation violates human nature depends entirely on what you consider human nature to be. For our part, while Marx's thinking is as least as good as anyone else's in making a "human nature" statement, we are not willing to drop our critical attitude and agree; we say that the point is controversial, at best.

But "alienation from human nature" was not Marx's only thought. He noted further that in European societies people often identified themselves with the work they did (that's why in all European cultures so many people's last name refers to an occupation, presumably held by a distant ancestor of the person so named: Bill (the) Farmer, Susan (the) Hunter, Fred (the) Baker, and so on). It matters not whether, working in a capitalist economy, one is distanced from one's human nature; one is distanced from the immediate and obvious identification with what one's does. One doesn't select one's work, or modify it based on one's engagement with it; instead, once again, you do as you're told or you're fired. One's job is just "what you do to pay your bills," to be tossed aside after the whistle sounds, after which you can be the "real" you. To put it bluntly but accurately, capitalism forces people to prostitute themselves to the will of an owner for at least a portion of his/her working day rather than engage in freely chosen activities. Thus, in addition to being alienated from our human natures, we are alienated from our work.

Marx went further. In "traditional" societies, not only were people often identified with their work, the products of their work (the fruits of their labours) were known to everyone. If someone made bread, or clothing, or a bow, or whatever, and it was traded for goods or services provided by other group members, then you knew who to go to for particular goods *and* you knew who to take questions or complaints to concerning those goods. Likely, if you bought a bow from Edna and it broke on first use, you would take it back to Edna *and she would make good on your complaint*. After all, she's known as Edna the Bow Maker, she takes pride in her work, and she wouldn't want a reputation for shoddy bow-making to begin circulating in the village.

Under capitalism, Marx noted, commodities are anonymous. The process of mass reproduction requires that any commodity be the result of tens, if not hundreds or even thousands, of people making a small contribution to the creation of the commodity. Who made the loaf of bread on the shelf in the store? The store owner doesn't know, neither does the driver of the truck who delivered it. In fact, if you went to the bakery you'd likely find many people doing many different jobs to ensure that thousands of loaves would be baked and shipped… but it's unlikely you'd find one person, "the baker," who would accept responsibility for a badly baked loaf. (And of course, nobody knows who grew or milled the wheat.) In other words, under capitalism, *nobody* did it, *nobody* accepts personal responsibility, and, although you might get a replacement loaf out of your complaining, the whole thing would leave you feeling a bit dirty.

There are deeper points that Marx makes (including competition between workers for jobs) about capitalism's influence on communities, but by-and-large they arise because of the inherent anonymity of commodities produced under capitalism. So, under capitalism, people are also alienated from their communities; think of this the next time you see an Xmas tree-lighting ceremony in a nearby big city and see 50 people (out of 50,000) attending.

Finally, Marx points out that the mass production of commodities requires that everyone look at the world differently. Rather than experiencing awe in natural beauty or feeling the majesty and mystery Nature commands, capitalism demands that you must see the natural world as primitive commodities that stand in need of being transformed into manufactured goods. There are mountains to be flattened, forests to be levelled, lakes and rivers to be diverted, drained, and polluted. And polluted they will be; cleaning up or even just behaving responsibly takes time (money) and effort (money); so businesses will divert effluent into tailing ponds or toss their garbage into the air because it is profitable for them to do so. Does the offhanded way which capitalism demands the destruction of the world offend you? No matter. Someone else will be desperate enough to do as they're told, even if she/he has to hold her/his nose while doing it. And you can keep your principles and lament the passing of Nature, while starvation or death from cancer competes for your corpse.

Rather than having a limited impact on a hypothetical feature (alienation from human nature), the destruction capitalism brings to societies can now be seen as pervasive. Human nature *may* be alienated under capitalism, but alienation *certainly* (1) impacts our notions of self, (2) affects our sense of community, and (3) influences our relationship with Nature. Marx's initial work on alienation has been greatly extended (e. g., Allen, 2011; Archibald, 1994; D'Amico, 1981; Forbes, 1990; Fromm, 1963; Schaff, 1980; Torrance, 1977; Wallimann, 1981), even to the point where some theorists (e.g., Schweitzer & Geyer, 1989; Geyer & Heinz, 1992; Geyer, 1996) wish to turn it into another individual, internal gremlin to be targeted it with therapy. But this is not at all how Marx invites us to see it: alienation is a structural feature of capitalism, an unforeseen by-product of increasing productivity by assigning to different people the specific components of the comprehensive goal of particular work.

We don't believe this concludes what is important about Marx's writing on alienation, but deeper analysis doesn't get us much further here. Suffice it to say: the form of life inherent in capitalism *is antithetical in every way to the various forms of life our Native nations pursued prior to the European invasion.*

We realize that Marx is a boogey-man that nearly everyone in the west has received warnings against even reading, and that, consequently, people reject his work out-of-hand without having any familiarity with it, whatsoever. If it makes you feel any better, you can assure yourself that his writing on alienation is *early Marx*, one that many Marxists themselves reject as being immature work and which they distinguish from the later Marx, the "real" one, who they find acceptable. Fine by us.

Finally, we've said that Canada's coercion to abandon our traditional forms of life and adopt their political economic system (or, just drop dead) should be regarded as a *double alienation*. What we mean is this: people everywhere, faced with the imposition of capitalism and the consequent alteration in their existing forms of life, resisted. But resistance to the incursion of the capitalist form of life required the maintenance of the previous form: first as a rallying point and second as a living template for how things could be different. In Europe, however, the form of life capitalism was replacing (feudalism) had been authoritarian to begin with; in many practical ways, capitalism merely changed those who ruled the roost (an hereditary nobility and rigid church hierarchy being replaced by wealthy people). The common people suffered various privations, such as loss of land security (via acts of enclosure), community security, and personal general competence (being forced to specialize in jobs rather than engage in the totality of actions that assured the well-being of her/his family). But, in terms of distance between the way things were and the way capitalism changed things, the indigenous peoples of North America had, and continue to have, to contemplate much starker contrasts and much greater divides between pre- and post-capitalism societies than the peoples of Europe contemplated.

Not just that; in North America, the templates and terrains for non-capitalist forms of life have remained available to indigenous peoples for a much longer time than European peoples had their own alternatives at hand. Authentic indigenous forms of life (and not the invented traditions still being manufactured by those engaged in the ongoing attack on our ways; Hobsbawm & Ranger, 1983) have remained in the living memories of many indigenous nations in Canada, all the way up to the present day. Part of this is because, when confronted with oppression, Native people could and did just get up and leave; that is, retreat more deeply into "the Bush," where Indian agents and missionaries feared to tread, thus keeping authentic indigenous institutions alive. Even once reserves began to be formed, they were often so remote and the attention of the Indian agent so casual that real indigenous ways could continue on the quiet.

The double alienation we continue to suffer is not just what must be endured by any people having capitalism imposed upon them; nor is it the frankly genocidal purpose and program that the Canadian government pretends is a way of "embracing his Red Brother." It is that, for those who know where to look and who can understand what it is they're seeing, enough of our own ways are still available to be seen. And so, like a feast laid out before a starving family, it is both a torment and an abiding hope.

Shed a Little Light

A life-long diet of pabulum makes digesting a real meal difficult. In a similar way, many people we've talked to, having spent a lifetime taking at face value the bald assurances of spin-doctors and apologists, have seemed unwilling to consume the proposition that governments, *their* governments, would willingly and with malice aforethought engage in what amounts to programs of *officially bullying* Indians. They grant the *possibility* that some policies may *amount* to that, but that if so, it arose unintentionally, as a sort of second-hand by-product of well-intentioned policy carried out, perhaps, by enthusiastic but ham-fisted governmental employees (and probably new ones, at that).

"Oppression" is something done by the Nazis, or the Russians, or people who hate other people's freedoms, but not by "our" side.

However, this is Bobbi/Bob once again, with "naive good intentions" inhabiting the heads of mainstream malefactors, explaining away what are nothing less than crimes. It's pure pabulum. Here's a pertinent example.

We owe Figure 9 to Churchill and Vander Wall (1990). Although it has been available for over a quarter century now, many of you will be seeing it here for the first time. It is a letter commissioned by the American Federal Bureau of Investigation (FBI), paid for by American taxpayers, and sent in 1964 to the then-recent winner of the Nobel Prize for Peace, Dr. Martin Luther King Jr. Please take a moment to read what you can of the letter now. Although it has been heavily censored by the FBI the intent of the letter is obvious from even a cursory examination: it was meant to induce Dr. King to kill himself.

In a day and age where the President of the same country claims the self-appointed power to blow to smithereens any human being on the planet for no reason whatsoever, that the FBI would engage in such "shenanigans" might seem amusing, at best. But consider for a moment that, at least back then, such things were not supposed to happen, and that Dr. King, if not his cause, then as now commanded near-universal respect (at least among thoughtful people). So: the FBI (1) decided, for reasons it has never chosen to share, that it didn't like Dr. King and/or what he was doing; (2) decided, in agreement with who-knows-how-many-other powerful politicians and governmental officials, that he had to be stopped; (3) worried about how it would look if they simply took out their guns and shot him; (4) consequently assembled a team of experts (presumably psychologists and psychiatrists, plus bullies, assassins, and blackguards, as deemed necessary); (5) then had that team compose the letter, which they then posted; and finally, (6) was so proud of what they had done, hid the fact for nearly 25 years, fought against the release of this letter down to the last possible moment, then released the mainly blanked-out letter you see here.

If this is the first you've seen of this letter, consider that, first of all, Dr. King *did not* go on to kill himself (nor did he give in to other strong-arm tactics the FBI employed, illegally, after this letter failed; Branch, 1998; Garrow, 1983). But do you think even for a moment that, had it succeeded, at some point the FBI would themselves have published this letter? Was this "their finest hour?"

Consider your own reaction. Do you accept this historical vignette at face value and move on, or do other questions come to mind? "Who did/does the FBI think it is? What was their attitude to race inequality in the US? Did they try to assassinate other people whose ideas they disagreed with? Who? Were they successful? Who approve this practice? How "high up" did it go? There are "*experts*" in doing things like this? Did those experts violate personal and/or professional ethics in participating in this reprehensible enterprise? What else is the government hiding?" Sure, you can close the door and walk away from this sordid history. But with a few moments of thoughtful reflection, the issues will keep right on coming.

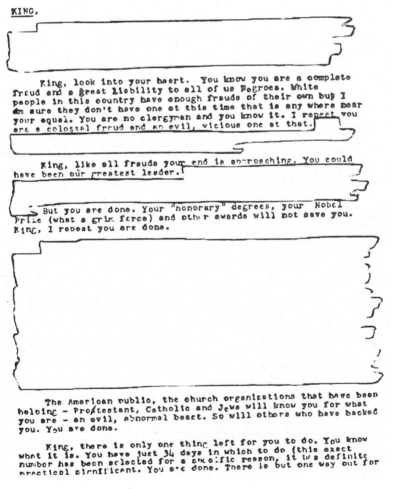

KING,

King, look into your heart. You know you are a complete fraud and a great liability to all of us Negroes. White people in this country have enough frauds of their own but I am sure they don't have one at this time that is any where near your equal. You are no clergyman and you know it. I repeat you are a colossal fraud and an evil, vicious one at that.

King, like all frauds your end is approaching. You could have been our greatest leader.

But you are done. Your "honorary" degrees, your Nobel Prize (what a grim farce) and other awards will not save you. King, I repeat you are done.

The American public, the church organizations that have been helping - Protestant, Catholic and Jews will know you for what you are - an evil, abnormal beast. So will others who have backed you. You are done.

King, there is only one thing left for you to do. You know what it is. You have just 34 days in which to do (this exact number has been selected for a specific reason, it is a definite practical significant. You are done. There is but one way out for

Figure 9. The United States Federal Bureau of Investigation anonymous fan letter to Nobel Peace Prize winner, Dr. Martin Luther King.

However, in writing a book on Native suicide and in making the case that *prolonged, systematic, discriminatory governmental oppression* must be considered a major cause of it, we have two observations to make. First: *the FBI did what it did because they expected that it could/would be successful.* That is, in a self-characterized law-abiding and freedom-loving country, official designates of an agency specifically tasked with "fighting crime" wrote a letter to a famous, popular, and internationally honoured citizen of that country which it believed would provoke him into killing himself. Nobody employs a weapon he or she doesn't think will work; that's why FBI agents carry handguns and not water-pistols. By whatever route (prior experience, experimentation, testimonials from other murderous spy agencies, etc.), they had concluded that a letter composed by their band of specialists had a reasonable chance of accomplishing their aim: Dr. King's death. So: at least one major government is of the opinion — and so is in agreement with our point — *that the powerful can compel the deaths of citizens by indirect, devious means.*

Second: we have been careful not to characterize Dr. King's anticipated actions as "suicide," because had the FBI's letter accomplished what it was sent off to do, Dr. King would *not* have committed suicide; *he would have been murdered by the FBI, with the letter as the murder weapon and Dr. King himself as the flunky just following orders; as the patsy shielding the higher-ups from scrutiny and disclosure.*

Had they thought him about to kill himself, the FBI wouldn't have bothered assembling their experts, composing the letter, and sending it. They would have just waited for it to happen. And, as we've already noted, had the letter in fact been successful the FBI would never had released it on its own. But without the letter, the rest of us would have been left only with the "inexplicable" mystery of why Dr. King had acted as he had: what "mental illness" or internal demons had tormented him into taking this action? Possibly, the cause for which he was fighting might even have been discredited: "The civil rights movement was being led by a nut-bar," and "The fight for civil rights is so stressful that it drives people to suicide," are two refrains we probably would have heard as a result.

But with the murder weapon in hand (the suicide letter) it's clear that, had it been successful the FBI would have been guilty of first-degree murder. As events ultimately played out, it was clearly *attempted murder.*

Is there any defense to these charges? However, we have been unable to locate any information on criminal prosecutions, license hearings, ethics boards meetings, etc., for the FBI flunkies who were responsible for this. If anything, those responsible probably were given medals.

In Canada, both provincial and federal governments now recognize that people can *bully people to death*. It has played out in the news as being related to social media on the internet, but does anyone consider that that's a serious caveat? "It's only *bullying on the internet* that can kill people!" Utter nonsense. "Only *individuals* can bully *individuals!*" Tell that to the warriors of the civil rights movement. Announce that to LGBT community. Look at the suicide rates for indigenous peoples and try to maintain that with a straight face.

Nor does any "susceptibility issue" provide any mitigation. Does anyone consider that, after an arrest for bullying someone into self-destruction, the defendant's claim that "Well, the victim had low self-esteem and a weak will!" would or should be considered a reasonable defense? Right… and rape victims dress "provocatively" because they want to be raped.

Isn't it time we all grew up?

That Which We Call a Suicide... Once it becomes obvious that people can set out to commit murder by inducing someone to kill him- or herself, the sensibility of reflexively calling any death a "suicide" logically must be called into question. Once it is clear that bureaucrats can, at the instigation of governments or powerful interests, or even on their own initiatives, establish and enforce programs aimed specifically at creating enough duress in entire populations that at least some of the people so targeted will kill themselves, does someone pretend there is a calculus that will allow us to derive what fraction of those deaths are murders as opposed to "real" suicides?

To say that all deaths by a person's own hand must reduce to the mental machinery to which that hand was attached is deliberate distortion. Bartolomé de las Casas (Hanke, 1959) provided an eyewitness account of Spanish soldiers "hearding" hundreds of Native women, fleeing with their children, to the tops of cliffs, thereby to entrap them and enslave both mothers and children. The mothers, with no chance of escape, threw their children onto the rocks below and then jumped after them, to their own deaths.

Just some of your average, everyday murder-suicides?

Or take a description from Borkin (1978) and ask, is the word "suicide" used appropriately by him here:

"Two physicians who studied the effect of the I. G. [Farben] diet on the inmates noticed that 'the normally nourished prisoner at Buna could make up the deficiency by his own body for a period of three months... The prisoners were condemned to burn up their own body weight while working and, providing no infections occurred, finally died of exhaustion'... An eye-witness reported, 'As a result it was practically impossible to sleep, since if one man was in a reclining position, the others would have to sit up or lie over him.' The simplest comforts were denied; even tables and chairs were almost unknown. Hygenic conditions were subhuman. In the summer the heat was oppressive, almost beyond endurance, and in the winter there was no heat at all... The working conditions at the Farben Buna plant were so severe and unendurable that very often inmates were driven to suicide by either dashing through the guards and provoking death by rifle shot, or hurling themselves into the high-tension electrically-charged barbed wire fences (p. 159 & 174)."

Well... how could the Nazis *have known* that the conditions they inflicted were enough to make prisoners crack?

In 1976 Nelson Small Legs, of the Piikani Nation of southern Alberta, wrote an indictment of Canada's treatment of Native peoples and then shot himself. Was it a political statement? A manifesto? A call to action? Maybe a plea from the heart, punctuated in the most forceful manner he could imagine? Or was it "the final self-destructive act of despair, committed while in a state of hopelessness and depression?" Nowadays we don't get to decide for ourselves: in 2000 the World Health Organization issued guidelines to the media concerning suicide stories: "Reporting suicidal behaviour as an understandable response to social or cultural changes or degradation should be resisted (Marsh, 2000, p. 45)." Why? Is it beyond our understanding that some might choose suicide as the sincerest form of protest he or she could imagine (when Buddhist monks protested repression by the South Vietnamese Diệm government in 1963, they did so by self-immolation; Goldstein, 2008)?

Exactly whose purpose does it serve, whom is it supposed to benefit, to suppress *what often are likely to be pertinent factors in the death of a human being?* Are we supposed to shake our heads when we hear about Mr. Small Legs' actions and then forget about him? By all accounts, that was not his wish.

There is nothing simple about the manifold uses to which the term "suicide" has been employed. We find it distressing that, in the literature on Native suicide, this incredible complexity has, again and again, settled around the notion that there has to be something wrong with us. To anyone comfortable there, our aim is to raise unsettling possibilities. Canada's policies have been and are, as the successive governments have admitted, designed to coerce indigenous peoples to disappear. Does anyone claim the Powers That Be have a "severity gauge" it applies to its policies concerning us, one calibrated precisely enough to know how crowded they can make our houses, how filthy they can make our water, how worthless they can make us feel, before it will drive some of us to self-destruction? If they did, would that alone stop them from ratcheting things up past that point?

If this was a murder trial, Canada has both motive and opportunity, and the murder weapon is now in plain sight. Unfortunately for the truth, the defendants control the courts and the media, and even the minds of many of its victims. Does justice have a chance?

DYING TO PLEASE YOU:

INDIGENOUS SUICIDE IN CONTEMPORARY CANADA

Chapter 6, What Is to be Done?

Raiders of the Temple Crusade

In our opinion the contrast between what modern mainstream suicidology offers as possible reasons for the indecent Native suicide rate in Canada and what we have here proposed as a substitute could not be greater. However, given that many specific points appear to be held in common between the two positions, it's likely that some of our readers won't appreciate just how drastic the contrast is. Mainstream suicidology has been engaged in ransacking the mental contents of suicidal Indians, like berserk Indiana Jones's of the mind, trying to penetrate our inner recesses, filch the golden artifacts within, and emerge triumphantly, holding aloft our most prized possessions to put on display for all the world to see. Or to sell them in Marrakech.[10]

We think they've all been looking in the wrong place (and it's somewhere they have no business being, anyway). To understand our high suicide rates, we think you must place it, first, in a material context: Canada's continuing need to exterminate aboriginal titles and rights; and second, in an historical context: Canada's consequent and continuing efforts at what it euphemistically refers to as its policy of assimilation of indigenous peoples. These are matters of public record, although it's likely that the complete history and full extent of Canada's concerns are hidden away in cabinet documents and top-secret files. What was going on in the heads of lesser functionaries implementing policy is largely irrelevant — *as long as the functionaries did what they were told to do.* Once more, is this sounding familiar? Nobody's recesses of anything need be violated: Canada is far from the only colonizing country in the world that has found the autochthonous population bothersome, nor was it the first to hit upon genocide as its preferred solution.

We see no possibility of an accommodation between our position and the positions we have criticized. Even should our efforts penetrate in some way the program of modern suicidology, suicidologists must warp what we're saying into something they're capable of comprehending. Thus, when we say *oppression kills and Canada oppresses Indians*, they say: "Oh! We get it now! What you're **really** saying is: Oppression kills! *And Indians **feel** oppressed! And this impacts their conscious or unconscious minds! And that makes them **feel** depressed! And **that's** why they kill themselves!*" And then they're off again. We would call it a wild goose chase, but only if the goose were invisible and a Yeti, instead.

10   Seriously, has *anybody* watched the first fifteen minutes of that movie??

Canada, Therapist or The Rapist? But why should anyone doubt them? They assure us that they're the experts: they get the grants; they do the research; they publish the papers; they give the workshops. They're concerned and caring and sincerely want Indians to stop killing themselves (at least, as much as their current high rates indicate). And it all sounds reasonable.

The acid test of these propositions is intervention. They're willing to intervene in Native individual's attempts in inflicting death upon themselves, to get between a person and the next world. Or they're willing to set out programmatic suggestions for us to follow, as best we can, with local approximations to their recommendations. If nothing else, they'll look over our shoulders from time-to-time. Governments are willing to fund their programs (at least to a point). And who among us at the local level wouldn't fight to get a chance to do this work, regardless of how bad the pay might be? For haven't we all been struck? Wouldn't we do anything to get a chance to strike back?

Imagine psychologists working inside a concentration camp, charged with the task of convincing Jewish inmates not to commit suicide. It didn't happen, of course, but Hilberg (1992) has documented that Nazis made real efforts to lower the suicide rates of the Jews elsewhere in the territories under their control, so here let's treat the possibility as a thought experiment.

Who would they be working for? Who would they tell the Jews they were working for? Who would be paying their salaries? Where would they sleep at night? Who would they hang out and party with, when the day's work was over? What would their "working theory" of Jewish suicide be? Would their work be conducted with compassion and the sincere hope that they could prevent Jews from killing themselves? Would their work, as psychologists, actually involve doing anything to reduce the Jewish suicide rate?

This is all hypothetical, of course, and you may answer accordingly. We say: They would be working for the Nazis, and might well be Nazis themselves. They would tell the Jews they were there to help *them.* The Nazi government would be paying their salaries. They would sleep at home, *outside the barbed wire.* Their friends and associates would be *not Jews.* Their working theory would be that some character flaw in the Jewish mind was responsible for them "taking the cowards way out;" their therapeutic target likely would be finding some method of inuring them against depression and despair (resilience). We can see no reason they wouldn't perform their work with care and diligence; after all, they've been told that it's important to stop these inmates from killing themselves. Finally, no: psychologists are not resistance fighters, gun runners, or even food smugglers; as psychologists, they would never be in doubt concerning who they thought the sick people were.

We don't care whether or not the parallels we imply are "fair." Even if they're not, isn't it clear that defining the issue of indigenous suicide as a "personal problem" immediately depoliticizes and decontextualizes it? Isn't it obvious that "successful" therapy is getting the client to accept the psychologist's a-historical and im-material interpretation of personal causation? This is why, earlier, we charged that intervention within the Broken Indian model devolved into (1) letting *"Nature take its course:"* where Nature was the Vanishing Indian and the Vanishing Indian was dead; (2) *drugs*: where inconvenient behavior can be chemically paved over; or (3) *Missionary Work*: convincing the client that the therapist's notions of what was happening and what the client should do about it was the correct appraisal.

The Broken Indian model is insidious. It sounds scientific; it sounds caring and concerned; but it is a hand where the deck has been stacked against us. "Nature taking its course" is, obviously, *indigenous people breaking*, because that's what pressure does when applied long enough and hard enough to anything or anyone. Drugs — even self-administered ones — cloud our capacity to think clearly, protest, resist, and organize ourselves. And "talk therapy" recruits us to the ideas that "the problem" lies inside us, is our fault, and that we're "cured" when *we, personally* feel better about things. This is why we call it "Missionary Work:" our personal salvation becomes elevated as the sole thing that therapist to client alike are trying to achieve. But where did all the other oppressed Indians go?

To the extent that indigenous peoples lose sight of what the struggle is — our rights to our properties, our forms of life, our ways of thinking and doing, our right to meet the eternal mysteries in our own fashions, our right to assert and defend who we are — we lose. It makes no difference whether that sight is lost because we adopt someone else's vision of who we are and what purpose we have; or because our intellects have been clouded by irrelevancies; or because our lives have been overpowered by the press of circumstances. To accept someone else's definition of the problem is to limit the range of possible resolutions. The mainstream would have us gone, and whether by death, irrelevance, or co-optation (submission) makes no real difference to them.

Resilience. Let's take this upbeat, harmless-sounding concept for a moment. In recent years it has been popular to see the "problem" of suicide intervention with indigenous peoples as one of identifying personal and/or social "structures" that inoculate Indians, as it were, from whatever negative influences there may be that infect us and drive us to suicide. As we noted earlier, Kirmayer et al. (2007) devoted a chapter to these issues, but that is only the tip of the iceberg. Regardless: despite its popularity and topicality, we don't believe it deserves prolonged attention.

Suppose you're the commandant of a concentration camp. Everything is running smoothly; the trains come in, a large fraction of incoming Jews are sent off to "selektion" immediately, and a smaller fraction retained, assigned barracks, and enslaved in work in nearby factories that helps maintain the Nazi war effort. One small glitch appears: some of the longer-term inmates don't seem to like starvation rations and 23 1/2 hour workdays, and they are committing suicide. This is impeding the war effort, because of course it's only the retained Jews, the ones assigned war-effort labour, whose suicides are mucking things up (who cares what the "selektion" Jews do before they're gassed?). You call in your camp psychologist and spit-ball possible interventions. He/she/it suggests that detailed statistics on individual inmates be recorded and analyzed, and that those characteristics that are eventually found to correlate with length of stay (that is, not committing suicide) either *become the basis for initial selection* into slave labour or *should be fostered/rewarded/reinforced* in the inmate population.

This is what *resilience* is.

If anyone believes that there is anything noble in selecting for or fostering characteristics that assure the victims of oppression will hold up against longer-lasting, more vicious abuses, without threatening to overcome their oppressors, so that they might become more useful slaves to their oppressors, we'd like to hear arguments. But we shall not be convinced.

An example of this kind of thinking is Chandler and Lalonde (1998). Full engagement with these ideas must await a work in preparation[11] but here we can be brief in our objections. It is their

11   Chrisjohn & McKay, *Autochthonology*, projected for 2018.

contention that it is the maintenance of "indigenous culture" on some reserves that inoculates those reserve's inhabitants against killing themselves, and they produce some extremely dubious statistical manipulations purporting to establish a correlation between degree of cultural continuity and suicide rate. The suicide rates for some of the more resilient communities are claimed to approach rates of non-indigenous communities in British Columbia. So... success!

Our case here isn't against either the methodological holes or the theoretical frailty of their argument. Rather, it's the depth of their misunderstanding of indigenous forms of life. We don't even have to make the point ourselves: Waldram (2004), whose own contributions we bypassed earlier when we reviewed theories of Native suicide, gives a perceptive appraisal of Chandler & Lalonde's work: "Their measures of cultural continuity, however, were *anything but* [our emphasis], and included such items as involvement in land claims, self-government, and control over police, fire, and health services... none of these demonstrates continuity with a cultural past in which such institutions were non-existent... (Waldram, 2004, p. 175)."

And we would go further. These indicators of "cultural continuity" are, in fact, indicators of the *destruction* of indigenous forms of life. At best these indicators reflect maintenance of the merest nod to cultural appearances (like tying a headband around a bust of Freud), and at worst they reflect the progress being made in imposing mainstream institutional forms within Native communities.

The aim of current governmental policy is to eliminate reserves and turn them into communities indistinguishable from any common rural municipality (Manuel, 2015). Yet, this is the logical terminus of the "therapeutic" process Chandler and Lalonde (1998) advocate; and with the success of that development, of course, why would anyone expect any difference in suicide rates between "reserves" and any other place... they're indistinguishable. What Chandler and Lalonde (1998) document, then, is the movement from reserve communities to... *just communities*. The success here, such as it is, is not "indigenous" in any sense, since "rural Indian communities" are no more "indigenous" than the "Indian reserves" were themselves ever intended to be (both of them being designed by the colonizing oppressors to accommodate the wishes of the oppressors, not the oppressed). We fail to see anything "indigenous" about any of these outcomes. Rather, whatever there was that was genuinely indigenous is slowly being strangled.

The point of Canadian policy toward Indians was/is the extinction of anything "Indian" about us. If accomplished while retaining peasants with permanent tans, well then, fine; if it necessitated hiding piles of dead people, well then, that was fine, too. But the agenda was/is absolute: either their victims learned to think and act like every other peasant or they were history:

> Peace, order, and good government in Canada depend ultimately on the deep acquiescence of the people in the idea that they have no inalienable rights; ultimately, the final decision rests with the cabinet... it depends, for it success, on a citizenry ready finally to accept Papa's definition of the situation and Papa's resolution of it, and persuaded, ultimately, that it has no right to ask questions that probe into matters it has been told are not its concern (Friedenberg, 1980, p. 55).

We are gone when we behave like everyone else and not like *Indians*; at that point, we will have arrived as Canadians.

Economic Development: Salvation or Salivation?

At least when dealing with mainstream therapeutic thinking issues can be kept human. Therapy providers have neither more or nor less the amount of "pull" as that of statisticians, theorists, and researchers; and as we said much earlier, this is not the level at which policy is made and programs are developed and funded. No, the "heavy hitters" organizing the authentic assault on indigenous peoples — the real possessors of the "oppression" aimed at bringing about the compliance or collapse of indigenous peoples — are those with hands on the economic levers of society. Those wielding economic power are not troubled by having to substantiate hypotheses, evaluate arguments, or consider logical progressions; as we've said, they've pretty well already made up their minds about what they're going to impose, and if they seek support from an academic literature it is support for a conclusion they've reached on obviously ideological grounds since long before.

We can only briefly summarize the issues here (Anthony Hall's work is recommended, and we're aware of several manuscripts in preparation by other authors that will greatly enlarge this discussion). In dealing with indigenous peoples the single constraint upon Canada's economic power-brokers has been the British North America Act, in direct and indirect consequences. One direct consequence, as we've noted, was removal of outright physical genocide as a strategy for resolving dispossession issues... which led, of course, to the indirect bureaucratic genocide all good mainstream Canadians are expected to participate in and that we have been writing about here. A second direct consequence was the signing of treaties with First Nations (international agreements that are the highest law of any land), undertaken because of the BNA requirement that the newly-formed Canada "treat fairly" in future dealings with us. Canada's subsequent mistake was to trust the USA's assurances that Indians were about to disappear; the Holy Grail of conservative economic forces in Canada has, since the signing of the last numbered treaty, worked every angle it could to get mainstream citizens and Indians alike to denounce treaty rights as "reverse discrimination" and an unfair advantage (and to ignore the fact that they're contractual obligations, the abrogation of which, were it between Keystone XL and Canada, would be considered legally actionable). The mystery that people with this "unfair advantage" managed nonetheless to become the poorest, most uneducated, most unhealthy, 3rd-world-like people in North America — "education" and "health" being two additional unfair advantages we secured in treaties — just goes to prove something... about indigenous people, or about Canadians?

A recent United Nations ranking on multiple indicators listed mainstream Canada as the third best place in the world to live — unless you mean "indigenous Canada," in which case you immediately dropped to sixty-third. The price of the enviable position of "real Canadians" has been stolen, of course, from indigenous peoples, at a rate and over a greater span of time than even Hitler managed to achieve with the Jews (Aly, 2005). This mouth-watering outcome didn't just happen; it has been accompanied by, if not accomplished through: (1) one-sided abrogation of treaty obligation (Canadian courts situate themselves to sit in judgment despite obvious conflicts of interest); (2) the persistent evasion of the duty to "treat fairly" (Canada stopped signing treaties when it finally realized the Indians weren't going anywhere); (3) creation of programs placing band-aids on the haemorrhaging arising in indigenous communities from multifarious oppressive attacks (conceived by bureaucrats and politicians to appease the WIMPs they obey; programs, we must stress, that economically and numerically benefit far more "real Canadians," living outside the barbed wire, than indigenous peoples); (4) the ever-increasing Canadian contribution to an already disproportionate share of global warming (the Alberta Tar Sands, for example, were known as the Athabasca Tar Sands, after the First Nation that owned it, until a way was found (with taxpayer's money) to make gasoline out of it and the land was expropriated); and lots of other interrelated specifics.

To this, we must add, those of us whose property stoked the prosperity and good fortune of our oppressors have been subject to the constant barrage of abuses posing as explanations for our privations and as starting points for interventions. We're stupid, we're lazy, we're drunks, we're irresponsible, we're depraved, etc., which is why we're so backward. But, whoopee!; now there's a new program, targeting our stupidity, our laziness, our drunkenness, our irresponsibility, our etc., which our betters will provide to us, rescuing us from our ingrained depravity.

The Satan Bug. If you think we're exaggerating, recent years have seen a new spin on the Broken Indian model. The source isn't really surprising, since ultimately it has been the real source of our difficulties all along. What is different is the kind of pitch being made. And it's coming from the WIMPs, themselves.

Let us be clear; the dispossession and elimination of indigenous peoples has *always* been the wet-dream of any WIMP, big or small, national or international, because indigenous peoples, our land title rights and our aboriginal rights (whatever they might be) get in the way of them just doing as they please (just ask, for example, the Keystone XL Pipeline people). But, until fairly recently, big business has been willing to let "Egghead" disciplines (psychology, sociology, education, medicine, etc.) do whatever bad-mouthing of Indians was deemed necessary to "justify" whatever programs and policies business demanded of governments. It wasn't Big Business who declared that Indians were congenitally stupid, were "right-brained," suffered from FASD, had the "thrifty gene," possessed a congenital predisposition to respiratory diseases, and so on. They merely benefited from the direct removal or indirect marginalization of these sub-humans, as instantiated in these attacks. (The Indian Act, for example, on the assumption that we were, essentially, children in grown-up bodies, placed the government in position of control of our economic resources. Search the histories of what royalty deals Canada, *in loco parentis,* made in our name with oil companies, and ask if you'd want *your* parents to behave like this).

Perhaps it was impatience at the slow speed of dispossession; or maybe it was the "protection money" that disciplines like psychology and education were demanding to keep Indians "in their place." Who knows? But by the mid-90's there was talk of indigenous peoples suffering from something called "dependency." It's odd, because it was economic conservatives doing the talking, and they weren't using dependency in any recognizable economic form (you know, as in seizing the assets and means of production of a whole people and determining the shape and direction of their fundamental economic activities, just as in concentration camps — Jews in Nazi Germany were very "dependent"). They applied it to us *as if it were a newly-discovered personal gremlin!* We were suffering from "dependency disorder;" or even, from the lack of an "entrepreneurial instinct," such as they themselves possessed. This defect accounted for our absence in the mainstream Canadian political economy, our economic backwardness, our relative joblessness, why we got fired a lot, and why we were always late for appointments. The cure (it will come as no surprise, again, considering the source) was "tough love," or the "sink or swim" approach: which consisted of cancelling all treaties, ending any social programs and subsidies, taxing Indian reserve lands (and seizing the lands when taxes weren't paid on time), and letting good old Mother Nature (red in tooth and claw, we hear) sort things out for us. Whoever or whatever was left after this blitzkrieg of Social Darwinism was unleashed would (like the vase that bounced on the asphalt in the Myth we created, earlier) be welcomed into the margins of "real" Canadian society; after all, who could care about what color their janitors, maids, and ditch-diggers were?

The self-serving circularity of the whole conception bypassed even a hint of science (heck, psychologists had to go through the whole rigmarole of inventing and administering tests before declaring, scientifically, that we were more stupid than everyone else): we obviously had the "inner, hidden trait" of dependency — causing laziness, lateness, unemployment, poverty, etc. — because we didn't work, didn't show up for jobs we didn't have, were poor, etc. (Circular arguments are fine, according to WIMPs.)

So far the only innovations in all this were (1) a brand-new, previously undetected indigenous defect, and (2) the removal of any veneer of pretend science to back it up. What was new was that, suddenly in the mid-00's, mainstream post-secondary institutions discovered that they were capable of curing this disorder! It had nothing to do with disasters in university funding (often associated with the incredible bloat of academic administrations), or the fact that Indian butts in post-secondary institutions were four guaranteed years of tuition and other educational cost spin-offs during a time students were beginning to question the relevance of academic gate-keeping. Or any other of that economic stuff. No, this was all purely Missionary Work. Indeed, the business community had identified a disease common in Indians that had slipped past the Eggheads, and fortunately at just the same time post-secondary schools realized they could cure it. "Historic" transfer agreements resulted (name one).

Is there a place for "Dependency Disorder" in the average mainstream Canadian's understanding of indigenous peoples? Of course. Because it's pure racism that, once more, blames the victim as it extracts by means of force something of what little remains of the victims' own forms of life. It is reminiscent of the scientific manifesto on Dysaesthesia Aethiopica — Black people's built-in laziness — and Drapetomania — their irrational desire to run away from their lawful masters and live like, well, *not slaves*. The cures for these disorders (to be applied at first appearance of sulkiness, unjustified dissatisfaction, uppitiness, and — in free Blacks — freedom) included copious administrations of whippings, strappings, long hours of work in the sunshine, and, to prevent running at all, the surgical removal of the big toes (if surgery can be done with an axe).

It is true: indigenous peoples are, on the average, confronted with the pains of economic extremity (to a magnitude similar if not surpassing the extremity of our suicide rates). Is a *personal defect* responsible? There is not a shred, a sliver, an atom of evidence that this is the case, and the people who tell you otherwise either do not understand what evidence is, or don't care to know (Blaut, 2000). They do not have the interests of indigenous peoples at heart, for their cures are no better than the abuses Black people suffered under slavery.

Capitalism is not our form of life, for any of us. Force-feeding it to us is oppression. Resisting the imposing of alienation upon us is the fight that has always been fought by those of us who have chosen to resist, whether or not we have been able to articulate it in these words. We have a human right to our own forms of life. Those who urge this "cure" upon us, again and again, in one disguised form or another, are not our friends. They are our oppressors.

Samson's Work. Producing anything like a complete survey of the connections between invasion, exploitation, expropriation, marginalization, and then intervention, stitched together with the underlying cables of capitalism, alienation, and oppression would be an enormous project, one that frankly eludes us, given that at best we are focused on how suicide is entwined within it all. But the time periods involved, the changes in governments and specific policies, the different personages passing through, and an uncountable number of details make even contemplating such work strain the heart.

Fortunately for us, someone has come close to doing this, at least for one region, Labrador. We became familiar with Samson's work in 1999, when a group of which he was a part issued a critical assessment of Canada's treatment of the Innu of Labrador (Samson, Wilson, and Mazower, 1999). The report had been released on the internet, so we read it on the same day it was formally announced. Our reaction was that the report was effective, devastating, and unanswerable by WIMPs, politicians, and bureaucrats alike. We waited for the firestorm to develop around it. But no firestorm happened. It became a "one-day wonder" news story, at least in Atlantic Canada, and the world of "real" Canadians went back to hockey, lottery ticket numbers, and Michael Jackson (or whatever it did in those days).

Samson was not to be put off, however. Four years later he released an entire book (Samson, 2003) giving even greater depth and breadth to his original appraisal and analyses. Labrador was and is home to Inuit and Innu peoples, the latter being speakers of an Algonkian language related to Mi'kmaq, Cree, and many others. For some time Labrador had been left largely on it own, to its aboriginal inhabitants and to traders, fishermen, and missionaries pursuing local interests that impinged only slightly on the real owners. Canada made no attempt to extend the treaty-making process to the region, first, since the Native peoples who they *had* made treaties with, elsewhere, didn't seem to be dying off on schedule, and second, because Canada couldn't imagine it could ever want anything the Inuit and Innu peoples possessed.

That situation changed. After World War II the lands were considered "perfect" for testing NATO's airborne arsenal in low-level flying, and Canada was happy to rent access to other people's living rooms to NATO allies from then until the present day — over the protests of the owner-inhabitants, of course, who found caribou and other animals they depended upon for sustenance driven into frenzies by the intrusion of fighter-jets, dog-fights, and missiles into their environment.

Advancements in remote sensing of resources soon afterwards led to the determination that, rather than being a flat, empty rock out in the middle of nowhere, Labrador was an untapped gold mine (more like a nickel mine) just waiting to be tapped. This led to an interesting dilemma, at least for Canada: on the one horn, Labrador was obviously unceded indigenous territory, since Canada had avoided signing treaties with Inuit and Innu when they could have had the normal Canadian advantage of getting Native people to sign something they couldn't read. Canada had even denied them services ordinarily available to "real" Canadians (and theoretically available to status Indians) because of that, telling the Innu and Inuit that if they wanted schools and hospitals and such-like, then they should start collecting taxes and build them on their own. The other horn of the dilemma was that, as we've said, during the period it was becoming clear that Labrador was a new and boundless source of natural resources, the real owners had, in that same interval of time, learned to read. And, if they didn't know the projected value of the land they and their ancestors had walked on since time immemorial, they could hire someone who did.

Canada's solution has been merely to go ahead and "develop" Labrador as they (or their industrial WIMP bosses) see fit; that is, as if the territory is theirs to do with as it pleases. Chanting the conservative mantra, "jobs, jobs, jobs" (a magical phrase said to have the capacity to deforest, pipeline, and frack the whole of Canada), it has released the forces of modern capitalism upon Labrador's inhabitants, with at least the non-Native ones applauding. "Native leaders" — the ones "empowered" by Ottawa to sign away the resources (but not address Native rights or aboriginal title), under the implied threat that if they don't agree Canada will appoint new leaders who will — are also on board. What about everyone else?

Samson (2003) provides not just a history of what has happened and an account of present events; it is the single clearest documentation of the destructive power of modern capitalism — acting within a focused area, within a relatively short period of time — that we've ever seen:

> Incentives were created, such as availability of goods and services long having been requested but denied, to discourage nomadic life and enforce a sedentary one;

The arrival of Christianity brought not only the denigration of previous spiritual ways, but the physical, emotional, and sexual abuses associated with missionary work and residential schools;

"Culture days" and similar vapid approximations to authentic Innu forms of life were introduced in schools, not only to give the appearance of continuity between formal education and Native practices, but to induce defiant children and parents to participate;

Alcohol abuse, drug abuse, gasoline sniffing, became national scandals, particularly with respect to children;

After "treatment" for these conditions elsewhere, recidivism rates or completed suicides reached 100%;

To live in the community, one has to depend on jobs and government transfer payments. Virtually all the wage labour available, however, consists in jobs servicing the assimilationist agenda, such as working in group homes, women's shelters, youth treatment center, and so on;

Innu communities achieved unemployment rates hovering about the 80% mark;

Innu are still capable of living in the country, but as unspoiled land disappears and necessary equipment changes to a higher level of technology, money... cash earned from a job... is quickly becoming indispensable;

If individuals want work they must travel outside their communities, there to assist in the destruction of the land that was the basis for their traditional form of life;

By the age of 30, 53% of Innu people are dead, as compared to 5% of Canadians in general;

The child mortality rate for Innu is roughly 5 times that of Canadians in general;

Labrador achieved the highest suicide rate in the world, one that was double that for other indigenous peoples in Canada and five times the Canadian national rate.

We could go on, because Samson (2003) goes on, but we will break off his description of this cataclysm and encourage you; buy the book and read it. We think it important not for the facts he had brought together and the power of his prose, though both are important. From our perspective he provides verification for Marx's analysis of capitalism and its relation to suicide. Samson worked as a concerned individual with no particular political axe to grind. Appalled, as any human should be, at what he was seeing, he made his observations about what was happening and who was responsible. The alienation from self, community, and Nature that Marx predicted, and its connection to suicide, is all established once you read Samson with the early Marx in mind.

It is important to realize: nobody who has ever made an "economic development" pitch to an indigenous community has ever explained the full consequences of accepting the proposal. There is not the remotest chance that either the person/company making the pitch, or the people receiving it, has ever heard of the alienation inherent in capitalism; of the impact on self, community, and relationship with Nature *implicit* in accepting this wholly foreign form of life as a replacement for their own.

It is a necessary part of any bargain struck with capitalism that what this bargain means is that it is only a matter of time before your form of life is destroyed. The obliteration of your form of life is part of what the government and the businesses it represents will extract from you; part of what, in addition to lands and rights, you must pay. This must be factored into any evaluation of the "bargain." What will remain, at best, will be the ornaments, the accessories, the marginalia of how you lived. These will be hung out on display, and perhaps even bring high prices when auctioned off to collectors. But what they betoken will be gone: how you and your people defended and asserted who you were, and how your ancestors found and kept the exquisite balance between the maintenance of tradition and the incorporation of innovation that is the hallmark of a form of life.

Of course, when it does happen that capitalism works its inevitable destruction, it will seen as, at worst, an unfortunate accident: as good intentions somehow gone awry. Or, if the inevitability is acknowledged, it will be presented as one inherent in the collision between the "savage" and "civilization," and not as one that was imposed by the "benefactor."

What Samson (2003) has shown most clearly is that *economic development has assumed priority as the central weapon of Canada's genocide machine.* What thanks awaited Samson from the publication of his revelations? The lead author, conducting a course in suicidology for an extension program in Labrador one summer, took along copies of *Canada's Tibet* as course materials but was surprised to find either that Samson's works were entirely unknown, or that students and service providers were openly hostile to them. Later, the two of us read reviews that excoriated Dr. Samson and disputed the accuracy of his every claim. They were, of course, uniformly produced by the comprador "Native leaders" who had signed away the resources for a song, or by the people who worked for them, picking up the pieces of a shattered people. So they had jobs.

The Elephant in Our Room

If the purely ideological nature of the Broken Indian model (which includes the absolute lack of evidence for it) has been mainstream suicidology's elephant in the room, ours has been setting out our suggestions about what should be done concerning the obscene levels of indigenous suicide. Many of the people we've reviewed and lots of people we've talked to on the subject have had ideas they wished to share, but until now wherever we've happened upon therapeutic recommendations we've veered away from the topic. Why we've done that should be fairly obvious by now: the mainstream has systemically, ideologically, and systematically misapprehended all along what "the problem of Native suicide" is. As well, we have charged that the interventions developed within the conceptual framework of the Broken Indian model constitute *recruitment into this warped view of circumstances*, regardless of how well-meaning and concerned service providers might be. What grounds could we (or anyone else, for that matter) have for believing their misunderstanding of the nature of the problem could lead to suggesting interventions destructive of our forms of life that nevertheless turned out to be the right thing to do?

The Freudians used to say that treating the symptoms of psychopathology would lead to their eventual reappearance, potentially in altered form, if the root causes weren't treated (with their own particular brand of mumbo-jumbo, of course). Discounting for the moment their mumbo-jumbo, they have a point. It isn't from out of the vortexes and lightning bolts of a malevolent unconscious mind that we say Native suicide originates, but rather from an alien, dehumanizing form of life imposed in an effort to recruit us into our own abuse while it legitimates our marginalization. There is nothing unconscious here, nothing invisible. When the smoke and mirrors have been removed: capitalism is alienation, alienation is oppression, oppression causes suicide.

The people who tell indigenous peoples what they must do to quell the suicide outbreak are either unaware of this (which we consider this most likely) or are consciously complicit in hiding this (which we consider unlikely, because it's complicated and would have required them to read and understand the early Marx). Either way, they benefit, personally and professionally, from maintaining the position they maintain. The sincerity of their beliefs is no proof of their correctness; the earnestness with which they intervene is no demonstration of their effectiveness. The therapists in the concentration camp would have been no friends of the Jews, and their actions would have done nothing to end their oppression. It was, in fact, Zhukov and Patton, and the forces they led, that ended Nazi oppression and ended the storm of suicide that engulfed the Jews.

Straight Therapeutics. Nevertheless, we think that people will be looking at our work with the expectation that we will make some suggestions about how to bring rates of indigenous suicide under some sort of control. We are also cognizant of the fact that, in taking the time and effort to come this far, many may have more than a detached, clinical interest in what we will say should be done to halt the Native suicide crisis. That is, at least some of you reading this will be doing so while facing your own, personal suicidal crisis. As you may infer from reading us, you are not alone. Please, read and consider what we have to say.

We will be brief. First, on a macro-level, it is clear indigenous peoples must come to grips with the domination of our lives by capitalism. Understanding how capitalism is the father of our oppression demands we find ways, both traditional and innovative, to endure (for that's what culture does: it finds the balance between continuity and change; Bauman, 1999). Those who benefit from capitalism show no inclination to alter it; but there are in fact viable alternatives to the present system. If nothing more, capitalism's implosion in 2008 and the continued rickety shambles that has been put in place since then has galvanized even mainstream economists into finding a way out of the mess (Rogers, 2014). We don't pretend to be economists, but the consideration of what capitalism *does* to us as human beings points the way to activities that oppose its tendencies. The building of local capacities for essential goods and services, job-sharing networks, responsible energy independence, and similar projects are in this vein (Restakis, 2004; Harrison, 2014; Blumenfeld, 2004). There are even suggestions by Marx himself, if that is your cup of tea (Hudis, 2013). In any event, positive moves toward getting off the treadmill of "Native leaders" signing away our rights to our lands and titles while gangster capitalism crumbles, taking the world with it, will soon have us recalling 3rd-World conditions as "the Good Old Days." As a counter, Idle No More has, in our opinion, the greatest potential to become *our* authentic alternative to modern capitalism.

Now, for those of you working in direct services, neither do we pretend this book substitutes for experience with suicidal individuals. If you want to become a specialist, go to university and specialize. Please keep this work in mind while you're studying there, however.

In the short term, if a person close to you gives an indication that he or she is considering suicide, the best thing you can do is not shy away from the topic, but rather discuss it, straight on. One of the things crisis intervention workers must do is learn to get past the urge to change the subject, leave the vicinity, or otherwise ignore the content of the conversation when even a hint of suicide arises. Being willing to treat suicide as a topic of serious conversation, among other things, puts you between the person considering it and death. If this is a safe place for you, then staying there will keep the next step from happening. If it is possible, bring in other friends and relatives to maintain death at a distance. It's possible that being treated like a grown-up and not a raving lunatic will help your friend and loved one endure.

In general, even before such situations arise, it's reasonable to have some familiarity with local facilities (hospitals, hot-lines, mentoring programs, etc.) that purport to intervene with suicidal clientele. These are often not readily available to reserve communities, and, given the ideology behind their therapeutic thinking, maybe that's not such a bad thing. But we realize that it is quite a burden for someone without training or support suddenly to find her/himself talking to someone who says they wish to quit this life. If you know there are nominal professionals at hand, or even if you're aware of a network of friends and loved ones you may call upon for help, you will be less likely to minimize the seriousness of your friend's communication.

Again, this is in no way intended as anything more than the roughest guidelines for people suddenly confronted with a suicidal friend or relative. Our hope here is that, when so confronted, our readership will be able to keep the other person alive long enough to follow our *real* recommendation.

Our Real Recommendation. Of all the blather we've had to read about what is going on in the mind of someone at the moment he or she takes the final step to suicide, the only one that has made sense to us is the person who compared suicide to someone trapped at the top of a burning building, having to make the choice between being burnt alive or jumping to his or her death on the ground below. "Why must there be something going on in one's mind when one is driven to the conclusion to jump?," she asked. We agree; whatever is in one's mind at that point, if anything, it is not the determinant of a person's behavior. It is the fire, it is the lack of rescue, it is the unavailability of any alternative that drives the behavior. This is what we wish to say about indigenous suicide: given the situation, it isn't a *thought*; it isn't a *choice*; it is an *inevitability*.

It is the inevitability that relentless oppression produces. It is designed to break us, either by driving us over a literal or metaphorical cliff, or by achieving our surrender. But now look back at Table 2. *Breaking* or *surrendering* are not the only options. We say there is *informed resistance*. One can look past the façade of bogus science and erased history and see the real process in action; and in seeing that, understand how it has come to dominate our situation. To put it another way, informed resistance demands that we learn who set the fire, why the ladders of the fire trucks don't reach high enough, why the building inspectors approved flammable building materials, and so on. In truth, it is the assertion of an intellectual process at a point well before the frenzy and confusion desired by our oppressors can take hold of our consciousness and erase it.

For anyone looking for our therapeutic recommendation: here it is. Become informed. If there is no one or no place to help guide you, we've recommended books to read; start there. Discuss them. Branch out from them. Involve the people around you. Regardless of whether it is you, yourself, that is poised at that metaphorical window ledge or someone near and dear to you, the alternative to breaking and surrendering is learning — as much as you can — what is happening to you and why. There is more.

Suicide typologies. We brought these up some time ago, primarily because suicidologists talk about different types of suicide. But when those suicidologists got to indigenous suicide, the subject was dropped like a hot bowling ball. In many ways this gave the impression that Native suicide is uniformly a pathological phenomenon. But that is the way mainstream suicidologists have treated it, and *not* the way we've understood it here.

Can a person intend her or his suicide as a political statement, like Nelson Small Legs? Certainly. Can it be offered and/or taken as an act of defiance? Of course. In the vignette with which we started this book, we noted that the Nazis intervened to reduce the Jewish suicide rate; when we've told people this, they find it confusing... didn't the Nazis want the Jews dead? Yes. But the Nazis wanted them dead when, where, and how *the Nazis* wanted them dead, and we have no doubt that a substantial fraction of Jewish suicides during the Holocaust were ways of saying: "Screw you, Adolph!" The Nazis certainly thought so.

Can someone receive a medical diagnosis entailing a life of unendurable pain without chance of cure, and decide not to put up with it? Yes. Can one look back at a long, full life and say, "I will leave on my own terms." Of course.

Have all indigenous people who have killed themselves done so for the same reason? Of course not.

Most importantly, at least for us: have some — all too many — indigenous people who killed themselves done so because the Powers That Be in Canada have arranged things so as to drive us to the edge of a precipice or the window ledge of a burning building, so that we either fall, or grasp the forlorn straw they offer, the "moderate livelihood" under the rules of their form of life?

Have some of us been the patsies for our own assassinations?

We say: "Yes."

Thomas Szasz, a man for whom we had great respect, argued, as related earlier, that terminating one's life was an enduring human right. Treatments imposed — drugs or restraint, for example — were not treatments at all according to him, but rather infringements by the state in a place it had no right to go: a person's right, for whatever reason, to end his/her own life.

For all the things he has taught us, we draw a line here. We agree: people have the human right to end their lives. We agree: the claim by the mainstream, that the person is "not in his or her right mind," or "they're in a midst of a depressive episode from which they will emerge, with proper treatment," is not based on substantive knowledge of the contents of another person's mind. If it interferes with a rational, fully-informed person's decision to end his or her life, it works an injustice.

But *this is our point*. Indigenous people in Canada are *not* fully informed. We are, rather, systematically *mis*-informed about the nature of the forces arrayed against us as individual human beings. We are told stories of this gremlin or that, with this power or that, which, collectively, creates our failures, erodes our happiness, and decides our futures. It is a lie. It is the confusion that must be created in our minds until we see only *different ways of breaking*, so that we choose one and accept the blame for whatever shreds of a human life wait upon that decision. And it is a revolver with six bullets, because sooner or later we realize that imitating our oppressor was its own form of suicide.

So, *pace* our departed friend, Dr. Szasz, we say that the human thing to do is to intervene, to get between a person and death, only because it is so highly unlikely that she or he has made her or his decision having *all* the information. Does the mass of Indians who "commit suicide" understand that this is a *murder*? Do they understand that their murder is being carried out by people under a façade of helping them? Do they understand that, in participating, even assisting them in this murder, they are giving their oppressors exactly what those oppressors were hoping to gain?

We Are One. When it has come up from time to time in this work we have uniformly been critical of Pan-Indianism: the tendency to believe that information concerning one indigenous nation or community tells us something about all indigenous nations or communities. We've said, and we still maintain, that we are very different peoples — more different than Hungarians and Spaniards — and that there's no reason to expect continuities between us.

But we also mentioned there was a reasonable sense in which we could be treated as very similar; it's just that, the people we examined didn't grasp that sense or recognize its importance. But that sense is this: the manner in which we have been treated by the oppressive mainstream forces coercing our assimilation. Here it makes no difference whether you're Onyota'a:ka or Mi'kmaq, Siksika or Passamaquoddy... we've all had an alien form of life shoved down our throat; we've all been told there is no incongruity in being both Canadians and "Whatevers" at the same time; and we've all been scolded that breakdowns within our ranks are attributable to our own internal failures and shortcomings. And the forcible application of this treatment has produced similar results across our nations; we are all equally confused about what is happening to us. We cast about for ways to deal with the chaos and all grab at the same straws offered us. We have all lived lives with "futures pitilessly blocked and passions violently choked by oppressive discipline... and... excessive physical or moral despotism..." and have all run up against "the ineluctible and inflexible nature of a rule against which there is no appeal."

Canada isn't necessarily trying to kill Native peoples; the necessity of our physical destruction was long ago obviated by the policy of bureaucratic genocide. No: they are satisfied with some of us killing ourselves, and with others of us helping to keep the great mass of Natives "in line," while the rest of us take (by various means) our places on the margins of Canadian society. Success in creating the Broken Indian — Native individuals destroyed by ignorance, alcohol, drugs, STD's, self-deprecation, and despair, and who thereby *validate* Canada's self-serving, self-aggrandizing, racist narrative of a brown hoard of sub-humans the Eurocanadians must tolerate, rescue, and reform — is more than enough of a victory for them.

But there is a reason for us to step back from death, because, as we've argued, to step back from death gives us the chance to step away from ignorance. To do that is to give ourselves time to work through *all* the reasons we believe we want to kill ourselves; and then, yes, with full information and due consideration, to complete that act as is our human right. As human beings, we each shall go when we decide it is time for us to go. But if we take the time to learn how and why we've been misled about what is happening to us, the opportunity is presented of doing something meaningful before that step is taken prematurely.

Schaff (1980) made the point that alienation is not a bad thing if it motivates you to overcome it. We have no doubt that the most positive ANTI-SUICIDE program for indigenous peoples that has been seen in Canada in the last few years is the Idle No More movement. After all, Indians behaving like Indians is the negation of what the moonshine of the Broken Indian model was designed to achieve, and can only be the scariest thing seen by the government in recent years. If anyone sincerely wants to see a decrease in or even the elimination of indigenous suicide, and they understand the arguments we have presented here, there is no serious *general* option. It has not escaped our notice that the Native peoples of Canada are not the only oppressed peoples in the world today experiencing their own suicidal crises. A partial list we have is: the Guarani Indians of Brazil, Argentina, Paraguay, and Bolivia; unemployed young males in Greece; dispossessed farmers in Chennai; veterans of the U. S. army who served in the Middle East; South Koreans; women with illegitimate pregnancies in India; rape victims; Sri Lankan refugees; Virginians; American farmers; unemployed British youth; the elderly in Greece; Pennsylvanian prisoners; Chinese factory workers; Canadian first-responders; and more. The capitalism-alienation-oppression-suicide progression explains much of what's happening in the world today, and we invite suicidologists to stop peering inwardly, start looking at the world around us, and see what's happening to us all, Indian or otherwise.

But indigenous peoples are nobody else's miner's canaries; some kind of expendable warning device that other, more important people can use to gauge their own, more portentous problems. There is nothing more important to us *than* us. We demand that we collectively step back from the precipice being urged upon us, if only to take the time to do what we do best: think, discuss, understand, share... then *act*.

The great Michael Collins urged his fellow oppressed Irish to stand up against a totalizing world power bent on their suppression. He proclaimed:

> They can jail us; they can shoot us; they can even conscript us. They can use us as cannon fodder in the Somme. But, we have a weapon more powerful than any in the whole arsenal of the British Empire. And that weapon is our refusal: our refusal to bow down to any order but our own, to any institution but our own.

"Our only weapon is our refusal." We ask that you refuse to die. (Rest, my dear old friend. Nyao-wen.)

144

REFERENCES

Aldrich, R. (1996). *Greater France: A history of French overseas expansion.* New York: Palgrave Macmillan.

Allen, K. (2011). *Marx and the alternative to capitalism.* London: Pluto Press.

Aly, G. (2005). *Hitler's beneficiaries: Plunder, racial war, and the Nazi welfare state.* New York: Henry Holt.

Archibald, W. P. (1994). *Marx and the missing link: Human nature.* Atlantic Highlands, NJ: Humanities Press International, Inc.

Anderberg, T. (1989). *Suicide: Definitions, causes, and values.* Lund: Lund University.

Baechler, J. (1979). *Suicides.* New York: Basic Books.

Baker, G. & Hacker, P. M. S. (1982). The grammar of psychology: Wittgenstein`s *Bemerkungen über die philosophie der psychologie. Language and Communication,* 2(3), 227-244.

Bauman, Z. (1989). *Modernity and the Holocaust.* Ithaca, New York: Cornell University Press.

Bauman, Z. (1999). *Culture as praxis.* New edition. London: Sage.

Beck, A. T. (1967). *Depression: Causes and treatment.* Philadelphia: University of Pennsylvania Press.

Bennett, M. R., & Hacker, P. M. S. (2003). *Philosophical foundations of neuroscience.* Oxford: Blackwell Publishing.

Blaut, J. (2000). *Eight eurocentric historians.* New York: Guilford.

Blaut, J. (1993). *The colonizer's model of the world: Geographical diffusionism and eurocentric history.* New York: Guilford.

Blumenfeld, Y. *Dollars or democracy: A technological alternative to capitalism.* World: Xlibris.

Branch, T. (1998). *Pillar of fire: America in the King years.* New York: Simon and Schuster.

Brant, C. C. (1993). Suicide in Canadian Aboriginal peoples: Causes and prevention. In *Royal Commission on Aboriginal Peoples: The path to healing.* (55-71).

Caplan, P. J., & Cosgrove, L. (2004). *Bias in psychiatric diagnosis.* Lanham, Maryland: Rowman and Littlefield.

Chandler, M. & Lalonde, C. (1998). Cultural continuity as a hedge against suicide in Canada's First Nations. *Transcultural Psychiatry, 35,* 191-219.

Chrisjohn, R., Young, S., & Maraun, M. (1997). *The circle game: Shadows and substance in the Indian residential school experience in Canada*. Pentincton, British Columbia: Theytus Press.

Chrisjohn, R., Pace, D., Young, S., & Mrochuk, M. (1997b). Psychological assessment and First Nations: Ethics, theory and practice. Appendix C in R. Chrisjohn, S. Young, & M. Maraun, *The circle game: Shadows and substance in the Indian residential school experience in Canada*. Pentincton, British Columbia: Theytus Press.

Chrisjohn, R., Wasacase, T., Nussey, L., Smith, A., Legault, M., Loiselle, P., & Bourgeois, M. (2002). Genocide and Indian residential schooling: The past is present. In R. Wiggers & A. Griffiths (Eds.). (2002). *Canada and international humanitarian law: Peacekeeping and war crimes in the modern era*. Centre for Foreign Policy Studies: Dalhousie University.

Chrisjohn, R. & McKay, S. (2018). '...and Indians, too:' Indigenous peoples and the Canadian form of racism. Forthcoming.

Churchill, W. J., & Vander Wall, J. (1990). *Agents of repression: The FBI's secret wars against the Black Panther Party and the American Indian Movement*. New York: South End Press.

Cole, M. (1999). Culture free versus culture based measures of cognition. In R. J. Sternberg (ed.) *The Nature of Cognition*. Boston: MIT Press.

Conklin, A. L. (1997). *A mission to civilize: The republican idea of empire in France and West Africa, 1895-1930*. Stanford, California: Stanford University Press.

Conklin, A. L., Fishman, S., & Zaretsky, R. (2011). *France and its empire since 1870*. Oxford: Oxford University Press.

Cronbach, L. J. (1971). Test validation. In R. L. Thorndike (Ed.), *Educational measurement* (2nd ed., p. 443-507). Washington, DC: American Council on Education.

Cuneo, T., & van Woudenberg R. (Eds.) (2004). *The Cambridge companion to Thomas Reid*. Cambridge: Cambridge University Press.

D'Amico, R. (1981). *Marx and philosophy of culture*. Gainesville, Florida: University Presses of Florida.

Daube, D. (1977). The linguistics of suicide. *Suicide and Life-Threatening Behavior*, 7, 132-182. (Reprinted from *Philosophy and Public Affairs*, 1972, I, 387-437).

Davenport, J. A., & Davenport III, J. (1987). Native American suicide: A Durkheimian analysis. *Social Casework: Journal of Contemporary Social Work, November,* 533-539.

Davis, R., & Zannis, M. (1973). *The genocide machine in Canada: The pacification of the north.* Montreal: Black Rose Books.

Douglas, J. (1966). The sociological analysis of the social meanings of suicide. *Archives of European Sociology,* vol. 7, 249-275.

Douglas, J. (1967). *The social meanings of suicide.* Princeton, NJ: Princeton University Press.

Durkheim, E. (1895/1982). *Rules of sociological method.* New York: The Free Press.

Durkheim, E. (1897/1966). *Suicide: A study in sociology* (J. A. Spaulding & G. Simpson, Trans.). New York: The Free Press. (Original work published 1897).

Einstein, A. (1922). *The meaning of relativity.* Great Britain: Science Paperbacks & Methuen & Co. Ltd.

Evans, A. (2004). *Chee Chee: A study of aboriginal suicide.* Montreal: McGill-Queens University Press.

Evenson, B. (2000, January 28). Suicide linked to defective gene: Suicidal tendencies treatable, Ottawa scientists say: Discovery raises concerns genetic marker will be used to stigmatize people who have it. *National Post.*

Fairbairn, G. J. (1995). *Contemplating suicide: The language and ethics of self harm.* New York: Routledge.

Forbes, I. (1990). *Marx and the new individual.* London: Unwin Hyman Ltd.

Friedenberg, E. Z. (1980). *Deference to authority: The case of Canada.* White Plains, New York: M. E. Sharpe, Inc.

Fromm, E. (1963/2004). *Marx's concept of man.* New York: Continuum.

Fusé, T. (1997). *Suicide, individual and society.* Toronto: Canadian Scholars.

Garrow, D. J. (1983). *The FBI and Martin Luther King, Jr.* New York: Penguin Books.

Geyer, R. F., & Heinz, W. R. (Eds.) (1992). *Alienation, society, and the individual: Continuity and change in theory and research.* New Brunswick, New Jersey: Transaction Publishers.

Geyer, R. F. (Ed.) (1996). *Alienation, ethnicity, and postmodernism.* Westport, Connecticut: Greenwood Press.

Goldstein, G. (2008). *Lessons in disaster: McGeorge Bundy and the path to war in Vietnam*. New York: Holt.

Hacker, P. M. S. (2007). *Human nature: The categorical framework*. Toronto: John Wiley & Sons.

Hacker, P.M.S. (2013). *The intellectual powers: A study of human nature*. Toronto: John Wiley & Sons.

Hanke, L. (1959). *Aristotle and the American Indians*. Chicago: Henry Regnery Company.

Harrison, R. (2014). *People over capital: The co-operative alternative to capitalism*. Ottawa: New Internationalist.

Hilberg, R. (1992). *Perpetrators victims bystanders: The Jewish catastrophe, 1933-1945*. New York: Harper Perennial.

Hobsbawm, E. J., & Ranger, T. (Eds.) (1983). *The invention of tradition*. Cambridge: Cambridge University Press.

Hudis, P. (2013). *Marx's concept of the alternative to capitalism*. Chicago: Haymarket Books.

Jennings, F. (1994). *The founders of America: From the earliest migrations to the present*. New York: Norton.

Kenny, A. (1971). The homunculus fallacy. In M. Greene (Ed.), *Interpretations of life and mind*. London: Routledge & Keegan Paul.

Kirmayer, L. J. (1994). Suicide among Canadian Aboriginal peoples. *Transcultural Psychiatric Research Review*, 31: 3-58.

Kirmayer, L. J., Brass, G., Holton, T. Paul, K., Simpson, C., and Tait, C. (2007). *Suicide among Aboriginal People in Canada*. Ottawa: Aboriginal Healing Foundation.

Kral, M. (1994). Suicide as social logic. *Suicide and Life-Threatening Behavior*. 24(3):245-255.

Krimsky, S., & Gruber, J. (2013). *Genetic explanations: Sense and nonsense*. Cambridge: Harvard University Press.

Kulchyski, P. (1994). *Unjust relations: Aboriginal rights in Canadian courts*. Toronto: Oxford University Press.

Lester, D. (Ed.) (1994). *Emile Durkheim: Le suicide one hundred years later*. Boston: Charles Press.

Levine, B. (2016). Proven wrong about many of its assertions, is psychiatry bullsh*t? Retrieved from http://www.alternet.org/personal-health/proven-wrong-about-many-its-assertions-psychiatry-bullsht.

Lewontin, R. D., Rose, S. & Kamin, L. J. (1984). *Not in our genes: Biology, ideology and human nature.* New York: Pantheon.

Lux, M. K. (2001). *Medicine that walks: Disease, medicine, and Canadian plains Native people, 1880-1940.* Toronto: University of Toronto Press.

Mann, C. (2006). *1491: New revelations of the Americas before Columbus.* New York: Vintage Books.

Manuel, A. (2015). *Unsettling Canada: A national wake-up call.* Toronto: Between the Lines.

Maraun, M. (1998). Measurement as a normative praxis: Implications of Wittgenstein's philosophy for psychological measurement. *Theory and Psychology* 8(4):436-461.

Maraun, M. (2014). The concepts of suicidology. In *A Wittgensteinian perspective on the use of conceptual analysis in psychology* (T. P. Racine & K. L. Slaney, Eds.) pp. 233-252. New York: Palgrave Macmillan.

Marsh, I. (2010). *Suicide: Foucault, history and truth.* Cambridge: Cambridge University Press.

Marx, K. (1867/1977). *Capital: A critique of political economy, volume 1.* (B. Fowkes, Trans.). New York: Vintage Books.

Marx, K. (1844/1988). *Economic and philosophic manuscripts of 1844.* (M. Milligan, Trans.). New York: Prometheus Books.

Meehl, P. E. (1973). *Psychodiagnosis: Selected papers.* Minneapolis: University of Minnesota Press.

Mercola, J. (2011, April 6). *Depression is not a chemical imbalance in your brain – here's proof.* Retrieved from http://articles.mercola.com/sites/articles/archive/2011/04/06/frightening-story-behind-the-drug-companies-creation-of-medical-lobotomies.aspx

Nishnawbe-Aski Nation Youth Forum on Suicide. (1996). *Horizons of hope: An empowering journey.* Final report. Nishnawbe-Aski Nation.

Noë, A. (2009). *Out of our heads: Why you are not your brain, and other lessons from the biology of consciousness.* New York: Hill and Wang.

Perelman, M. (2000). *The invention of capitalism: Classical political economy and the secret history of primitive accumulation.* Durham, North Carolina: Duke University Press.

Pickering, W. S. F., & Walford, G. (2000). *Durkheim's suicide: A century of research and debate.* New York: Routledge.

Plaut, E. A., & Anderson, K. (Eds.). (1999). *Marx on suicide.* Evanston, IL: Northwester University.

Pope, W. (1976). *Durkheim's suicide: A classic analyzed.* Chicago: University of Chicago.

Racine, T. P., & Slaney, K. L. (Eds.) (2014). *A Wittgensteinian perspective on the use of conceptual analysis in psychology.* New York: Palgrave Macmillan.

Ratner, C. (2012). *Macro cultural psychology: Its development, concerns, politics, and direction.* Oxford: Oxford University Press.

Restakis, J. (2010). *Humanizing the economy: Co-operatives in the age of capital.* Gabriola Island, British Columbia: New Society Publishers.

Robinson, E., & Quinney, H. B. (1985). *The infested blanket: Canada's constitution - genocide of Indian nations.* Winnipeg, Manitoba: Queenston House Publishing Co. Ltd.

Rogers, C. (2014). *Capitalism and its alternatives.* London: Zed Books.

Rogers, J. (2001). Theoretical grounding: The "missing link" in suicide research. *Journal of Counseling & Development,* Winter, (79), 16-25.

Rogers, J. R. & Lester, D. (2010). *Understanding Suicide: Why we don't and how we might.* Cambridge, MA: Hogrefe Publishing.

Ross, A. (Ed.). (1996). *Science wars.* Durham, North Carolina: Duke University Press.

Ross, C. A., & Pam, A. (1995). *Pseudoscience in biological psychiatry: Blaming the body.* Toronto: Wiley and Sons.

Ryan, W. (1971). *Blaming the victim.* New York: Pantheon Books.

Ryan, W. (1981). *Equality.* New York: Pantheon Books.

Samson, C. (2003). *A way of life that does not exist: Canada and the extinguishment of the Innu.* London: Verso.

Samson, C., Wilson, J., and Mazower, J. (1999). *Canada's Tibet: The killing of the Innu.* London: Survival International.

Schaff, A. (1980). *Alienation as a social phenomenon.* Oxford: Pergamon Press.

Schweitzer, D. & Geyer, R. F. (Eds.) (1989). *Alienation theories and de-alienation strategies.* Northwood, Middlesex: Science Reviews Ltd.

Shewell, H. (2004). *"Enough to keep them alive": Indian welfare in Canada, 1873-1965.* Toronto, Ontario: University of Toronto.

Shneidman, E. S. (1985). *Definition of suicide*. New York: Wiley.

Shneidman, E. S. (1996). *The suicidal mind*. Oxford: Oxford University Press.

Smith, A. O. (2002). Bearing the burden of proof: Theory and practice in First Nations suicidology. Undergraduate thesis: Department of Native Studies, St. Thomas University, Fredericton, New Brunswick. Infra.

Smith, G. W. & Bloom, I. (1985). A study of the personal meaning of suicide in the context of Baechler`s typology. *Suicide and Life Threatening Behavior,* Spring, 15(1), 3-13.

Sokal, A. & Bricmont, J. (1998). *Fashionable nonsense: Postmodern intellectuals' abuse of science.* New York: Picador.

Syer-Solursh, D. (1987). *Report of the National Task Force on Suicide in Canada.* Ottawa: Health Canada.

Szasz, T. (1961). *The myth of mental illness: Foundations of a theory of personal conduct.* New York: Hoeber-Harper.

Szasz, T. (1970). *The Manufacture of Madness: A comparative study of the inquisition and the mental health movement.* Syracuse, New York: Syracuse University Press.

Szasz, T. (1987). *Insanity: The idea and its consequences.* Syracuse, New York: Syracuse University Press.

Szasz, T. (1999). *Fatal freedom: The ethics and politics of suicide.* Westport, CT: Praeger.

Szasz, T. (2002). *The meaning of mind: Language, morality, and neuroscience.* Syracuse, New York: Syracuse University Press.

Szasz, T. (2007). *The medicalization of everyday life: Selected essays.* Syracuse, New York: Syracuse University Press.

Szasz, T. (2011). *Suicide prohibition: The shame of medicine.* Syracuse, New York: Syracuse University Press.

Thatcher, R. W. (2004). *Fighting firewater fictions: Moving beyond the disease model of alcoholism in First Nations.* Toronto: University of Toronto Press.

Titley, E. B. (1986). *A narrow vision: Duncan Campbell Scott and the administration of Indian Affairs in Canada.* Vancouver, British Columbia: University of British Columbia Press.

Torrance, J. (1977). *Estrangement, alienation and exploitation: A sociological approach to historical materialism.* New York: Macmillan Press.

Valenstein, E. (2002). *Blaming the brain: The truth about drugs and mental health.* New York: The Free Press.

van Hooff, A. J. L. (2000). A historical perspective on suicide. In *Comprehensive textbook of suicidology* (Eds. R.W. Maris, A. L. Berman & M. M. Silverman), pp. 96-126. New York: Guilford.

Vygotsky, L. (1986). *Thought and Language (2nd ed.).* Boston: MIT Press.

Wallimann, I. (1981). *Estrangement: Marx's conception of human nature and the division of labor.* Westport, Connecticut: Greenwood Press.

Waldram, J. B. (2004). *Revenge of the Windigo: The construction of the mind and mental health of North American Aboriginal Peoples.* Toronto: University of Toronto Press.

Wekstein, L. (1979). *Handbook of Suicidology: Principles, problems and practice.* New York: Brunner/ Mazel, Publishers.

Wittgenstein, L. (1951/2009) (4th ed.). *Philosophical investigations.* (Trans. G. E. Anscombe, P. M. S. Hacker, & J. Schulte). London: Blackwell.

Appendix 1

BEARING THE BURDEN OF PROOF:
THEORY AND PRACTICE IN FIRST NATIONS SUICIDOLOGY

by

Andrea Odessa Smith, M. Sc.

and

Roland D. Chrisjohn, Ph. D.

Cassius. I know where I will wear this dagger, then;
Cassius from bondage will deliver Cassius:
Therein, ye gods, you make the weak most strong;
Therein, ye gods, you tyrants do defeat:
Nor stony tower, nor walls of beaten brass
Nor airless dungeon, nor strong links of iron,
Can be retentive to the strength of spirit;
But life, being weary of these worldly bars,
Never lacks power to dismiss itself.
If I know this, know all the world besides,
That part of tyranny that I do bear
I can shake off at pleasure.
Casca. So can I:
So every bondman is his own hand bears
The power to cancel his captivity.

Shakespeare. *Julius Caesar*, Act I, Scene III

CHAPTER 1

Suicide is clearly one of the most urgent problems. Too many Aboriginal youth and young adults are pointing shotguns at their heads, putting ropes around their necks, destroying their powers of reason with fumes of gasoline and glue. Even one such death or serious injury would be too many. It is hard to imagine a public responsibility more pressing than stopping them. -- Royal Commission on Aboriginal Peoples, *Choosing Life.*

Introductions

A sudden rash of people dropping dead is likely to arouse consternation in any society. Regardless of *who* is dying, the question of *why* they are dying arises. Any inability to render immediate sense from the situation leads us to try to figure out just what is going on. Studying the patterns of the deaths seems a reasonable initial strategy, if perhaps a formal one. Looking at such things as similarity between the victims, the differences between those who died and those who lived, and the correlation of individually-indexed variables all appear to be reasonable attempts to obtain answers.

Consequently, Canadian society is justly concerned that one group of people within its geopolitical borders, indigenous peoples, seem to be dying disproportionately from self-inflicted deaths. A quick survey of the relevant literature of Native suicidology presents a grim picture: the generally acknowledged figures of suicide rates on reserves is held to be between three to five times higher than those for non-Native people. A mass of media coverage, government reports, research publications, and program initiatives serve as a reminder of the seriousness of First Nations suicide, and so we will take it for granted that readers are acquainted with the issue (or that at least the issue is familiar).

Following the established pattern, mainstream Canadian society has undertaken to come to grips with the phenomenon of indigenous suicide by following the procedures sketched out above. The "mysterious and inexplicable tragedy" of aboriginal suicide seems beyond us, and in our attempts to understand why it occurs we search for what *causes* indigenous people to behave in such an extraordinary manner. Calls for more research and for funding suicide prevention programs are consistent with a *common sense* formulation: when we have an understanding of the *causes* of suicide, we then have at least an idea about how to *interfere with* that causation (should we be so inclined). (By common sense we mean, following Pleasants (1999, Ch. 2), sense that is common, not meaning sense that is "universal," "natural," or "right.") Thus, the matter of *why* is central to the search for effective means of preventing First Nations suicide. Public and mental health professionals design intervention strategies in accordance with and based upon, however loosely or solidly, formal explanations and theories of suicide. Theories and explanations, by establishing the causal mechanisms that account for the incidence of suicide amongst Native peoples, identify which causal links can serve as possible sites of intervention.

The fact that, despite intervention, First Nations people are still killing themselves points to the limited success of prevention programs and the theoretical framework upon which they are based. If existing theories and explanations were accurate, some diminuation of rates might have been expected in the last 20 years of intervention. This cuts both ways, however, for the obvious lack of success health professionals have had can be (and has been) used to argue for more of the same; rather than rejection, the limited success has suggested the further *refinement and elaboration* of existing theories and explanations.

It is our thesis that the limited success of current intervention programs makes the case for their rejection rather than for their refinement and elaboration. The "mystery" of indigenous suicide is, in our view, impressed upon us by the manner in which we (and our professional designates, the suicidologists) investigate the issues. We argue that research into the causes of indigenous suicide suffers from the conflation of empirical and conceptual issues (Cf. Baker and Hacker, 1982); that this conflation arises in part from the Western ideological commitment to empiricism and its drive to provide generalizable causal explanations of predictive value; and that dominating present day approaches to understanding this issue cannot, in principle, provide what it purports to be able to provide. That is, there are no experiments, no cohort studies, and no data manipulation techniques that could (even if funding was sufficient) eventually draw a complete picture of, and thus a complete blueprint for, intervening with indigenous suicide. Thus, a commitment to a standard, mainstream methodological approach to the investigation of Native suicide is, in fact, a commitment to its perpetuation.

More than this, however, we demonstrated that First Nations suicide is not mysterious at all. An alternative frame of reference (a non-Western ideological commitment, if you prefer) is readily available which, if taken seriously, would shed an entirely different light on the issue and lead to interventions with real chances to end, or at least drastically curtail, the "epidemic." Rather than examining First Nations suicide and its causes as a set of empirical relations, we describe how we can seek intelligibility by looking at conceptual relations. The meaning of suicide stems not from its reference to some sort of objective, mind-independent reality, but instead from grammatical uses in our lives. Yet this should not be interpreted as an attempt to develop a new theory or method of indigenous suicide intervention. At best, it is a cry to halt: to show how deep are the muddles in our thinking and in the thinking of well-intentioned people, who expound causes and solutions as they trip over their own feet.

The real problem, we argue, is the ideological divide that legislates the irrelevance (even harmfulness) of existing approaches, for the ideology that makes the positivist approach almost inevitable is the same ideology that has been the driving engine behind Canada's assimilationist attack on indigenous peoples. Theories of First Nations suicide contribute more to our understanding of Canadian society than to solving its occurrence. Thus we maintain that indigenous suicide come down to a final irony: existing mainstream approaches to the problem are a continuation of the assimilation attack that constitutes a major factor in creating the "Indian suicide problem" in the first place.

CHAPTER 2

> If somebody's belief is such that the reasons
> he can produce for it are no more certain than
> his assertion, then he cannot maintain that he
> knows what he believes. -- Michael ter Hark,
> *Beyond the Inner and the Outer*

Ideology and Methodology

Regardless of intentions, well-meaning people fall into dangerous lines of thinking and doing. As the saying goes, "the road to hell is paved with good intentions." While our argument does rest on a thoroughgoing refutation of explanations of suicide, it does not constitute a personal attack on the professionals and lay people working in Native suicide prevention. It is precisely because public and mental health professionals and suicidologists are concerned and trying to change the situation with respect to First Nations suicide that they comprise our target and our audience. The aim is not to offend, but neither is it not to offend; such a dimension is irrelevant for judging a serious argument. Thus repudiating the thinking on this issue should not be confused with repudiating the thinker. Exception to our manner of presentation only serves to distract from a true examination of the unspoken core tenets of explanations of First Nations suicide. If the analysis provided provokes, it is because the limits of intellectual horizons are being tested.

For present purposes, the most dangerous line of thinking adopted by professionals engaged in suicidology is the presumption that the individual person (that is, "what individuals think, choose, and do;" Bhargava, 1992, p. 1) is the locus both of understanding the problem of indigenous suicide and intervening with it. Methodological individualism (MI), the technical name of this presumption, is rarely if ever explicitly addressed outside of academic philosophy departments and is consequently never treated by more "hands on" disciplines as the ideological commitment it is.[1] As an ideology, however, it has no more claim to "truth" status than any belief, however fervently held; as a grounding for methodology, research, and theory construction, it is subject to the same justificatory criteria as, say, choosing linear regression over monotone regression in statistical analyses.

Consequently, that the thinking around suicide and its causes is so confused stems not from the personal intellectual predilections of social scientists, but is symptomatic of their (and our) immersion within a western worldview, individualism. As the dominant ideological framework of western civilization, individualism is an ideology that "serves mainly to obscure the realities and sources of oppression and to give the experienced realities of living the appearance of naturalness and inevitability (Bleier, 1984, p. 163)." The pervasiveness of this explanatory framework is so great that the majority of people, academics and otherwise, play by these rules, doing so (for the most part) without intention: "one's methodological views are rarely consciously held: methodology is nowhere explicitly taught in modern curricula; rather, the modern scientist learns his methodology by plying his scientific trade (Caldwell, 1983, p. 3)." Elucidating the basic assumptions of this explanatory framework is important, for such an analysis reveals; (a) the unquestioned dominance of individualism and its methodological concomitants (together known as methodological individualism) and (b) the role methodology plays in prescribing what is to be considered an acceptable scientific explanation (Caldwell, 1983, p. 2).

An examination of evidentiary standards clearly establishes how MI, as a methodology and ideology defines scientific method.[2] In determining what constitutes "evidence", limits are also placed on what is considered "real;" the west has been distinguished in this regard, clearly placing primacy on scientific knowledge, dismissive at best of other modes of explanation (religious, cultural, etc.). Empiricism, a methodology which takes sensory data (that is observation) as evidence dominates scientific practices, including suicidology. But whose sense data, whose observations are being used? The reliance on personal experience reflects a commitment to individualism, for it is individuals who experience, who see, who conduct experiments, and so on (Easton, 1983, Ch. 1). Hence, within MI, individuals are given ontological and epistemic priority.

Individualism has several other corollaries, including reductionism. Cartesian reductionism is deeply entangled within science, manifest in how understanding of the whole is sought by understanding the parts that are constitutive of the whole, and so the task of science becomes one of explaining what is observable by referring to latent, constitutive properties (Levins and Lewontin, 1985, Ch. 1). This has lead (historically, not necessarily) to the adoption of a mechanistic picture of society, one that responds to why is society the way it is by saying it's because people are the way they are; more specifically, in the form of methodological individualism, the personal, internal properties of individuals serve as explanations of social conditions. Explanation within this ideology is the construction of the putative causal mechanisms and general laws that account for why individual people commit suicide.

Empirical and Conceptual Distinctions

Consistent with methodologically individualistic practices, existing theories of suicide develop hypotheses and compare them with systematic observations concerning suicide among Native peoples. Indeed, these practices provide a picture, presented to us in the form of a causal model that (supposedly) represents what is going on and why. As empirical propositions, it is possible to evaluate theories, at least in principle, by comparing the correspondence between propositional content and external criteria. One consequence of this is that, for something to be an empirical investigation, it must be sensible for a proposition to be other than the condition it asserts: if *only* blonds were *ever* capable of having fun, then "blondhood" and "fun-having capacity" would be synonymous, and it would not be possible to "investigate" whether blonds did or did not have "more fun."

But the workings of the world are not fully encompassed by empirical propositions alone. Observations about the nature of the world must also recognize non-empirical, or *conceptual* content. Certain analytic statements, for example, are void of content (it is nonsense to wonder whether or not bachelors are married). Quite distinctly from empirical issues, conceptual issues are not and cannot be resolved, nor defended, by citing empirical data like facts and figures. They are not descriptions of an objective, external reality, but in fact delineate the bounds of reality, in that they provide the conceptual framework in which empirical statements can be made (Baker and Hacker, 1982). One thus decides conceptual issues in a fashion wholly distinct from empirical issues. Furthermore, careful attention is demanded to distinguishing empirical statements from conceptual ones, since the manners in which they are to be evaluated differ completely. Treating an empirical statement as a conceptual one, or *vice versa*, is perhaps the fundamental confusion found in suicidology literature.

As previously stated, we reject the notion that by gathering and analyzing data suicidology can, in principle, construct a comprehensive explanation of why Native peoples kill themselves; we must systematically ignore certain kinds of factors necessary for fully understanding First Nations suicide when we treat the problem as a purely empirical one. However, in that, it must be made clear that we are not trying to *prove* that the causal models built by suicidologists are wrong, but rather that talking about suicide solely as a set of empirical relations is incoherent and self-defeating (if understanding is one's goal). Thus, we are not making an empirical argument but rather a conceptual one, and the standards which we must satisfy are not those of the empiricist. What may seem a disinterest in addressing a statistically significant correlation between, say, racism and Indigenous peoples' self-inflicted death is not a weakness or omission on our part: facts and figures do not bear upon the conceptual clarification of First Nations suicide. Instead, what may or may not be meaningful about such a correlation depends on having a conceptual framework within which the correlation may be understood. Seeing indigenous suicide wholly as a branch of empirical science is in fact an ideological commitment to methodological individualism, one that limits our understanding of the phenomenon and thus circumscribes ultimately what we decide to do about it. By embracing empirical science as its enterprise, suicidology has in effect committed itself to advancing by gathering data and making certain kinds of arguments. However, as we shall see, suicidology has run into a self-constructed roadblock, for it does not and cannot meet the standards of evidence its own method requires.

Theories of Suicide

Regardless of whether the analysis is quantitative or qualitative, which level of analysis is adopted, or the disciplinary focus, understanding First Nations suicide is approached as necessitating a demonstration of empirical causes. This is an uncontroversial claim; suicide in general has attracted the attention of people from numerous disciplines and theoretical positions, resulting in a large body of literature on the subject as well as the formation of a separate discipline, suicidology. Suicidologists include, among others, psychologists, neurologists, molecular biologists, psychotherapists, sociologists, epidemiologists, and public and mental health professionals. The assertion that epidemiology and public health are scientific disciplines should elicit no reaction. Even within the social sciences, it is generally accepted that there are analogies between the "hard" or "natural" sciences and the social sciences, including the notion that the scientific method is applicable to the study of humans. Though the transferability of methods is sometimes controversial (e.g., are there quantitative methods useful for analysis of social phenomena?) it is, for the most part, accepted that the social sciences deal with matters of fact, and are involved in making and evaluating empirical propositions about human activity. Arguments as to the level of analysis at which the "true" explanatory bedrock resides appear to be a result of major disciplinary differences, but such differences are remarkably trivial upon closer examination. Theories of indigenous suicide,[3] though seemingly diverse, reflect the generic philosophical commitment to empiricism and, as we shall see, share its philosophical confusions.

Committed to positivism and empiricism, suicidologists take it that *understanding* suicide is equivalent to *explaining* suicide by constructing generalizable models that replicate what *actually* causes indigenous peoples to commit suicide. According to the National Task Force on Suicide in Canada:

> Identifying the chain of causal and triggering factors, which may in any event be highly individual, and deriving from this an overall prevention and treatment strategy is one of the most vexing problems facing professionals in the health sciences (1986, p. 3).

Although written in 1986, clearly the work of suicidologists remains unfinished, evinced by the subsequent Update of the National Task Force. In 1994, the Task Force offered these above comments again in their preface (Health Canada, 1994, p. ix). Their presumed starting point for investigating suicide etiology is epidemiology, the study of the statistical distribution of health indicators; their assumption is that statistical correlation between indices indicate associations, which can, in turn, be used as grounds for inferring causal relationships. Epidemiology's:

> main focus is on identifying certain sociological characteristics and attributes of suicide such as age, gender, occupation, residence, marital status, education, religion, race and ethnicity, means of suicide and/or motives to pin-point... target populations and high-risk groups (Fusé, 1997, p. 5).

But this is a misnomer, as the variables identified, such as age and marital status, are not features of Canadian society (society cannot be said to have a job, live at 34 Huntington St, and be single; only an individual fits such a description). As Levins and Lewontin aptly point out,

> while we ordinarily think of statistics as an analysis of populations, the basis of the statistical approach to inferring causes is a model of the individual and it is an explanation of the properties of the individual that is being sought (Levins and Lewontin, 2000, p. 874).

The statistical approach commits us to a model of understanding society by an empirical analysis of the personal characteristics of individuals, and thus is consistent with methodological individualism. Nothing exemplifies this more in suicidology than the work of Durkheim.

Suicide and Durkheim

As Plaut (1999) recently observed, "the twentieth century... has not produced either insight or methodology that has greatly increased our understanding of suicide beyond that contained in [Durkheim's] work (p. 29)." The approach of analyzing statistical data in hopes of discovering patterns of suicide causation and incidence was initiated by Durkheim back in 1897, when he sought to establish the social causes of the statistical differences between the suicide rates of different social groups. Durkheim was reacting against the prevalence of what he called the "cult of the individual," and went to great lengths (some say too great) to stress the social character of seemingly individualized things (Thompson, 1982, p. 51). Interesting enough, he also was one of the first to conceive of sociology as a science, and his work *Suicide: A Study in Sociology* is the first practical demonstration of his sociological method. One of his reasons for selecting suicide as the subject of investigation was that it was characterized as an individual act. Thus, a successful defence of its social character would easily extend to other less individualized aspects of human activity.

Being scientific, the sociological study of suicide was (and is) held to be an "objective" and "rigorous" investigation. Anderberg notes Durkheim was himself a social realist, believing that the scientist had only to come across and accurately describe the real state of affairs out there (1989, p. 117)." Objectivity required that sociology:

(a) define its objects of study theoretically, (b) that the objects have external characteristics, and (c) that they be observable. Sociological characteristics, what he termed "social facts," therefore needed to be treated and conceived as *things* in order to be subject to the scientific method (Thompson, 1982, p. 101).

Hence, suicide was depicted not as a characteristic of individuals but of society, and Durkheim attempted to specify a definition avoiding reference to intentions: "the term suicide is applied to all cases of death resulting directly or indirectly from a positive or negative act of the victim himself, which he knows will produce this result (Durkheim, 1951, p. 44)." Avoiding a discussion of private experiences and mental states was necessary in order to pursue an analysis of suicide that was not at the level of the individual. Durkheim attempted to demonstrate the causal impact of social facts on individual behavior. In doing so, he committed himself to designing general laws covering the nature of the empirical causes of suicide.

Using national suicide data, Durkheim argued that the differences between group suicide rates pointed to a causal agent that originated outside of individuals. He reasoned that since groups with similar religious and occupational affiliation, marital status, and other indices, were associated with similar suicidal behavior, the causal agent must be external to individuals for individually located causes could not account for such similarities. Though he did not disregard the existence of individual reasons for committing suicide, he theorized that those individuals who were either too little or too much integrated into or regulated by society were at greater risk for suicidal behavior. His presumption (an unfounded explanation) is along these lines: "when society is strongly [though not overly] integrated, it holds individuals under its control, considers them at its service and thus forbids them to dispose wilfully of themselves (Durkheim, 1951, p. 209)." In this vein, Durkheim classifies the causes of suicide into four categories: egoistic, altruistic, anomic, and fatalistic; the first two are related to the level of integration of the individual into society, the latter two the degree of regulation.

According to Durkheim, egoistic suicide is caused by the insufficient integration of the individual in society, a form of excessive individualization. In such instances, individuals, "so far as they are admitted masters of their destinies, it is their privilege to end their lives. They, on their part, have no reason to endure life's sufferings patiently (Durkheim, 1951, p. 209)."

The opposite of egoistic suicide, altruistic suicide occurs when the individual is too integrated into his society, thus lacking a sense of personal identity. "To all intents and purposes indistinct from his companions, he is only an inseparable part of the whole without personal value... [so] that society should not hesitate, for the very slightest reason, to bid him end a life it values so little (Durkheim, 1951, p. 221)."

Orthogonal to a society's characteristic integration is the regulative force it exerts. When society lacks regulation, characterized by normlessness and rootlessness, individuals are given to "appetites" which are boundless and insatiable:

> Irrespective of any external regulatory force, our capacity for feeling is in itself an insatiable and bottomless abyss. But is nothing external can restrain this capacity, it can only be a course of torment to itself... How could the desire to live not be weakened under such conditions (Durkheim, 1951, p. 247)?

Mentioned only in a footnote, Durkheim identifies a fourth type of suicide caused by the over regulation of individuals in society, fatalistic suicide. "It is the suicide deriving from excessive regulation, that of persons with futures pitilessly blocked and passions violently choked by oppressive discipline (Durkheim, 1951, p. 276)." Thompson (1982, p. 110) illustrated the relationships between the types of suicide and degrees of regulation and integration (see Figure 1):

See our Figure 7 on page 76 of the main text.

What the terms integration and regulation mean, and importantly, how the differ, is not made apparent by Durkheim. Although he categorically and rhetorically emphasizes their importance and their distinctiveness, he fails to conceptually clarify the concepts (Pope, 1976). This omission is particularly significant given that Durkheim defined these forms of suicide as "social facts" — as observable, empirical phenomena. For we can ask, how could one tell whether someone had committed anomic as opposed to egoistic suicide? What evidence could be provided to settle the matter one way or another? Durkheim himself had something to say on the identification of the cause of an individual's suicide:

We should add, to be sure, there they are not always found in actual experience in a state of purity and isolation. They are very often combined with one another, giving rise to composite varieties; characteristics of several types will be united in a single suicide. The reason for this is that different social causes of suicide themselves may simultaneously affect the same individual and impose their combined effects upon him... Two factors of suicide, especially, have a peculiar affinity for one another, namely, egoism and anomy. We know that they are usually merely two different aspects of one social state (1951, p. 287-288).

Here we are presented with a contradiction in Durkheim theory, in that he sets out to classify suicide "by the [social] causes which produce them (1951, p. 147)," yet he himself describes suicides as having multiple causes, which are indistinguishable in the individual case. If the causes of suicide are indeed empirical, then they should be identifiable through observation, or measurement. Instead of following through with a demonstration of his theory's explanatory power, Durkheim implies that he cannot account for actual cases, which are too complicated, begging the question as to the utility and accuracy of his initial explanation.

Moreover, by depicting social facts as having a causal impact on the individual, and being unable to provide empirical verification, he resorted to providing a metaphysical description of social forces, indicated in Durkheim's use of the language of "forces," "powers," and "passions." For example, in speaking about the social facts which restrain individuals' "appetites," he writes:

Either directly and as a whole, or through the agency of one of its organs, society alone can play this moderating role; for it is the only moral power superior to the individual... It alone has the power necessary to stipulate law and to set the point beyond which the passions must not go (Durkheim, 1951, p. 249).

Durkheim's use of the organic analogy (that society is conceived of as a body which possess different parts or "organs," each playing a different function) is indicative of the influence of the biological sciences on his development the sociological method (Thompson 1982, 94 – 96). The important thing to note is that this is an *analogy*; that is, that society is *like* a body, not that it *is* a body. In the above quote, Durkheim is speaking *metaphorically*, yet his commitment to empiricism means that he did not intend it as such; he meant quite literally there are parts of society that play a moderating role. Even though they are so described, social facts are not objective, external conditions of reality. We are unable to subject Durkheim's theory to comparison with reality, nor does he cite evidence of where this spoken-of "power" is located, what it consists of, or when it occurs, and so he leads us into metaphysics.

Similarly, it can be said of his use of the concept of social solidarity, which he describes as playing a decisive role in the occurrence of suicide:

> There is, in short, in a cohesive and animated society a constant interchange of ideas and feelings from all to each and each to all, something like a mutual moral support, which instead of throwing the individual on his own resources, leads him to share in the collective energy and supports his own when exhausted (Durkheim, 1951, p. 210).

Though it is clear from reading Durkheim that he intended to explain suicide in terms of social factors as opposed to psychological, hence, individual ones, his search for hidden causes leads him to develop an explanatory model that is committed to individualism. Such an analysis is likely to evoke protest, particularly considering critics of Durkheim have taken objection to his "extreme sociologism [that] neglects the role of the individual in suicide (Fusé, 1997, p. 100)." Yet for all his use of language of social relations ("public life," "social forces," "collective life," etc.), Durkheim describes the causal impact of the level of integration and regulation as effecting individuals' psychological states. That is, social facts affect individuals' psychological states, which in turn, explain why they committed suicide. Rather than containing his analysis of suicide in terms of society (as he intended), Durkheim reduces social facts to a discussion of individuals' mental states and values.[4] "Anomy," he writes, "begets a state of exasperation and irritated weariness (Durkheim, 1951, p. 209)," and people "cling to life more resolutely when belonging to a group they love (Durkheim, 1951, p. 209)." But are such propositions *veridical* or *conceptual*? Do individuals really "cling to life more resolutely when belonging to a group they love?" Could we *prove* that individuals really "cling to life?" Durkheim again comes up empty-handed in demonstrating that anomie results in individuals experiencing "exasperation" from insatiable "appetites," and nowhere does he offer evidence of these emotional and mental states causing individuals to take their lives.

> Instead of contenting himself with metaphysical reflection on social themes, the sociologist must take the object of his research groups of facts clearly circumscribed, capable of ready definition, with definite limits, and adhere strictly to them (Durkheim, 1951, p. 36).

Taken from the preface to *Suicide: A Sociological Analysis*, the above quotation conveys Durkheim's dedication to see sociology develop as a rigorous scientific discipline. Though an admirable attempt to develop a scientific theory of the social causes of suicide, Durkheim's work fails to live up to its task, its shortcomings stemming mainly from confusion between conceptual and empirical issues. Durkheim takes social facts such as anomie, integration and regulation to be empirical, but no psychical entities so defined exist. In addition, the metaphysical acrobatics he performs using "collective consciousness," "forces," and "powers" end up being the causes of the private experiences of individuals, and so in his explanation, social facts are reduced to individual facts. The work of Durkheim, as we will see, is central to the literature on First Nations suicide, and in failing to distinguish between conceptual and empirical propositions, carries over the same philosophical confusions.

Suicide after Durkheim

Much of the literature on First Nations suicide cites Durkheim's important theoretical contribution to suicidology (Johnson and Tormen, 2001; Middlebrook, LeMaster, Beals, Novins, and Manson, 2001; Novis, Beals, Roberts, and Manson, 1999; Brant, 1996; Health Canada, 1994). Using Durkheim's concept of social solidarity as a causal agent of suicide, it is asserted that Native people lack social integration into either their own societies, western societies, or both. It is generally regarded that Native people commit *anomic* suicide, characterized by normlessness and social disintegration that occurred after "contact" with Europeans. Indigenous peoples "experiences rapid socio-cultural change", and in conflict with, and overwhelmed by, dominant non-

Native society, Native people have "lost" their traditional cultural ways, resulting in social disintegration. The lack of firm cultural and spiritual foundation has resulted in indigenous peoples feeling hopeless, helpless, and lacking self-esteem, which when compounded by stressful life events, including poverty, and the history of colonial relations, leads to suicide. For example, in its discussion of Native Suicide, the National Task Force on Suicide on Canada writes: "many of these conditions [alcoholism, poverty, lack of education] have developed as a result of the difficulties of integration into white man's society (1986, p.33)." In a similar vein, the Native Psychologists of Canada articulate the philosophy of their Focus Group on Suicide Prevention:

> Suicide is a serious problem in our Native communities. It has reached epidemic proportions. It is the final self-destructive act of despair, committed while in a state of hopelessness and depression. The hardest hit are our young men between ages of 15 and 24. They are unable to find meaning in their lives. They feel abandoned by their culture and rejected by the larger society. They turn to substance abuse to ease their pain and frustration, and, in the process, simply worsen their mental state (1995, p. 5)

The concordance between this statement by the Native Psychologists of Canada and Durkheim's theory of suicide should be apparent. Differences between disciplines is of little concern, for, as the analysis of Durkheim's work indicated, the methodological tendency is to discuss suicide as being the end result of internalized, individualized causes (even if the causal factors had an external origin). Studies of Native suicides, whether they are psychological, biological or sociological, are individual-level analyses that depict the causes of suicide as residing within First Nations.

In 1995, the Royal Commission on Aboriginal People (RCAP), after consultations with members of various Indian reserves, published their findings as *Choosing Life: Special Report on Suicide among Aboriginal People*. The following passage articulates how considerations of political, economic, social causes of suicide are reduced to a discussion of Native peoples' mental states:

> Like other forms of violence and self-destructive behaviour in Aboriginal communities, it [suicide] is also

the expression of a kind of collective anguish – part grief, part anger – tearing at the minds and hearts of many people. This anguish is the cumulative effect of 300 years of colonial history: lands occupied, resources seized, beliefs and cultures ridiculed, children taken away, power concentrated in distant capitals, hopes for honourable co-existence dashed over and over again (RCAP, 1995, p. x).

And, from another passage:

Racism, loss of culture, physical and mental abuse, family discord, feelings of boredom, loneliness and powerlessness all contribute to the personal pain that leads these young people to choose suicide. Drug and alcohol abuse tends to exaggerate the problem (RCAP, 1995, p. 8).

That is, after citing economic or social factors as contributing to aboriginal peoples' higher suicide rates, it is immediately posited that the social processes of acculturation and anomie have a causal, mechanistic impact on the psychology of individuals. Wein gives a *pro forma* account of this mystical enterprise: "externally derived shocks" lead to "community and family disintegration" which in turn has "individual level consequences," and together with "triggering and release mechanisms," will cause suicide (Wein, quoted in Davis, 1986). Social factors such as racism, colonialism, and historical political relations are taken into consideration only insofar as they affect individual First Nations feelings (since feelings are property of individuals, not societies, it is incoherent to speak of a sad culture, or of "collective anguish"). Our objection here is not that racism and colonization do not affect individuals. Rather, it is that such factors, when conceived of only as the "felt experiences" of individual persons, fail to provide us with a sufficient account of what these (and other) forms of marginalization accomplish (but see below).

Hence, Native youth are depicted as killing themselves because of their "deep psychological pain," "lack of identity," and "lack of meaning in their lives." Yet the experience of existential or emotional crisis does not alone account for why someone kills themselves. Several theorists have asserted the interaction of several causal factors; that together, account for why Native people commit suicide. For example, Johnson and Torman (2001) write:

This set of relationships is composed of underlying causes that are generally circumstances in the individual's environment, precipitating stress events, with personal feelings such as alienation, anomie, helplessness, hopelessness, and despair. These personal feelings are places into motion by stressful life events, which are manifested by the development of suicidal thoughts and gestures, the culmination being the successful suicide act (2001, p. 238).

In a similar vein, Brant (1996) articulates the different agents that interact to cause suicide:

The triad of poverty, powerlessness, and anomie produce the triad of alcoholism (and other substance abuse), suicidal ideation (and attempts), and depression. The first triad is neither sufficient, nor necessary, to produce the second triad of symptoms but must be liberally sprinkles [sic] with disturbing childhood experiences and usually a recent separation or loss (1986, p. 176).

With only slight modification, these assertions are mirror images of one another. What causes someone to commit suicide may be the result of several causal interactions, (the individual's social situation, their mental state, and some form of external trigger mechanism, such as a recent loss or separation). As the bulk of the explanatory power resides in such concepts as hopelessness, helplessness, and feeling anomie (that is, in emotional states) it is clear that theories of the causes of First Nations suicide locate the difficulties as properties of First Nations individuals: since they "contain" these problems more frequently than mainstream individual Canadians, they have a correspondingly higher suicide rate as a people.

Let us take a closer look at these explanations, bearing in mind that they are purported to be veridical descriptions of the causes of indigenous suicide. Psychological or psychosocial explanations identify the causes of suicide as being individuals' personal emotional/mental experiences, even when external factors are seen as contributing. External factors are held to have an effect on the individuals' private experiences, such as "stressful life events" putting "feelings into motion." But assertions of this kind, as objective causal models, cannot be placed alongside the reality they are supposed to describe, and therefore cannot be subject to the empirical verification they purportedly embrace. Asserting that we could conduct an experiment where we could observe the speed and direction of a feeling would likely bring some skepticism as to what we were doing in our research laboratory all day other than research.

See our Figure 2 on page 40 of the main text.

Allow us to be more specific. Figure 2 is Fusé's (1997) model of suicide (his figure 9). Although his discussion does not make it clear whether he conceives of his depiction as a simple but overgrown regression model or as a higher-order latent variable model, the issue is irrelevant for the present discussion. Putting aside (for the moment) purely technical difficulties, what are the conceptual limitations? They are legion. What grounds does Fusé have for the universality of his model (and universality is, explicitly, or implicitly, a claim, since *only* Figure 9 is given and not countless different figures; either some claim of universality is being made, or the positivist, empiricist position must admit to the *particularity* of its description, demonstrating our point)? Certainly not empirical ones, since no data is offered (and exactly what *kind* of data could be presented bearing on a claim of universality?). But then the generic applicability must somehow be conceptual, and what possible conceptual grounds could there be for the universality of concepts like "bankrupt," "unemployed," "divorced," etc., that are features of western protestant capitalism, and certainly not descriptive of universal human conditions?

What can be said of Fusé's sociological factors can also be said of his list of psychological and biological factors. Distinguishing between helplessness, hopelessness, depression, suicide ideation, and suicide may be a claim to be "carving Nature at Her joints," but such a claim is certainly not empirical (that is, no "joints" are presented) and runs afoul of objections that any such distinction are similarly culturally bound and arbitrary. The same holds for the superficially more concrete biological factors; illness (mental and otherwise) varies across culture and within the same culture over time. The inclusion of such explanatory variables as serotonin deficiencies (and the even more recent notion of a "suicide gene") violates the self-imposed positivist criterion: they do not hold up empirically.[5] Finally, the very concept he is trying to explain, "suicide," can only be culturally bound (or we would, in principle, be committed to explaining the purported practice of elderly Inuit floating off on ice floes in terms of "bankruptcy," "absence of support groups," and so on).

The status not only of his explanatory variables, but the variable he hopes to explain, turns what seems like a precise scientific statement into a salmagundi. As if that were not enough, consider the *form* of the model: the variables are *associated*, but what that association *is* and how it is to be modeled is neither empirically supported (how could it be, anyway?) nor conceptually prescribed. Is it rectilinear, monotonic, or curvilinear; parametric or non-parametric; cumulative or discrete; etc.? Selecting and using any particular index of association commits one to an answer to these (and many more) questions, but these questions are largely, if not exclusively, conceptual rather than empirical ones.

There is also a conceptual problem in making sense of the purported explanatory power of such a model. Think of, for example, "despair" as mediating between "unemployment" and "suicide." Social facts cause someone to be unemployed, which in turn causes him/her despair, which in turn causes him/her to commit suicide. The "despair" is proffered as a concretizing of the process by which "unemployment" leads to "suicide."

However, does it, in fact, actually clarify any process? How does drawing directional arrows and calculating associational coefficients demonstrate or clarify or concretize "unemployment" turning into "suicide?" Putting "despair" into the middle of the sequence, or lots and lots of other things, too, does nothing in the way of unfolding an empirical process, but is a misdirection that convinces the inattentive observer that he/she has actually seen "unemployment" straw being spun into "suicide" gold. And note, finally, that "it just does" neither is an argument nor provides a justification for thinking so.

Lest anyone think we are picking on Dr. Fusé, he merely provides a convenient formal depiction of the approach. The conceptual difficulties raised here (and elsewhere in this work) are applicable regardless of which particular model is examined. The variable and properties postulated in these theories are not detectable or observable, and are therefore inferred as a result of it being necessary to explain theoretically the known and observable features of indigenous suicide. By failing to distinguish what is empirical (and thereby verifiable) from what is conceptual, theories of First Nations suicide just cannot be talking about what they purport to be talking about. This critique of suicide research as an empirical endeavour is not an attack on empirical investigations as such. The point being made rather is that there are limits to its application, for an intelligible empirical analysis requires that the matter under study is in fact empirical. Without clarifying what are the subjects of investigation we get into the sort of cloudy thinking that characterizes Native suicidology. Research into the facts of First Nations suicide presents us with a picture: "they are reified representations of states of affairs which cannot really be pictures at all (Pleasants, 1999, p. 34)." We are left with model building as a stand-in for sense.

CHAPTER 3

Philosophers constantly see the method of science before their eyes, and are irresistibly tempted to ask and answer the questions in the way science does. This tendency is the real source of metaphysics, and lead the philosopher into complete darkness. --Wittgenstein, *Culture and Value*

An Incomplete Picture

In adhering to methodological individualism, suicidologists are ideologically wedded to discussing what are construed as social problems by looking for systematic association between individually-referenced variables. The bedrock of explanation is taken to be what "individuals think, choose, and do," a preference embedded within the empiricist's explanatory strategy. We have seen how the failure to discriminate between conceptual and empirical issues and afford them separate treatment characterizes theories of the causes of First Nations suicide. And it should also be clear that such confusions reduce the epistemic status of these theories from science to pseudo-science. Now we will demonstrate that *even if* the conceptual issues previously identified were remedied, empiricism *itself* poses limits to our understanding of First Nations suicide. Researchers, theorists, and policy makers alike, by taking First Nations suicide to be explainable by pointing to verifiable causes are left with an incomplete, and consequently inaccurate, picture of what is going on. "Draw a lion incompletely," as the ancient Chinese proverb says, "and it looks like a dog."

Our argument that empiricism *necessarily* leaves out conditions or factors that are real but not amenable to analysis as variables has two facets. The first is an analytical point, one that illustrates the confusion around only accepting the "observably measurable" as evidence. Positivist and empiricist standards of evidence legislate that only what is observable in the *present* counts as evidence. This is, however, analytically meaningless. "Present," as a concept, requires that there exist other temporal realities — the "past" and the "future." The meaning of the present is contingent upon its conceptual relationship with other temporal concepts. So the positivist's claim that the present is the only "real" reality is illogical; the present cannot be isolated as the only reality (Hacker, 1989, Ch. 9).

Secondly, empiricism necessarily excludes what it cannot incorporate within its methodological scheme. Bauman (2000) illustrates this schematic difficulty with an example from Holocaust research. Reviewing a study conducted by Fein, which Bauman calls "the most notable among the distinctly sociological contributions to the study of the Holocaust (2000, p. 4)," he writes:

> She defined her task as that of spelling out a number of psychological, ideological and structural variables which most strongly correlate with percentages of Jewish victims or survivors inside various state-national entities of Nazi-dominated Europe. By all orthodox standards, Fein produced a most impressive piece of research. Properties of national communities, intensity of local anti-Semitism, degrees of Jewish acculturation and assimilation, the resulting cross-communal solidarity have all been carefully and correctly indexed, so that correlations may be properly computed and checked for their relevance. Some hypothetical connections are shown to be non-existent or at least statistically invalid; some other regularities are statistically confirmed… Without revising some of the essential yet tacit assumptions of sociological discourse, one cannot do anything other than what Fein has done; conceive of the Holocaust as a unique yet fully determined product of a particular concatenation of social and psychological factors, which led to a temporary suspension of the civilizational grip in which human behavior is normally held… Having processed the facts of the Holocaust through the mill of that methodology which defines it as a scholarly discipline, orthodox sociology can only deliver a message bound more by its presuppositions than by 'the facts of the case': the message that the Holocaust was a failure, not a product, of modernity (Bauman, 2000, p. 4).

The point Bauman makes, which is applicable to theories of suicide, is that the discovery of causal laws and statistical probabilities must necessarily omit important factors from consideration. In terms of the Holocaust, sociology's commitment to methodological individualism means that *modernity* must be left out of the analysis, for there is no personal, internal representation of modernity to be found within individuals, or even within groups of individuals. Another way to put this is in terms of mathematical constants; factors which apply to all cases alike have a mathematically undefined relationship to each other. As Bauman is pointing out, the factor he wishes to emphasize as a determining condition for the Holocaust, modernity, cannot be analyzed as a "cause" and therefore must be treated like an "effect," if at all. Like the Holocaust, the empirical approach understands indigenous suicide as an outcome of a predisposing condition it cannot include in its analysis.

Theories of suicide, in taking their unit of analysis to be the individual, commit further logical fallacies. For starters, existing theories commit the compositional fallacy, which is the assumption that the properties of the composite are reflected in the properties of the sub-groupings that comprise the collective. Regardless of whether one takes an individual indigenous person as a collectivity comprised of his/her physical-psycho-social subsystems, or "indigenous peoples" as a collectivity comprised of different specific Native subgroups, there is no logical ground for presuming correspondence between these different levels of organization (Copi, 1986). That is, what accounts for "First Nations" suicide has no necessary relation with what accounts for a particular instance of suicide, even if committed by a First Nations person. Related to this is what is known as the psychologistic fallacy, the presumption that individual level outcomes are explainable exclusively at the level of the individual. For, "although the level at which data are collected may fit the conceptual model being investigated, important facts pertaining to other levels may be ignored (Diex-Roux, 1998, p. 220)." Such is the case with empiricism.

Explanation and Prediction

> People who are constantly asking 'why' are like tourists who stand in front of a building reading Baedeker and are so busy reading the history of its construction, etc., that they are prevented from seeing the building. (Wittgenstein, 1985, p. 40).

Suicidologists fail to see the difference between *explanation* and *prediction*. In offering explanations, demonstrating the causal between variables is seen as offering a deeper understanding of where to intervene. It is assumed that there is symmetry between *explanation* and *prediction*. But this is not the case. Prediction and explanation are not merely "different sides of the same coin," for the difference is more than temporal (Caldwell, 1983, p. 29). The ability to predict does not mean that the explanatory model being used is right, as Harré (1972) points out. Medieval barbers could accurately predict the course of the disease of someone displaying the early symptoms of bubonic plague, but were nowhere near the truth in the explanations they gave as accounts of disease onset and development.

Even were the explanatory model "correct" in some sense, it does not follow that such a model would provide a blueprint for how to intervene successfully in the system so described. A correct model would, at best, be a model of how *that* system operated. There is no justification for assuming that altering the world so that the model was no longer descriptive of the world would eliminate a problem; it would merely assure that the model would no longer be valid. Thus, if availability of shotguns was demonstrably related to suicide rates, destroying all known shotguns and preventing their further manufacture would be at best only assure that people would no longer be able to commit suicide with shotguns; there is no reason to assume suicide would have been done away with.

Even more defeating is that the ability to predict does not mean that anything consequential will follow. For example, socio-economic conditions have long been identified as having an impact on suicide rates; yet the recommendations of, for example, the Royal Commission of Aboriginal Peoples (1995) and the National Task Force (1986) suggest nothing to intervene in these material conditions; their recommended interventions are primarily therapeutic and, hence, individualistic.

Wittgenstein describes the building of causal models as an "architectural requirement" — that they are built "for the sake not of their content, but of their form (Pleasants, 199, p. 64)." In other words, the need for explanation is a requirement brought about by the strategy itself, not by any purported material reality. Theorizing inherently obfuscates understanding because theories are essentialist; they necessarily select (though not arbitrarily) one or a small set of feature as underlying causes, and thus, are necessarily a distortion (Pleasants,

1999, p. 24). Wittgenstein tried to "show that transcendental reference to hypothetical cognitive powers and tacit rules — as entities which must exist in order to account for the meaningfulness of human action and experience — give a wholly delusory sense of adequate explanation (Pleasants, 1999, p. 62)." We take this as bearing on an empirical analysis of suicide: within MI, the suicidal person is conceived as an individual who is separable from his/her material and social relationships, for the concern is only with how such factors "play out" in what he/she thinks, chooses, and does. This analytical separation involves an abstraction, a reification of both the suicidal individual and the act of suicide. Because of this slip (that is, we fail to appreciate conceptual problems that must be addressed), we draw an empirical relationship between the two — soliciting the use of the concept of causation, applied to a set of background conditions which, in total, we consider necessary and/or sufficient. On the imputation of causation, Hart and Honore (1985) wrote:

> We must take care not to be deceived, by the language used, as to the character of these issues... These questions look like questions of fact to be answered by reference to general principles or definitions telling us in what the relationship of cause and effect consists, or what a superseding cause is (1985, p. 4).

The concept of cause in theories of indigenous suicide is used in an empirical sense; it serves to establish a relationship between individuals and their "inner" (mental states) or their "outer" (social relations). But such relations as defined in the suicidology literature do not withstand empirical verification.

Lacking a perspicuous presentation of the uses of our language, we take the way we talk about suicide as offering a theory of suicide; how we talk is seen as actually corresponding to how and why we act. This strategy falls into essentialist lines of thinking, the search for what lies behind, for the real causes (those of explanatory value) are never readily apparent. We must, like treasure hunters, scour the human condition for the truth. The concepts, such as suicide, hopelessness and isolation seem to us to function as a name, that they refer to private states, or something (an event, object, mechanism, process). Hence it seems reasonable, if not demanded, that we formulate propositions that represent the essential properties of what causes suicide. But while we easily and sensibly speak of a particular instance of suicide, "it is chimerical to believe that one could say something both true and *interesting* about social phenomena [such as suicide] *per se* (Pleasants, 1999, p. 17)." The difficulty, we contend, is that suicidologists do not have a clear grasp of the meaning of suicide itself, and in misunderstanding the usage of the concept, are lead to assert all sorts of empirical relations where there are none. Now we afford these confusions philosophical treatment, by proceeding to conceptually clarify the concept of suicide.

CHAPTER 4

Philosophical Treatment

When the suicides of Indigenous people are explained within a methodologically individualistic framework, the resulting picture is one in which the putative causes of suicide are individuals' psychological characteristic, such as feelings of hopelessness and alienation, lack of purpose in life, and low self-esteem. In taking metaphors too seriously, suicidologists end up describing individuals as being driven by internal engines, not unlike Descartes' homunculi (located in the pineal gland and acting as an intermediary between mind and body); agency is attributed to peoples' psychological conditions (e.g. Joey's "aggression" turned "inward" and so he killed himself) but not to the persons themselves.

Treating the meaning of suicide as an empirical relation, we are left building a bridge between the act of suicide and the mental state which resides behind it, a bridge without substance, and "confusion is created by advancing causes where reasons should be given (ter Hark, 1990, p. 29)." In the suicidology literature, suicide is identified by pointing to the regular occurrence of intentional mental states. However, we propose that intentions are *constitutive* of the meaning of suicide; that is, the relationship is a conceptual, not empirical, one. Now we will elaborate.

The problems encountered in attempts to define suicide in general also surface with the identification of any particular death as suicide. Such a task can be approached as the investigation of external criteria of the causes of the death, but with regards to suicide, this is far from straightforward, as indicated by the distinctions between "actual" and "reported" suicide, and the category of "parasuicide." The difficulty mainly stems from the fact that we can give multiple descriptions of a behavior that are consistent with that behavior; in other words, the class of things called "suicide" cannot be characterized by a set of necessary and sufficient conditions.

As suicide can be accomplished by all sorts of means, the criterion that distinguishes them from other forms of death is the intention, which is held to reside behind the act. So, to establish if a particular death should be classified as a suicide, we look for external, observable evidence of the intention: a note, conversations with friends and relatives, preparations such as writing a will or giving away cherished belongings. Some evidence solicited will be more convincing that others. "Psychological autopsies," advanced as "a set of procedures for revealing the state of mind of a deceased person prior to his or her death (Johnson and Tormen, p. 240)," are but a means of systematizing this guesswork; but such technical procedures do not clarify the *meaning* of suicide.

Psychological autopsies and courtroom procedures for determining the presence of *mens rea*, the intent that corresponds with the criminal act (the *actus rea*), are similar in their grappling with the difficulties in establishing firm ground for the designation of intentions. This convergence points to the significance of intentions within both arenas. Courts, to determine criminal responsibility, must establish whether the accused acted with intention; lack of intention, as evinced by the insanity defence, serves to exculpate a person's actions. Similarly with suicide, it must be established that the person "meant to" in some sense, that the actions leading to death were intended, voluntary, and conscious; in sum, knowingly decided upon (Duff, 1990).

This is where the confusion begins. It is taken that the meaning of suicide is the presence of intentional mental states, which are the private experiences of the individual who engaged in the suicidal behavior. Desiring, realizing, consciousness, and decision making are all taken to be things or processes occurring "north of the neck" and as having empirical content, and so definitions of suicide focus on getting the right concoction of mental states. To illustrate, here are several definitions:

> A suicidal act is any deliberate act of self-damage which the person committing the act cannot be sure to survive (Hodson, p. 16).

> The term suicide is applied to all cases of death resulting directly or indirectly from a positive or negative act of the victim himself, which he knows will produce the result (Durkheim, 1951, p. 44).

> Suicide is a conscious act of self-induced annihilation, best understood as a multidimensional malaise in a needful individual who defines an issue for which suicide

is perceived as the best solution (Shneidman, cited in Leenaars, Sakinofsky, Wenckstern, Dyck, Kral, and Bland, 1998, p. 460).

Or a person has committed suicide when:

he has instigated a course of events, of which he is an active or passive participant, where the great majority of his simple actions (or action-constituents) are performed wit the intention to shorten life, for whatever motive, good or bad, and from which death follows in the way he had planned or at least in a way he could accept (Anderberg, 1998, p. 56).

Yet, despite their apparent precision, definitions of suicide remain fallible: (a) such definitions are necessarily culture-bound (as discussed earlier); (b) their meaning relies on the usage of concepts such as "deliberate," "conscious act," and "multidimensional malaise" whose meaning in turn remains unspecified; and (c) all rely on some form of mental state, which does not clear up the initial problem of identifying its presence within the suicidal person. We must pose the question: is our understanding of what we are talking about really challenged by the lack of a definition or the variations in different definitions? The vagueness of a concept is characteristic, and does not entail incomprehension or confusion concerning its meaning (Wittgenstein, 1951). Our use of psychological predicates such as intention, desire, motive, planning, decisions, and foresight are concepts with a "family resemblance." They serve to render human activity — that is, voluntary human behavior — intelligible to us, and their meanings are public. Their meaning comes from their application: meaning is neither hidden, nor referential (Grounds, 1987). The act of suicide and its history (by history, we mean not life history or the personal narrative of the individual) are mutually constitutive.

For if we cannot speak of the causes of death as being self-inflicted or intended then we cannot say reasonably it was suicide; perhaps parasuicide, or an accident, maybe manslaughter, or even murder. That suicide is intentional is not an empirical proposition, but a *grammatical* remark. Taking it as an empirical proposition leads to conceptual confusions that take us beyond the bounds of sense.

An illustration provided by Anderberg to justify his definition of suicide is a prime example of the confused thinking around the meaning of suicide. Taking the identification of suicide to be the presence of intention, Anderberg confronts the issue of how much of the act must be intentional or voluntary. He concludes that "exact limits cannot be drawn, but as a rule of thumb one could say that at least two-thirds [sic] of the simple actions that together add up to the complex action 'a suicide' ought to be voluntary for that description to be acceptable (Anderberg, 1998, p. 34)." His logical proof is the example of "Dionysios":

> A chronic alcoholic, *Dionysios*, is told by his physician to quit drinking; if he continues this dangerous habit he will most certainly die within a few months. In fact, one single bout of heavy drinking would be fatal. Shaken up by the news, Dionysios enters the nearest pub and orders a glass of liquor. Being used to alcohol, one glass does not noticeably change his state of mind. But, remembering the warning just issued from his physician, he suddenly gets depressed, and decides that life is not worth living. So, instead of leaving the pub to follow the narrow path of sobriety and ordered living, he orders more liquor, meaning to die in the easiest way possible. He gulps down a second glass, then a third, a fourth… and so on. Naturally he gets more and more dizzy, and after the tenth drink he is barely conscious of the surroundings. After the twelfth glass he collapses on the floor and dies (Anderberg, 1998, p. 32).

Though we should, according to Anderberg, conclude that the above passage describes a suicide, the last actions of Dionysios, when he was consuming his last drinks, cannot be said to be intentional because he was drunk. He could not be said to be conscious or acting voluntarily after his tenth drink, but since the actions prior to that point were voluntary, we are justified in determining that it was a suicide (Anderberg, 1998, p. 32-33).

Such are the cases that suicidologists and others must invent in order to justify their particular definitions of suicide. Anderberg's definition is no more precise than others he reviews, for he assumes that how we talk (and hence think) about suicide necessarily relates to some objective thing called "suicide," which possesses characteristics called "simple actions" and "intentions." Asserting that there is an equation to help clarify whether a particular death was a suicide ("2/3 of the simple actions must be voluntary") gets us nowhere in relation to these conceptual issues; instead of sense making, it serves to mystify them.

More than this, these examples involve an abstraction; the cases are extracted from our social practices. Upon closer examination of the case of Dionysios we find the presence of two other people, the doctor who offered the diagnosis of a terminal condition, and the bartender who served the last fatal drinks. Only in a philosopher's parlour game could such a situation be described, for in our society, doctors and bartenders are both subject to laws and codes of professional conduct. In the case of Dionysios, it can be argued that these professional codes were violated. How is it that a doctor, knowing of his client's condition — a severe alcoholic with a failing physiology — could give a diagnosis and then let his patient walk away? Must not counselling services, medical services (such as admittance to a detoxification center or hospital), be provided? And what about the bartender? Did he or she have a responsibility under existing liquor laws to stop serving drink after drink after noticing that his/her customer had become severely intoxicated?

Such considerations may not alter the description of Dionysios' death as a suicide, but may include an inquiry into negligence or malpractice on behalf of the doctor's behalf and/or the bartender and the drinking establishments' ownership. In any event, there is a need to question the responsibility of the doctor and bartender in the death of Dionysios that is not admitted in the description provided by Anderberg. Since there is no necessary relationship between how we talk and the way the world is, we can offer several descriptions of the behavior that are seemingly incompatible.

This highlights the importance of the conceptual relationships between suicide and intentions, for to speak of suicide is to imply that the person her/himself is responsible for her/his death. Intention, like suicide, is a concept that renders sense out of our lives. For when we come upon someone who has, say, hanged him or herself, we are forced to come to grips with the situation, and offer some form of explanation for his or her death. How else can we explain such otherwise mysterious behavior? Indeed, in Agatha Christie novels, mysteries often have story lines about murders (for instance frauds, or to prevent a revelation, etc.) that are disguised as suicides. That is, the murderer creates the circumstances such that subsequent investigators would conclude that suicide is the only way the deceased could have died, and doing so entails attempting to pass it off as an intentional act. Yet, suicide is not a characteristic of the deceased individual, nor of the act, but of those of us left behind to make sense of it.

CHAPTER 5

"The difficulty is, e'en on the face of 'em the
facts are dark – doubly so if you grant, as wise
men must, than an ill deed can be done with
good intent, and a good with ill..." -- John
Barth, *The Sot-Weed Factor*.

A Broadening of the Circumstances

Thus far we have argued that an ideological commitment
(methodological individualism) on the part of suicidologists has given
rise to a particular form of analysis, one which locates putative *causes* of
suicidal acts in the personal and internal machinery that makes people
go. The analogy to "mechanism" is appropriate, since suicidologists,
as we have seen, draw pictures of these machines (causal modeling),
modify the pictures in light of information (empiricism), and concern
themselves with how to prevent the machines' effective operation
(intervention). The problem is, however, that such an approach does
not and cannot meet its own burdens of proof: the mechanisms
depicted *must* be incomplete and therefore inaccurate; features with
undeniable impact cannot be incorporated into the mechanisms and
the system dynamics therefore *must* be misspecified; the hypothesized
mechanism(s) *cannot* be shown and thus their empirical status and
importance is, at best, an act of faith; and, the variables within the
hypothesized mechanism, while not being identifiable within the
mechanism depicted, *can* be shown to be part of the conceptual
network we use to make sense of our world. These are not failings
of a *particular* statement by a *particular* theorist or practitioner, but
arise of necessity once the presumption is made that a suicide must be
explained by the inner dynamics of the person who committed it. In
sum, methodological individualism may allow us to draw a dog, but
something else is needed to get us to the lion.

In casting about for additional directions it would be useful to
incorporate viewpoints that explicitly recognized the limitations
imposed by MI, and such a viewpoint is provided in the works of
Karl Marx. Marx was perhaps the first philosopher to recognize MI
as an ideology and gave an early practical demonstration of its generic

problems in his analysis of alienation (Marx, 1844). In 1845, Marx translated, edited, and wrote a commentary on Peuchet's (1838) *Memoires tires des archives de la police*, a bureaucrat's account of 20 years of suicide investigations in Paris. From his selection, organization, and emphases, it is clear that Marx was applying the conceptual processes forged in his analysis of alienation to the task of understanding suicide:

> How is it that people commit suicide, despite such great anathema against it? The blood of the despairing does not flow through the same arteries as that of those cold beings who have the leisure to debate such fruitless questions. Man is a mystery to man; one knows only how to blame him, but one does not know him. Has one noticed how mindless the institutions are under whose rule Europe lives? ... When one has noted all these things, one cannot comprehend how, in the name of what authority, an individual can be ordered to care about an existence that our customs, our prejudices, our law, and our mores trample under foot (Marx, quoted in Plaut and Anderson, 1999, p. 49).

There are many noteworthy ideas in his work in general (which appeared in limited circulation more than 50 years before Durkheim's) and this passage in particular. In the passage, Marx levels a connected series of charges: that the theorists of his day were uselessly spinning their wheels in wondering why people were committing suicide; that the factors giving rise to suicide were clearly observable and obvious; that the factors arose from the material conditions of existence of "the despairing," the group giving rise to greater number of suicides; and that the "authority" that demanded the misery of the oppressed had no authority to demand the misery be endured. In the overall work, as Anderson (1999) pointed out, "Most of the examples of suicide that Marx draws from Peuchet could be linked to the core issue in Durkheim's fatalistic suicide, excessive regulation (p. 21)."

This warrants a closer look. As we have already noted, Durkheim's discussion of fatalistic suicide is limited to a single footnote in which he dismisses it as "useless to dwell upon" because it has "little contemporary importance" and "examples hard to find" (Durkheim, 1951, p. 276). To hold that "excessive regulation and "futures pitilessly blocked" are not descriptive of much of contemporary 1897 human existence bespeaks an incredible ignorance and/or arrogance on Durkheim's part. Remember, this is the Europe that was in the process of expanding physically into the African, Australian, Asian, and American continents, which had been running world-wide slavery operations for 400 years, that had killed perhaps 20 million enslaved peoples in Central and South American mines alone, that had forced, as a matter of economic policy, opium addiction on millions of Asian peoples, and had performed other inhuman depredations too countless to number (Stavrianos, 1981). Marx certainly had no problem adducing examples of "excessive regulation" and linking them to suicide, and to do this he did not need to step outside the limits of his own mid-1800 Eurocentrism.

We could speculate endlessly on the inner dynamics of Durkheim's blindness but there would be little point. Once we follow Marx's lead there is no lack at all of examples of the kind of suicide Durkheim so blithely dismisses[6]: mass suicides by the Caribbean indigenous peoples Columbus enslaved and tortured (Zinn, 1995); remarkable suicide rates in, for example, Home Children packaged out from England to various colonies (Bagnell, 1980), Pacific Islanders whose lands were expropriated by various Western powers (Cockburn, 1988), and Australia Aboriginal Peoples under "management" by an immigrant European mainstream (Tatz, 1999); and perhaps most tellingly, a suicide rate for German Jews during the Nightmare Years that was, at various points in time, 5 to 50 times the rate for non-Jewish Germans (Hilberg, 1992).

Consider for a moment, what an MI interpretation makes of the last example given above. Is the Jewish suicide rate during the Holocaust difficult to understand unless we translate it somehow into the mental contents of perpetrator, victim, and bystander? Should we entertain, even for a second, the notion that, say, a generalized serotonin deficiency was the "real" reason the Jews were killing themselves? That "a gene" just decided to "kick in" in 1933 and phase itself out in 1945 (when the suicide rate began to drop toward pre-war levels)? Or that depression and anomie in concentration camps were the causal agents for the Jewish deaths by action or omission of action? To entertain seriously any of there suggestions entails the notion that the "real" problem" with the Holocaust was the primitive state of psychoactive medications, the absence of access to therapists, or the lack of funding for such interventions, and that the material circumstances of existence of Jews in occupied Europe be completely ignored.

This reveals, we believe, the blindness to material conditions imposed by a methodological individualist ideology. Those dedicated to the MI position (psychiatrists, psychologists, social workers, etc.) have nothing to do, as members of their disciplines, in regard to the material conditions of oppressed peoples; that is, Jews in concentration camp did not need better medications or someone to talk to. The people who acted most directly to eliminate the "Jewish suicide problem," Marshall Zhukov and General Patton, acted not as *therapists* but as *liberators* (and even *that* action depended in no way on Zhukov's and Patton's *personal* knowledge of or attitude toward the Holocaust). In fact, action *as* a medical officer or therapist would only mask and perpetuate the oppression the medical officer or therapist was ostensibly designated to address. To put it bluntly, there is no long-term job growth potential for methodological individualist interveners who recognize the central role of oppression in the production and maintenance of human misery.

Indigenous Peoples and Fatalistic Suicide

Though the extremity of the situation of North American indigenous peoples is certainly not equivalent to the examples cited above, the direction in which they point is comparable. That such a parallel is not recognized by Canadian society is a further indication of the predominance of methodological individualism. A brief examination of Native peoples' material conditions lays open the grounds for comparison; Native peoples are "second-class" citizens, even by the Canadian governments' own standards (Galabuzi, 2001). First Nations communities are characterized by high rates of unemployment, poverty, and lack of access to such basic serviced as education, housing, and health care. Fifty-four percent of indigenous people over age 15 do not have a high school diploma, compared with 34% of the general population. One-third of indigenous people are employed in the service sector, confirmed in the average annual income ($17,382) being one and a half times lower than the national average ($26,474). Those who live on reserve earn even less, with one out of five people receiving or living on social assistance. Though indigenous peoples comprise only 3% of the total Canadian population, they account for 15% of sentences to federal correctional facilities, and in some provinces up to 76% of the inmates are First Nations individuals. In spite of improvements in health care delivery made since the 1940's,

First Nations peoples have markedly higher prevalence rates than non-Natives for HIV/AIDS, tuberculosis, type II diabetes, and infant mortality (Medical Services Branch, Health Canada, 1999).

This is but the tip of the iceberg. Canadian government policy, past and present, functions to limit the roster of those indigenous people who are entitled to receive the benefits required by Canadian treaty obligations. Indian residential schools were operated by the Canadian governments in partnership with the major churches (Anglican, United, Presbyterian and Catholic) from Confederation until 1996. Under the pretence of "education," the schools were mandated to "beat the Indian out of the Indian" — to "civilize" Native children for their assimilation into Canadian society. To do this, children were forcibly removed from their families under penalty of law and placed under the absolute care of the churches, sometimes for as long as thirteen years. Over 15,000 law suits have been filed against government and churches for specific cases of abuse by those responsible for the schools' administration. Though little formal documentation exists, Native women were known to be sterilized without their knowledge or consent, in accord with acknowledged genocidal and eugenical Canadian policies and legislation (McLaren, 1990. These atrocities are far from isolated; for example, it is not widely known that since 1948 Indian residential Schooling constituted genocide, as per the U.N. Convention (Chrisjohn, Young, and Maraun, 1997).

There is more than can be said in a similar vein, but the point can perhaps best be summarized by noting, as did *The Globe and Mail* (October 1998), that, while Canada ranked first in the United Nations' list of "best countries to live in," indigenous Canadians, considered as a group, ranked 63rd (behind Indonesia, North Korea, and many other notably impoverished countries). Methodologically individualistic accounts draw a picture of these circumstances which place a defective, incompetent, and degenerate indigenous horse in front of a cart pulling a load of economic, legal, moral, social and psychological troubles (including suicide). It is our suggestion that such pictures should locate the economic and legal factors in the horse and place the troubles in the cart following behind. It may have required the benefit of 60 years, a World War, and an international war crimes trial to correctly draw the picture for Jewish suicide in Nazi Germany, but as scientists we are supposed to learn from our mistakes.

CHAPTER 6

Conclusions

The Royal Commission on Aboriginal Peoples commented that "attention to Aboriginal suicide cannot wait until the foundations of a renewed relationship between Aboriginal and non-Aboriginal people in Canada are in place (RCAP, 1995, p. 18)." At odds with the critical analysis developed here, those officially designated to address First Nations suicide continue to see the suicide as one issue and colonialism/genocide as another. That is, somehow the task of dealing with marginalization and oppression is a different task from preventing people from taking their own lives. Methodological individualism requires that what are political, economic, legal, social, or moral issues be depoliticized, deeconomized, delegalized, desocialized, and demoralized. The residue of such a filtering is an overweening emphasis on the personal and internal qualities of individual indigenous peoples, an emphasis rightly recognized as racism when detached from the here and now of a caring Canadian society.

Hence, treating the solution to Native peoples' suicide as something to be revealed through science is part of the problem. To recapitulate, approaching suicide as something to be studied through the construction of empirical propositions that model reality is part of an ideological commitment to individualism. In treating concepts as things, grammatical and conceptual statements are presented as if they had empirical import, creating conceptual confusion that lead to the search for intention where there is no thing that corresponds to them. Causal models accounting for the psychosocial mechanisms that cause someone to take their life cannot be compared, not even in principle, with reality; they are more like elaborate Rube Goldberg machines, ridiculously complicated ways of doing something simple. Moreover, even if concepts were clarified, the empirical study of suicide necessarily leaves out factors that cannot be discussed as a property of individuals, factors which we argue are crucial for rendering First Nations suicide intelligible.

If the goal of suicidology remains to provide a highly generalized theoretical account of the mechanisms and structures that are the underlying causes of suicide, we cannot see how such practices will assist in the prevention of self-inflicted deaths. How is it possible that intervention strategies based on this philosophical foundation will address suicide, when they do not even allow a serious discussion of the issues? We concur with Tatz in that "the vivid display of pyrotechnics does not alleviate suicide any more than does the pathologizing of suicide as a psychiatric disorder (Tatz, p. 125)." That advocates of a discipline take the bedrock of explanation to be what "individuals think, choose, and do" is *a preference*; the entrenchment and compelling force of this dominant picture in the social sciences conveys its ideological character. Native suicidology is not a far cry (if at all) from eugenics: First Nations are depicted as suffering from personal predilections that increase their susceptibility to pathological behaviors, including suicide. Thus, it is their own "nature" (fault) that accounts for their inferior position in society.

Put this way, it is likely that people will object. Recollect from the previous discussion of intentions and ideology: we do not claim that suicidologists and mental/public health workers act maliciously with racist aspirations. However, such an ideological position is necessary, for if we do afford our analysis serious consideration, it becomes clear that the remedy for the suicide "epidemic" among First Nations is not to be found neither by science nor by therapy. Rather, what is needed is something along the lines of Zhukov's and Patton's intervention in Jewish suicide; the fundamental assault on indigenous peoples within Canadian society must be stopped. It is relatively pointless to say that this is far from easy.

But as pointless as it may be, there may be controversy concerning what, exactly would make it difficult to stop. We agree with those (e.g., Chrisjohn, et al., 1997; Churchill, 1994) who contend that in order for Canada to remain Canada (geographically, politically, economically) it must legitimize its claim to the land by extinguishing Aboriginal title, and to do this requires the elimination of indigenous peoples (by a "paper" genocide, if not a physical one). For justice to be served and for First Nations to reconstitute their forms of life, massive restructuring of what is currently called Canada would be required. And this, not the lack of resources (financial and otherwise) or commitment (moral, professional, and otherwise), is the real impediment.

ENDNOTES

[1]   It is true that there are exceptions to this. However, the discussions that do occur are often disjointed and scattered, focusing on the methodological difficulties, which are treated as technical limitations as opposed to philosophical presumptions. Hence it is fair to conclude that in the sciences there lacks a sustained and systemized analysis of MI in most disciplines.

[2]   To speak of the scientific methods makes it sound as though we are referring to one thing. We acknowledge the lack of unanimity in what is science, and what are the shared traits of its method. Instead of looking at it in this way, we prefer to see scientific method as practices within a "family resemblance" (Wittgenstein, 1951). In other words, the scientific method lacks necessary and sufficient features for its identification, but the different practices share characteristics, though not all the same ones.

[3]   It is not necessary (nor possible) to detail the entirety of suicidology literature: several authors (Fuse, 1997; Leenaars et. al., 1998) have already covered this ground, and we refer readers to these works.

[4]   He himself wrote: "we see no objection to calling sociology a variety of psychology, if we carefully add that social psychology has its own laws which are not those of individual psychology (Durkheim, 1951, p. 351)."

[5]   Biochemical speculations about what causes Native people to kill themselves are based on correlations between serotonin, genes, and suicide; and in spite of being amongst the "hard" sciences, they are also afflicted with philosophical confusions. Biological explanations of suicide rely on positing an intermediary link between the biological or chemical component possessed by an individual and the manifest disposition of the individual. In the case of neurotransmitters, the intermediary is aggression. Studies purport to demonstrate the relationship between the serotonin metabolite (neurotransmitter) 5-hydroxyindoleacetic acid (5-HIAA) and suicide; it is claimed that individuals who have less 5-HIAA have little control over their will and aggressive actions. As a result, they are more prone to commit suicide, and using more violent means (Fusé, 1997, p. 136-148).

Research of this kind conceives suicide as an act of aggression against the self, consistent with Freud's psychological theory of suicide as aggression turned inward (Fusé, 1997, p. 144-115). This conception of suicide is used to support the findings, which are in turn used to support the conclusion. Aside from being circular reasoning, how does 5-HIAA, a bio-chemical, become equivalent with "aggression," a behavior? The justification for equating the two is not found within any evidence. In clinical settings, which are the norm of biochemical research, we do not have access to drawing a comparison between the theoretical causal variable, such as aggression, and the observable world, 5-HIAA. And even if significant correlations are found within experiments that support the researchers' hypothesis, the conclusions are not generalizable to human beings as a whole. Moreover, aggression is subject to the same defeating skepticism as are other psychological concepts.

As suicide is seen to run in families, researchers have been searching for the genetic basis of suicide, and the results of twin studies are held up as evidence that there does exist a gene for suicide (Fusé, 1997). Some even spin a wonderful fable about the evolutionary purpose of suicide. Very briefly, what such rationalizations assume is that it is possible to figure out the arithmetic that allows one to determine which percentage of out behavior is genetic and which is environmental. This is not done through twin and adoption studies as claimed, which are plagued by hidden variables such as the fact that families often share the same environment (Lewontin, 1990). As race is not a useful or valid biological concept (Lewontin, 1990), research explaining Native peoples' higher rates of suicide as the end result of genetic programming constitutes ideology, not science. And even more detrimental to the assertion of a biogenetic factor to suicide is that just because something is genetic does not mean that it is unchangeable. Linking genes with behavior is sociobiology and rests upon an ideological, not scientific understanding of what genes do. In sum, inferences drawn from the evidence are unfounded and, despite efforts to construe them as such, do not prove that there is a biological basis for suicide.

Far from being conclusive, drawing such conclusions as suicide is in the genes or the result of biochemical imbalance remains sheer speculation. Moreover, the identification of physiological causes of suicide offers little in terms of augmenting our understanding of why First Nations commit suicide. Rather than our objection being the conclusion of each hypothesis, the problem is the very manner in which the question is phrased and approached. The attempt to investigate the whys of Native suicide by establishing the chain (or web) of causal interactions, regardless from which level the purport to originate, is a misguided endeavour.

[6]   "So, for completeness' sake, we should set up a fourth suicidal type. But it has so little contemporary importance and examples are so hard to find aside from the cases just mentioned that is seems useless to dwell upon it. However, it might be said to have historical interest. Do not the suicides of slaves, said to be frequent under certain conditions... belong to this type, or all suicides attributable to excessive physical or moral despotism? To bring out the ineluctible and inflexible nature of a rule against which there is no appeal, an in contrast with the expression "anomy" which has just been used, we might call it *fatalistic suicide* (Durkheim, 1897; 1966; p. 276)."

REFERENCES

Anderberg, T. (1989). *Suicide: Definitions, causes, and values.* Lund: Lund University.

Bagnell, K. (1980). *The little immigrants.* Toronto: Macmillan.

Baker, G. & Hacker, P. M. S. (1982). The grammar of psychology: Wittgenstein`s Bemerkungen über die philosophie der psychologie. *Language and Communication,* 2(3), 227-244.

Barth, J. (1966). *The sot-weed factor.* New York: Grosset & Dunlap.

Bauman, Z. (2000). *Modernity and the holocaust.* (Rev. Ed.) Ithaca; NY: Cornell University.

Bhargava, R. (1992). *Individualism in social science: Forms and limits of a methodology.* Oxford: Clarendon.

Bleier, R. (1984). *Science and gender: A critique of biology and its theories on women.* Oxford: Pergamon.

Brant, C. C. (1996). Suicide in the North American Indian: Causes and prevention. In J. Morgan (Ed.), *Suicide: Helping Those at Risk, Proceedings of the Conference, King's College, London, Ontario, May 28-30, 1996.* (pp. 175-184). London: King's College.

Caldwell, B. J. (1983). *Beyond positivism: Economic methodology in the twentieth century.* London: Billing & Sons.

Chrisjohn, R., Young, S., & Maraun, M. (1997). *The circle game: Shadows and substance in Indian residential school experience in Canada.* Pentincton: Theytus.

Churchill, W. (1994). *Indians are us? Culture and genocide in Native North America.* Toronto: Between the Lines.

Cockburn, A. (1988). *Corruptions of empire: Life studies in the Regan era.* New York: Verso.

Coulthard, G. (1999). *Colonization, Indian policy, suicide, and Aboriginal peoples.* Retrieved 3/6/02 from http://www.ualberta.ca/~pimohte/suicide.html.

Davenport, J. A., & Davenport III, J. (1987). Native American suicide: A Durkheimian analysis. *Social Casework: Journal of Contemporary Social Work, November,* 533-539.

Davis, C. (1986). *Suicide among Native people in the Atlantic provinces.* Report prepared for Medical Services Branch, Health and Welfare Canada, Halifax.

Diez-Roux, A. V. (1998). Bring context back into epidemiology: Variables and fallacies in multilevel analysis. *American Journal of Public Health,* 88(2), 216-221.

Duff, R. A. (1990). *Intention, agency and criminal liability*. London: Blackwell.

Durkheim, E. (1951). *Suicide: A study in sociology* (J. A. Spaulding & G. Simpson, Trans.). New York: The Free Press. (Original work published 1987).

Easton, S. M. (1983). *Humanist Marxism and Wittgenstein social philosophy*. Manchester: Manchester University.

Fusé, T. (1997). *Suicide, individual and society*. Toronto: Canadian Scholars.

Galabuzi, G. E. (2001). *Canada's creeping economic apartheid: The economic segregation and social marginalization of racialized groups*. Canadian Social Justice Foundation for Research and Education.

Globe and Mail. (1998). *Aboriginals live in third world conditions, says government report*. October, National Edition.

Grounds, A. (1987). On describing mental states. *British Journal of Medical Psychology, 60*, 305-311.

Hacker, P. M. S. (1989). *Insight and illusion: Themes in the philosophy of Wittgenstein*. Bristol: Thoemmes.

Hart, H. L. A., & Honore, T. (1985). *Causation in the law*. (2nd Ed.). Oxford: Clarendon.

Health Canada. (1994). *Suicide in Canada: Update of the Report of the Task Force on Suicide in Canada*. Ottawa: Health Canada

Hilberg, R. (1992). *Perpetrators, victims, bystanders: The Jewish catastrophe, 1933-1945*. New York: HarperCollins.

Hodson, D. (1996). The Native belief system: Explaining suicide. In J. Morgan (Ed.), *Suicide: Helping Those at Risk, Proceedings of the Conference, King's College, London, Ontario, May 28-30, 1996* (pp. 185-192). London: King's College.

Johnson, T., & Tomren, H. (2001). Helplessness, hopelessness, and despair: Identifying the precursors to Indian youth suicide. In C. E. Trafzer & D. Weiner (Eds.), *Medicine ways: Disease, health, and survival among Native Americans.* (pp. 234-250). Walnut Creek, CA: Altamira.

Kunz, J. L., Milan, A., & Schetagene, S. (2001). *A Canadian profile of racial differences in education, employment and income*. Canadian Council on Social Development. Report prepared for Canadian Race Relations Foundation.

Leenaars, A. A., Sakinofsky, I., Wenckstern, S., Dyck, R. J., Kral, M. J., & Bland, R. C. (Eds.). (1998). *Suicide in Canada*. Toronto: University of Toronto.

Leonard, P. (1984). *Personality and ideology: Towards a materialist understanding of the individual.* Houndsmill: Macmillan.

Lewontin, R. C. (1990). *Biology as ideology: The doctrine of DNA.* CBC Massey Lecture Series.

Lewontin, R. D., Rose, S. & Kamin, L. J. (1984). *Not in our genes: Biology, ideology and human nature.* New York: Pantheon.

Lux, M. K. (2001). *Medicine that walks: Disease, medicine, and Canadian plains Native people, 1880-1940.* Toronto: University of Toronto.

McLaren, A. (1990). *Our own master race: Eugenics in Canada, 1885-1945.* London: Oxford University Press.

Marx, K. (1999). *Marx on suicide.* (E. A. Plaut, G. Edgcomb, & K. Anderson, Trans.). E. A. Plaut & K. Anderson (Eds.). Evanston, IL: Northwestern University.

Marx, K. (1977). *Economic and philosophical manuscripts of 1844.* (Trans.). Moscow: Progress.

Medical Services Branch, Health Canada. (1999). *A Second Diagnostic on the Health of First Nations and Inuit People in Canada.* Retrieved 06/03/01 from www.hc-sc.gc.ca/msb/fnihp/index_e. htm.

Middlebrook. D. L., LeMaster, P. L., Beals, J., Novins, D. K., & Manson, S. M. (2001). Suicide prevention in American Indian and Alaskan Native communities: A critical review of programs. *Suicide and Life-Threatening Behavior, 31*(Suppl.), 132-149.

Nader, L. (1995). Civilization and its negotiations. In P. Caplan, (Ed.), *Understanding disputes: The politics of argument.* Berg: Oxford Providence.

National Task Force on Suicide in Canada. (1986). *Report of the National Task Force on Suicide in Canada.* Ottawa: Health Canada.

Native Psychologists of Canada. (1995). *Focus group on suicide prevention: Presentations.* Ottawa: Native Psychologists of Canada.

Native Psychologists of Canada. (1995). *Focus group on suicide prevention: Executive summaries.* Ottawa: Native Psychologists of Canada.

Nishnawbe-Aski Nation Youth Forum on Suicide. *Horizons of hope: An empowering journey.* Final report. Nishnawbe-Aski Nation.

Novis, D. K., Beals, J., Roberts, R. E., & Manson, S. M. (1999). Factors associated with suicide ideation among American Indian adolescents: Does culture matter? *Suicide and Life-Threatening Behavior, 29*(4), 332-346.

Pleasants, N. (1999). *Wittgenstein and the idea of a critical social theory: Giddens, Haberman and Bhaskar.* New York: Routledge.

Pope, W. (1976). *Durkheim's suicide: A classic analyzed.* Chicago: University of Chicago.

Royal Commission on Aboriginal Peoples. (1995). *Choosing life: Special report on suicide among Aboriginal people.* Ottawa: Minister of Supply and Services.

Stavrianos, L. S. (1981). *Global rift: The third world comes of age.* New York: William Morrow.

Stevenson, M. R., Wallace, L. J. D., Harrison, J., Moller, J., & Smith, R. J. (1998). At risk in two worlds: Injury mortality among Indigenous people in the US and Australia, 1990-1992. *Australian and New Zealand Journal of Public Health, 22*(6), 641-644.

Strickland, C. J. (1997). Suicide among American Indian, Alaskan native and Canadian Aboriginal youth: Advancing the research agenda. *International Journal of Mental Health, 25*(4), 11-32.

Tatz, C. (1999). *Aboriginal suicide is different: Aboriginal youth suicide in New South Wales, the Australian Capital Territory and New Zealand: Towards a model of explanation and alleviation.* A Report to the Criminology Research Council. Centre for the Comparative Genocide Studies: Macquarie University.

ter Hark, M. (1990). *Beyond the inner and the outer: Wittgenstein's philosophy of psychology.* Dordrecht: Kluwer Academic Publishers.

Thompson, K. (1982). *Emile Durkheim.* New York: Routledge.

Wittgenstein, L. (1951). *Philosophical investigations.* (Trans. G. E. Anscombe). London: Blackwell.

Wittgenstein, L. (1960). *The blue and brown books* (2nd Ed.). New York: Harper & Row.

Wittgenstein, L. (1982). *Culture and value.* (Trans. P. Winch). G. E. Anscombe (Ed.). Chicago: University of Chicago.

Young , T. K., Malchy, B., Enns, M. W., & Cox, B. J. (1997). Suicide among Manitoba's aboriginal people. *Canadian Medical Association Journal, 156*(8), 1133-1138.

Zinn, H. (1995). *A people's history of the United States, 1492-present.* (Rev. ed.). New York: HarperPerrennial.

Appendix 2

An Historic Non-Apology, Completely and Utterly Not Accepted
A Response to Harper's Statement of June 11, 2008
(prepared and circulated Friday, June 13, 2008)

Roland Chrisjohn

Andrea Bear Nicholas

Karen Stote

James Craven (Omahkohkiaayo i'poyi)

Tanya Wasacase

Pierre Loiselle

Andrea O. Smith

The Maze of Rhetoric

We hope our title is sufficiently unequivocal to convey our reaction to the events of Wednesday June 11, 2008. Maybe by example we can show how one must approach issues which require the utmost clarity. On the other hand, this probably won't work, especially when it's clear the predominant intention behind a communication is to obscure. Whatever… in any event, for us, sitting on a spiky metal fence is an uncomfortable posture.

We listened with attention to what Stephen Harper had to say yesterday, and we did not hear what we needed to hear. Instead, again we watched and heard one more opportunity being thrown away, this one with more ceremony than those preceding it. We watched and heard the studious avoidance of truth, in what we can only regard as the hope that the repetition of a lie will somehow substitute for reality, a concept now reduced to another mantra (as is nowadays the case for, for example, "truth" or "reconciliation").

To those surprised or appalled by our reaction, or to people who simply have no idea that there's an issue here at all, let us begin by pointing to at least a few of the facts we had to keep in mind when listening to the statement of the current head of a political process that has, since it origin (Confederation in 1867), had the elimination of aboriginal peoples as its consistent policy:

(1) the "settler" population of Canada has had, from the point of its inception, a qualitatively different relation with indigenous peoples than the remote colonial bureaucracy that preceded it: for England, the Indian Nations were allies (who, arguably, saved Canada on more than one occasion); for the settlers of newly-formed Dominion of Canada, they were impediments to expansion, like swamps and vermin. However, in the transfer of authority, the Dominion was honor-bound to respect them, their rights, and their historical status.

(2) with legal and ethical limits placed upon their treatment of indigenous nations (so that, for example, the Dominion couldn't just set out to slaughter them all, as became the policy in the United States), tactics had to be adopted that had the effect of extermination without

giving its appearance (and the British empire had many models to emulate, particularly Tasmania). A simple but accurate characterization of the array of government programs, policies, and laws aimed at indigenous peoples and nations, then, is that they were a range of "carrots" and "sticks" deployed to turn those of us (if any) who survived these artifices from "Indians" into "Canadians" (or, after the era of multiculturalism began, "Indian-Canadians"). Residential school was only one of those programs, one that was heavy on the "stick" and light on the "carrot."

(3) church officials and government officials have, from time to time since the mid-1980's, offered what they (and others) have characterized as "apologies." These have not been apologies. An apology is not made an apology by the person offering it *saying* it is an apology; it is only an apology when those who have been offered it *accept* it as an apology. The fact that the rhetoric of pseudo-apologies has become more twisted as time has gone on should make all of us vigilant against immediately accepting *what sounds like an apology* without careful examination of exactly what was said, how it was said, *and what was not said*. And *repetition* is not an argument.

So, what happened Wednesday afternoon? Stephen Harper described the history of actions undertaken by the government of Canada against the children of indigenous peoples, specifically, their forcible removal from their families and communities and their placement under the unsupervised control of four major Canadian churches. Various aspects of these actions, characterized as "abuse" (including physical, mental, and sexual abuse), were enumerated, followed by variations on the refrain of "for this, we apologize" (or "we are sorry") and "we were wrong" (or "this should never have happened"). That it happened was attributed to bad, arrogant attitudes of superiority. Finally, when mention was made concerning where "we" go from here, the upcoming work of the so-called "Truth and Reconciliation Commission" was proffered as the most appropriate forum. Afterwards, this performance was, by-and-large, repeated by the leaders of the other political parties.

The presentation was offered with every indication of honesty and sincerity. We do not doubt the honesty of what was said, for reasons we will give below. But for those who take honesty as evidence of truth, it would be good to remember what Marx once said: "The secret of life is honesty and fair dealing. If you can fake that, you've got it made." Groucho Marx, that is.

So what's our problem? Actually, we have several: we did not hear an apology, we dispute characterizations that were made, and we do not believe that the putative mechanism of resolution (the "Truth and Reconciliation Commission") will resolve anything useful.

An apology has at least three characteristics (some people will say there are more, some will list more specific traits... this doesn't matter for present purposes). The absence of any of these three characteristics immediately disqualifies a statement as an apology: a sincere expression of remorse for the behavior, the promise never to repeat the behavior, and the undertaking to undo, as far as possible, the damage done by the behavior.

"Well," we hear some say, "the first conditions was obviously met... we all heard Mr. Harper recount a comprehensive list of offenses, halting at each one and saying 'Canada apologizes' and 'it was wrong,' didn't we?"

Suppose, after beating his wife to the point of hospitalizing her, a man attempted to make amends in the following manner: "I'm sorry I gave you a black eye... it was wrong; I'm sorry I chipped your teeth... it never should have happened; I apologize for breaking your arm... it never should have happened; I apologize for bruising your ribs... it was wrong;" and so on.

Does this sound odd to you? It does to us. Why would anyone choose to express his remorse in such a fashion? In "apologizing" to his wife, has the man adopted this manner of speaking, perhaps, to be more thorough (the list could go on and on...)? We think not. In this instance, the specificity of the list helps him *avoid* saying something, something more comprehensive, something more general, but in this case, something much more accurate: "I'm sorry *I physically assaulted you. It was a criminal action on my part.*"

We don't believe Prime Minister Harper adopted this obscurantist form of address to be more comprehensive; we believe he did so to *avoid* saying *I'm sorry the Canadian government committed genocide against you. It was a criminal action on our part.* (Of course, Mr.

Harper was unauthorized to avoid saying something similar on behalf of the churches; they've been doing their own artful dodging for years.)

Consequently, if we're right the sincerity of what was said evaporates *as an apology for residential schooling*. Thus it was no apology at all, but bluff and continued evasion. We believe he said what he said *honestly*; that is, that he sincerely *believed* in what he was saying, but only because, for the governments and individuals he was representing (past and present), he had to craft *an evasive statement* that he could, in all sincerity, endorse. Did Mr. Harper, all on his own, come up with this muddied, tortured declaration right off the cuff, or perhaps just a few minutes before he came down the stairs with his escorts in tow? Well, since Indian Affairs Minister Strahl has been telling us for weeks now what Harper was going to say, we doubt it. We also doubt that the Conservative party didn't have a team of lawyers, rhetoricians, and spin doctors, if not writing the statement, at least agonizing over every phrase, every word, every revelation in the evolving document, considering in detail every implication and weighing each possible consequence. Someone was even counting the number of words. No, what we saw was *carefully considered*, and when such a carefully prepared and comprehensively vetted document does some things (and not others) it is no accident.

So then, is our "belief" about what Mr. Harper was evading correct? We had no trouble seeing through the Prime Minister's tortured prose because we're well aware of related issues (such as the ones we began this essay with) that are no part of what the average Canadian is supposed to know and what government and church officials know all too well: the United Nations Genocide Convention and Canada's role in it.

Take a moment and judge for yourself: go online (if you're not online already) and find the text of the UN Genocide Convention. If you know anything about the internet you'll have no trouble finding it; we give the text of Article II below:

> **Art. 2.** In the present Convention, genocide means any of the following acts committed with intent to destroy, in whole or in part, a national, ethnical, racial or religious group, as such:
>
> (a) Killing members of the group;
>
> (b) Causing serious bodily or mental harm to members of the group;

(c) Deliberately inflicting on the group conditions of life calculated to bring about its physical destruction in whole or in part;

(d) Imposing measures intended to prevent births within the group;

(e) Forcibly transferring children of the group to another group.

Many of you will be reading this for the first time. You aren't supposed to be reading it at all. We call attention to sections (b) and, especially, (e), which we call the "Slam Dunk." If pressed we'd be willing to argue the entire list, but we don't have to: the Article says *any*, not all. Even Mr. Harper in his statement comes perilously close to the Slam Dunk a couple of times:

> "...very young children were often forcibly removed from their homes..."

and

> "...it was wrong to forcibly remove children from their homes and we apologize for having done this."

Was he, in subconscious guilt, aping a phrase he had read a million times before with the understanding he must avoid it at all costs? ... or, perhaps, intentionally teetering along the edge of a precipice, in order to mock the dozen or so of us who were waiting to see if he used the correct word? We don't know. He creeps into another neighbourhood (b) once again when he mentions:

> "...emotional, physical and sexual abuse and neglect of helpless children..."

But that's as close as he gets to any of the other categories of acts constituting genocide in international law. It isn't crucial, however; we already have the Slam Dunk.

Well, isn't there some way around this... this... embarrassing fact? No. One of the contributors to the current document wrote a book 14 years ago that established the genocide that was Indian residential schooling, and the absence of ways around it was thoroughly dealt with there. However, no one read it then and no one is going to read it now,

215

particularly when we've gone and spoiled the ending for everyone.

But then, is there no "responsible" authority (not just a dozen or so Indians, and worse, Indian-lovers, who can read and add and reason) who can tell you, our present readership, whether our "interpretation" is right or wrong? (Over the years, time and again, work on this issue has been slighted by phrases like "Roland *believes* that the residential schools were genocide," or "In Roland's *opinion*, Canada and the churches are guilty of genocide," like it was some disputable quirk on Roland's part that is at issue. Well, it's the United Nations "opinion," as expressed in the black-and-white of the Convention, that Canada and the churches committed genocide, and the UN is the body that in 1948 got to say what genocide was.) Okay. In support of our "interpretation," we call what all must agree is a "responsible" authority... the government of Canada.

Also available on the above web site is a paper that provides more detail and references concerning Canada's disreputable collusion with the United States in gutting a form of the genocide convention that would have been much more explicit with respect to the point we're making. The current convention is a watered-down version of the proposals of Raphael Lemkin (the man who coined the term "genocide" in 1944), but even watered down it is sufficient. So sufficient that, when it came time to implement the Genocide Convention in Canada's criminal code (which was what each nation of the United Nations was supposed to do), Canada omitted entire subsections of the UN Convention (by 1970, (b), (d), and (e) were gone, Canada telling anyone who asked that the laws against murder and manslaughter already banned genocide — reducing genocide, as they discussed in the early 50's, to outright killing). No less an authority than eventual Prime Minister Lester Pearson had suggested that surgery had to be performed on the UN Genocide Convention, or otherwise Canada and its churches would be in violation of it... and, for heavens' sake, Indians might someday learn to read!

It's true that even the Convention as articulated provided sufficient wiggle room to allow countries to adopt modified versions of it. But, as remarked by a commentator who first encountered the Convention last Wednesday, Canada's excisions and elisions betoken a guilty conscience about what it had been up to. After all, this is what the US, with Canada's aid, had forced through the conference dealing with this particular issue, and if it was good enough in principle for everyone else in the world, why was it inappropriate for Canada?

Finally, sometime in the late 1990's, Canada quietly, surreptitiously, and without ceremony removed genocide as a chargeable offense from its criminal code, leaving mention of it now solely in the provisions against hate crimes.

We find it interesting how closely the vaporization of genocide in Canadian law coincided with rising consciousness in Native America on the distance between what international law said and what governments had done, and with a government-commissioned secret study that warned the Chrétien government that Canada was liable with respect to the "genocide issue" and recommended it bite the bullet and 'fess up. As always, Canada provided itself with some explanatory "wiggle room" about why they did what they did, but we would certainly like to ask some direct questions of the officials involved, as well as examine documents and internal correspondence on these subjects (but see below). But, to summarize in a fashion both short and blunt, the history of Canada's involvement in the creation and implementation of genocide law, nationally and internationally, betokens an overriding concern with its culpability and liability with respect to its treatment of indigenous peoples in general, and its operation of Indian residential schools in particular.

So, Canada itself agrees that our reading of the UN Genocide Convention is correct, and that it accurately characterizes its behavior towards Native Peoples.

Okay, you might say, Canada's behavior is at variance with international genocide law... but didn't implementing what they did, however maimed and deformed, into Canadian law remove all future problems? After all, aren't their actions simply a version of what the United States, also worried about the possibility of being charged with genocide, undertook... adopting a limited version of the Convention, finally, at the end of the Regan administration, and then subjecting it to interpretation by American courts?

It's true it was pure evasion, but it isn't true that it lets Canada off any hook. Apart from the "guilty conscious" their behavior evidences, putting aside any question of legal liability that might or might not be attached, and forgoing any discussion of what jurists have long ago established concerning the priority of international law (e.g., that countries and government officials can't exempt themselves from accountability to international law); instead of all that, just ask yourself: was it merely the failure of the corrupt powers of Rwanda (or Slobodan Milosevic) to exempt themselves (or himself) from the Genocide Convention that got them (or him) into trouble? Suppose the Genocide Convention was in force during the Holocaust… would Hitler's declaring himself and his chums "immune" have rendered it inoperative? Is that the length the average Canadian is willing to have her or his government go to avoid having to deal with its genocide of indigenous peoples?

It has taken us some time, but Mr. Harper's statement:

> "…it was wrong to forcibly remove children from their homes and we apologize for having done this."

…must be amended to say:

> "…it was wrong *for the government of Canada* to forcibly remove children from their homes and we apologize for having done this. *And it was a crime.*"

Bank robbers, thieves, drunk drivers… all criminals, in fact… don't get to erase their crimes by saying "I'm sorry," regardless of how sincerely they might say it.

Genocide on the Table

A television snippet from country-wide reaction on Wednesday featured Diane Blair crying out "It was genocide! Why not just admit it?!"

A fair question, and one well-put. As we have seen, Mr. Harper *could* have used the term, and it was a deliberate act *not to*. What motivated him? Without too much thought we can see several reasons, grounds sufficient for us to have anticipated long before Wednesday's circus that what we weren't going to hear would be a genuine apology. To answer the woman's question, first, keep on reading the Convention; immediately you will find:

Art. 3. The following acts shall be punishable:

(a) Genocide;

(b) Conspiracy to commit genocide;

(c) Direct and public incitement to commit genocide;

(d) Attempt to commit genocide;

(e) Complicity in genocide.

Art. 4. Persons committing genocide or any of the other acts enumerated in Article 3 shall be punished, whether they are constitutionally responsible rulers, public officials or private individuals.

So we have Reason 1: rulers, public officials, and private individuals, criminals all, prefer to avoid being punished for their actions. It is very common, we think, for criminals to not want to be punished. In most cases, however, and unlike the case under consideration (i.e., the Indian residential schools), criminals are not in charge of the political, economic, legal, and journalistic controls of a nation. Journalistic control, of course, is particularly necessary if one is going to maintain the manufactured ignorance of multiple millions of Canadians.

Reason 2: Canada has held other nations accountable to a standard of international law that it has itself evaded. That is hypocrisy. Canada wants to complain to China about its human rights abuses; it does not want its own abuses thrown back into its face.

Reason 3: Assaults, rapes, and every other form of abuse expire in national law, perhaps even in international law, according to their Statute of Limitation. Genocide has no Statute of Limitation.

Reason 4: Canada presents itself as a good world citizen, a paragon of virtue. However, a country that bears comparison with Nazi Germany is a paragon of virtue like Charles Manson is a boy scout leader.

Reason 5: Speaking like a psychologist for a moment, abusers frequently tell themselves they have good grounds for the abuses they perpetrate. Often they repeat the lie to themselves with such regularity that they come to believe it.

Reason 6: This is a reason the head of the United Church gave us in a public meeting in 2002: "genocide" is such a harsh word that the membership of his church would be upset by its use, however appropriate. Thus, it's better to *perform* genocide than give it its proper name. So perhaps Canada is similarly just thinking about the tender sensibilities of its real citizens, and not those of its pseudo-citizens against whom the genocide was implemented.

Reason 7: The lengths Canada has gone (first, to limit the definition of genocide, and second, to obstruct every way there might have been for indigenous peoples to even raise it as an issue) shows the fear that, if the governments and churches show "weakness," Indians will treat them with the same rapacity Westerners show weaknesses detected in one another. That is, that Indians will behave like Westerners (the irony that this transformation is what the residential schools were trying to institute has not escaped our notice). It is to our credit that there is no evidence at all that we would behave in such an inhuman manner. More than for any other reason, the moves that have been made toward litigation have been motivated by the government and churches *closing off* any other ways of seeking redress. From the beginning, all the survivors wanted was *a genuine apology*, along the criteria we've mentioned at the beginning of this commentary.

Reason 8: For us, Reason 1 and its first cousin, Reason 7 are is the overriding motivations behind avoiding the word "genocide." But it takes not a moments reflection to appreciate that, once "genocide" is on the table, its application across the entire range of policies and programs affecting Native Peoples, historically and contemporaneously, must be considered.

Let's briefly look at some specific cases in light of Reason 8. So; how well does "genocide" fit the various incentives manufactured over the years for Indians to enfranchise themselves or to be enfranchised? Perfectly, we think. So; how descriptive is "genocide" concerning the 60's and 70's Scoops, where uncounted numbers of indigenous children were adopted out, some overseas, to non-Native foster parents? Flawlessly, in our opinion. (Sterilization? Who said that?) Or, can "genocide" accurately characterize the current status of suicide in aboriginal communities? It can and it does, we would argue.

And on and on. Maybe some of you would prefer to argue the point, but that's *our* point: the Indian residential schools were not isolated idiosyncrasies of a few members of a governmental department or two. Genocides involve a host of interrelated and interwoven policies and programs, the understanding of which requires sustained effort and the application of all 5 of the specific headings given under Article II. The Nazis, for goodness' sake, made it illegal for Jews to own parrots!

Bringing genocide to the table would take the churches, but more centrally the government of Canada, into the exhaustive examination of additional regions of its policies and programs with respect to indigenous peoples, regions that, up until now, it has successfully avoided (or at least, as it is now trying to do with residential school, managed to isolate from other policies). And, what is perhaps even more important, establishing that Canada's policies toward indigenous peoples constitute *an historic and ongoing genocide* rules out Mr. Harper's statement *as an apology*, since such would violate the second feature of a genuine apology; someone who is *still doing it* can't be promising not to do it again.

If Genocide, Why?

So far we have only dealt with why what Mr. Harper said on Wednesday was not an apology (to summarize, he meticulously avoided using the proper term "genocide" to characterize Canada's actions, thereby impugning the sincerity with which he had worked so hard to infuse his words). But at the outset we objected to more than the non-apologetic nature of his statement; we took exception with characterizations he made of the actions of the churches and governments.

We don't dispute his repeated assertions that "it was wrong." For us, this was a no-brainer: **genocide is wrong**. Mr. Harper's pathetic attempt to insinuate mitigating circumstances ("While some former students have spoken positively about their experiences at residential schools…"), another evasion which disqualifies his statement as an apology (just try to apologize for killing someone while driving under the influence of alcohol by saying "I always do silly things when I'm drunk"), also boomerangs when we consider the irrelevance of the specifics of a genocide to decide upon its "wrongness." After all, some Jews learned a useful trade working as slave labor in concentration camps; some made new friends; many lost weight; and some even had their metabolisms re-set, so that they were able to maintain a healthy weight for the rest of their lives! But when you make the moral decision that **genocide is wrong**, you don't have to listen to sophistry that tries to turn the task of making moral judgments into an accounting of the "goods" and "bads" of a particular program.

There are numerous other places we could be picayune. Calling residential schools "educational institutions" grated on us, for example. But in at least one more point the presentation descended much too far into pure fiction for us to leave it uncommented. With genocide now revealed as the accurate term to characterize the governments' and the churches' actions, the question of *why* arises. Even Mr. Harper, in evading the issue of genocide, still felt compelled to provide his listeners with an historical vignette of the underlying cause of creation and operation of the schools:

> Two primary objectives of the residential schools system were to remove and isolate children from the influence of their homes, families, traditions and cultures, and to assimilate them into the dominant culture. These objectives were based on the assumption that aboriginal cultures and spiritual beliefs were inferior and unequal.

There you have it; the objective was to assimilate Indians, because we were believed to have inferior cultures (spiritual beliefs are an expression of culture, and thus redundantly included in Mr. Harper's statement). This was "wrong," "caused great harm," and has "no place in our country."

We have no doubt about the "great harm" part of his statement; however, you should notice how it leaves the agents of all this misery unnamed. It was "the residential school system" that had objectives (and not *people* working for the churches and governments), and the "inferiority assumption" apparently just hung in mid-air during the years of operation of residential schools, unattached to anything identifiable as a human being wearing a frock or business suit.

Are things any better when we supply warm bodies to this dodge? Well, inserting human beings into all this would at least make explicit that it was *people* who had the objectives of (1) removing Indian children from their forms of life and (2) insinuating them into mainstream culture, and that *people* had the (now more obviously racist) assumption that Indians were inferior. So now, our agreeing that this was "wrong" allows us to encapsulate and restate this part of Mr. Harper's little history lesson into "*people* did harmful things to Indians because those *people* were racists."

But anyone who thinks we are satisfied with this rendering is much too used to bad movie scripts, where bad people do bad things because they are bad. As if the clergy and governmental officials responsible were all wearing black hats. Life is not so simple.

First, the image that in Indian residential schools an "inferior" culture was being replaced with a "superior" culture (which thinking, thanks to the P. M., we now know has "no place" in Canada) is simply wrong. Indian children were not being taught to drink tea with their pinkies extended, speak with an affected English accent, or appreciate poetry and opera; they were being taught to perform as menials (domestics, farm hands, cooks, etc.) for members of the superior culture (and even the not-so-elevated members of that culture). If they were expected to learn anything in residential schools, it was to *learn their place*; to perform, without question and with dispatch, the commands of their betters. If this was assimilation into "dominant culture" it was into its lowest, most wretched, most disposable stratum, where the inhabitants moiled to eke out a marginal existence. It was alright that these serfs would be Indians; after all, our "betters" have never really concerned themselves with the color of their peons.

Second, attributing this all to "the racists" (who, thank heaven, no longer have a place in Canada) erects a faceless, nameless straw man we're all supposed to take a turn at pummeling. But this piece of misdirection insinuates that ideology determines actions, rather than actions determining ideology. This is too big a subject to go into here, but ideologies of race, race inferiority, and sub-humanity *arise from* the material needs to dispossess and expropriate, and not *vice versa*. Canada's wealth has arisen from the willingness of the settler society to simply take what they want from indigenous populations (just ask the Lubicon, the Cree of Northern Quebec, and the Labrador Innu, for recent examples). It's in casting about for some excuse to justify satisfying a *material* agenda that Canadians have had to create and then invoked the non-humanity of the real owners of Canada.

Consequently, holding anonymous racists responsible for the woes of Indians and assuring us they no longer abide here is nothing but additional falsification on a heroic level. For banishing faceless and nameless spirits to some vasty deep does no such thing as long as the material need to do away with Indian rights and claims continues to abide here. Thus Mr. Harper's history lesson is nothing more than another kind of bribe... like the forthcoming Truth and Reconciliation Commission. "Just let us insinuate a comic-book version of Canada," it says. "We don't have to *name* the ghosts in the story; we all know who they were anyway. We'll just pretend they're all gone now, so you can sleep better at nights. And we get to pretend there's a clean and complete split with this admittedly reprehensible past." But the past is present, and it seems, the future.

Resolving *Anything* Useful?

For a "clean break" the events of Wednesday leave an enormous number of loose ends (some thicker than the Atlantic Cable) flailing around, at least for us. Even several of the leaders of the other political parties, in their responses to Mr. Harper's statement, noted on Wednesday that it was short on detail. That may be true; however, directly by Mr. Harper's words and indirectly by implication the upcoming Truth and Reconciliation Commission has been accorded the task of sorting out the remaining specifics.

Is it up to the task? Not even in the cartoon world Mr. Harper has created, much less in the real world.

As already mentioned the statement not only said things we dispute, it left unmentioned a host of issues we needed to see addressed. Let's run through a few of the omissions:

(1) **Genocide**. Is the commission going to bring this up? And so what if it does? Canada has already demonstrated it will simply ignore the charge if it's made, and has been careful to eliminate any possibility of treating the matter in a serious way. Minister Strahl, for example, stated repeatedly in the run-up to Wednesday that nothing Mr. Harper would say would prohibit an ongoing, aggressive investigation into crimes associated with the residential school. But he knew, as we did, that the central crime had already been removed from consideration. Even if Indian after Indian stands before the commission and charges genocide, nothing will happen about it. Most of all, such repetition will only dispose the "average" Canadian, who is supposed to be getting an education on these things, into the familiar stupor of "there go those damned Indians again, always complaining about something."

(2) **The Cover-Ups**. Once "wrongs" are correctly identified as "crimes," can anyone else see that Canada and its churches have been covering up the crimes of the residential schools for quite some time now? The pattern of responding to charges made by former prisoners of Indian residential schools was predictable and familiar: stonewall, then impugn the testimony and motives of the victims ("those troublemakers just like to make noise, or they're looking for another handout"), then admit that maybe, just maybe there was a "bad apple" here and there in a gigantic barrel of nice apples ("some bad things may have happened, but it was all done with the best of intentions"), then throw a sacrifice

(preferably one already dead) to a dissatisfied and growing crowd of lawyers, and then go back to stonewalling ("Hey, enough already! The issue has been settled!").

Canada and the churches have worked long and hard to avoid admitting anything (in 1998 it was estimated that the Anglican Church, for one, had spent the overwhelming bulk of their budget for dealing with residential schooling on advice from publicity agencies), much less general and specific criminal acts. As anyone paying attention could probably guess, here the government has long ago moved to limit its own possible damages from colluding in knowingly hiding crimes and hindering investigations, so that, for example, while it's illegal in Canada to destroy documents needed for criminal investigations the people who do the destroying can't be charged with anything (the "Naughty-Naughty" Principle).

But the churches have long looked out for their own, with known pedophiles in their ranks given a "time out" and then transferred to a new assignment without the inconvenience of having to face a criminal charge. By the way, isn't this what Becket and King Henry were arguing about back in the 13th century? Eventually, didn't English law come down on Henry's side? We have to agree with Henry on this one.

The victims of abuse at residential schools have had to endure not only the original abuse, but the vituperation and calumny of criminals and those assisting criminals in evading disclosure and prosecution. And, for parliamentarians and bureaucrats, even if they've removed themselves from the possibility of formal criminal charges under the existing criminal code, justice demands an accounting and acknowledgement of the cover-up as much as it demands them of the original crimes.

(3) **The Secret Histories**. Attention has been focused so much on church and governmental abuses that there is a clear and present danger that an additional unknown number of malefactors will slip through the cracks. It has already been acknowledged that, for example, in the 50's the Canadian Medical Association asked for, and received, permission to study the distribution and growth of tuberculosis in "human" populations by giving unpasteurized milk to the children in residential schools. Around the same time, the Canadian Dental Association asked for, and received, permission to study the lifelong development and growth of caries (tooth decay) in "human" populations by giving

"sham treatments" to Indian children in residential schools. Here, not only are the people who "authorized" these child abuses culpable, so are the people who ask for them. Both these cases, of course, took place long after the Nuremburg Protocols for ethical research with human beings had been articulated and accepted.

Nor does it end here. The notorious Dr. Donald Ewan Cameron, who, while in the pay of the Central Intelligence Agency, used electroshock and mind-altering drugs to experiment on innocent Canadians (a chapter in Canadian history immortalized, so to speak, in a CBC movie), also had some kind of involvement with Indian residential schools, mainly in the Prairie provinces. Rumors abound (since at least the early 90's), but there has never been enough hard evidence to sustain charges. Doesn't this bear investigation?

In fact, with a captive population and a supervening authority at best indifferent to their well-being and without any mechanism of complaint or due process available to the victims, what *could not* have happened? On this subject our imaginations have already been far outstripped by what everyone admits actually did happen; what a broadly-thrown finely-gauged net might dredge up is, in our opinion, anybody's guess. The (now, finally, at last) movement to start digging in church graveyards and remote, unmarked locations is merely the tip of an iceberg, one that could well nail, even for those Canadians at the utmost levels of denial, the concept of genocide to Canada's treatment of indigenous peoples.

There's more (Sterilization? Who said that?), but this is enough for now. These three loose ends, rather than "details" that can be dealt with summarily, are, we predict, Hydra's Heads that will sprout hundreds or even thousands of additional inquiries if pursued with due diligence. We have a number of problems with the upstart commission, but our question here is: Is the "Truth and Reconciliation Commission" equal to this task?

This commission can (1) subpoena no witnesses, (2) compel no testimony, (3) requisition no document. It cannot find, charge, fine, or imprison. Thus far, the only ones lining up to testify are members of groups who have already testified (the Royal Commission on Aboriginal Peoples generated thousands of pages of testimony from school survivors, a corpus, we must add, that has not in the slightest way entered into the consciousness of the average Canadian in the 12 years since its publication) and those who still maintain sufficient plausible deniability to publicly defend its inactions (the RCMP, for example). Those most obviously culpable have already stated their intentions *not* to bother showing up.

Will, somehow, the victims of residential schooling show up dragging bales of documents proving abusive actions, abusive policies, collusion, cover-ups, etc. on the part of ministers, bureaucrats, clergy, professors, bag-men, pedophiles, and the full host of assorted miscreants? They'd better, for the "Truth and Reconciliation Commission" won't have them.

Or maybe we just need to pray for our own version of a governmental or ecclesiastical "Valachi," who will show up and rat out the Dons, all the way up to and including the *Capo de Tutti Capi*. However, not only is this an extremely thin thread upon which to hang our hopes for truth (and more importantly, JUSTICE); what "witness protection program" is going to protect him or her?

"Truth" is an odd name for a body that can trade not at all in that particular commodity. "Reconciliation," too, is an odd word for five years of allegations that can be either scorned or ignored, according to the tastes of those who are its subject. It invokes the same fantasy world Mr. Harper constructed, where Canadian and indigenous peoples are returned to that happy state of mutual respect and cooperation that existed before the bad old residential schools came along and ruined everything. In "truth," however, there never has been any "conciliation" to "re."

Conclusions

We don't know about you, but we've been unable to swing a dead cat since Wednesday without whacking someone telling us about how the "apology" has "closed a painful chapter" and signals "a new beginning in relations" between "Canadians and Indian-Canadians" (sic). Like someone tearing apart a picture of a former boyfriend or girlfriend, spitting on it, and walking away from the pieces tossed over the shoulder, however, we've been witnessing a made-up ceremony, one where the participants, for various reasons, are trying more to convince themselves they've dealt with all the serious issues rather than actually putting an end to them.

Canada has, once again, *missed* a truly historic opportunity, putting paste on display rather than an authentic diamond, because the diamond, in someone's estimation, would have been far too expensive. Already, after the patina of ceremony has worn off, there have been some rumblings, primarily around the fact the Mr. Harper's statement was long on being sorry and short on being active. And as we pointed out at the start, a real apology promises to undo, as far as possible, the damage done. But now that the statement is revealed as just another evasion, we must caution against whatever action the governments of Canada would propose; as we've tried to make clear, the "action" Mr. Harper's statement endorses, the "Truth" and "Reconciliation" Commission, is no action at all. And someone who steals your car, wrecks it, and is unrepentant about his/her actions is most definitely *not* the person you'd choose to repair it or replace it.

But that person most certainly at the very least would be responsible to pay the costs of repair or replacement. If this be genocide, the role of Canada's government (and churches) is to make it possible for us to once again make ourselves whole, nothing more and nothing less. How should we do this, how long it will take us, where do we start... these questions and more crowd in on us all. But they are questions we must identify, discuss, and answer ourselves.

Those of you who saw clearly and immediately the farce that was being played out; those of you who felt in your heart of hearts that the whole orchestration was out of tune but couldn't identify the offending instruments until now; and those of you who were misled until you brought the powers of your own intellect to the examination of this exercise in rhetorical excess; whatever your history is that led you to complete this overlong commentary; we invite you to join in the task of building what ultimately must replace this charade, some kind of response authentically committed to truth in this history and justice in its resolution.

Roland Chrisjohn
Andrea Bear Nicholas
Karen Stote
James Craven (Omahkohkiaayo i'poyi)
Tanya Wasacase
Pierre Loiselle
Andrea O. Smith